Causality and Narrative in French Fiction
from Zola to Robbe-Grillet

Causality and Narrative in French Fiction from Zola to Robbe-Grillet

Roy Jay Nelson

Ohio State University Press   *Columbus*

Library of Congress Cataloging-in-Publication Data

Nelson, Roy Jay.
    Causality and narrative in French fiction from Zola to Robbe-
Grillet / Roy Jay Nelson.
        p.   cm.
    Bibliography: p.
    Includes index.
    ISBN 0-8142-0504-6 (alk. paper)
    1. French fiction—20th century—History and criticism.   2. French
fiction—19th century—History and criticism.   3. Causation in
literature.   4. Narration (Rhetoric).   5. Zola, Emile, 1840–1902—
Technique.   6. Robbe-Grillet, Alain, 1922–   —Technique.   I. Title.
PQ637.C37N45   1989
843.009′23—dc20   89-34065
                                                                              CIP

Printed in the U.S.A.
9 8 7 6 5 4 3 2 1

For Anita

Contents

Preface

Although it is a primary connector in the long, linear "syntagmatic" dimension of stories, causation in fiction has attracted only passing attention from theorists. Despite the illuminating pages on the subject by Genette, Todorov, Prince, and others which enrich this study, no attempt has yet been made to construct a unified theory of the causal concept in narrative. Among the many reasons for the dearth of etiological theories, two, I think, deserve mention at the outset. First, the causal dynamic remained largely invisible to the relatively static visions of literary structuralism, which dominated early theoretical exploration. Second, well-founded contemporary doubts about the real-world truth value of the causal concept raise questions about the validity of causal statements concerning fiction.

The pages that follow are organized partly in response to these problems. A brief introductory summary of philosophical views of "real-life" causation, from Hume and Kant, through Nietzsche, Bergson, and Russell, to Mackie and Anscombe, leads among other things to the observation that causation is indeed not a truth but a hypothesis, not an entity to be found in nature, but rather a useful perceptual grid in the minds of human observers. This finding leads me to postulate that the reader serves as the "human observer" of fiction, and that causation arises most basically in stories from readerly perception. Thus the principles of reader-response criticism open doors that were closed to structuralist poetics. Chapter one then evokes briefly the notions of causal "functions" in narrative as developed by modern narratologists and seeks to show how this approach, eliminating the human observer (reader) from analyses, erroneously seeks "true" logical connections between events. Yet causes are present only in the discourse of a text, in the unavoidable causal implications of language, not in the events of the story itself. This long-established distinction between "story" and "discourse" leads me to adapt for analytical purposes Genette's three-tier model of narrative, which includes a "narration" level as well, referring to the inferred author's "production" of the text.

Inductive analysis of four relatively traditional French novels serves to demonstrate how causality—or readerly inference thereof—operates on all three levels, each of which assumes a dynamic role. At this early stage of causal research, it seems both prudent and honest to derive elements of causal theory chiefly by induction, through observation of existing fiction, rather than to propose a system apparently *ex nihilo* and to attempt to show subsequently that real texts exemplify it. Near the end of part I, I advance a three-level provisional model of the causal dynamic in "standard" novels and seek to demonstrate that the levels of narrative are actually definable by causal operations.

Part II of this study attempts to apply this matrix, no longer to traditional fiction, but to a series of French modernist narratives. These further inductive analyses suggest that the twentieth-century French novelists in question have become increasingly unsure of the objective existence of real-world causality, or at least of human ability to observe it. They are less likely than traditional writers to seek to imply its existence between events of their stories, but they must nonetheless use language, with all the causal expression that entails. They employ therefore various strategies of blocking and indeterminacy to eliminate from readers' constitution of the "story" level whatever causation may remain operative in the discourse. In the most recent Robbe-Grillet text analyzed, all "real-world" referentiality is effectively eliminated, thus making it impossible for readers to draw causal inferences about the story. On the basis of strengths and limitations now apparent in the provisional three-tier model, my conclusion proposes a more complex and uncertain one as applicable within limits to both traditional and modernist texts.

Thus my response to the first problem—the inability of theory to observe causality in fiction—is an approach founded upon readerly response to texts. To the second problem, I reply that causal statements are not intended to be true: they are hypotheses. But they are inferences of such power that they inform the metonymical dimension of traditional stories and require those modern texts that would prefer to banish causal connections to adopt strategies of particular sophistication.

In an effort to make these pages readily accessible to all readers of

English, I have provided translations for the substantive quotations in other languages. Unless otherwise indicated, translations are, for better or worse, my own.

To Anita, for her patience, help, and unfailing support; to my University of Michigan colleagues, for their interest and longanimity; among whom to Marcel Muller, for his numerous useful references; and among whom especially to Ross Chambers, who read the penultimate version, for his uncommonly valuable insights, suggestions, and encouragement: my warmest thanks.

Introduction

There are neither causes nor effects. Linguistically we do not know how to rid ourselves of them. But that does not matter.

—FRIEDRICH NIETZSCHE
(trans. Kaufmann & Hollingdale)

Tu causes, tu causes, c'est tout ce que tu sais faire.

—Queneau's "Laverdure"

C ausality is fundamental to human thought and activity. Our every action implies a grasp of its practical application, and elements of its principles are inherent in all our decisions. From traffic lights to birth control devices, our precautions affirm our belief that causation is not simply a notion, but a reality. The affirmation is hardly new. The first human fire builders were obviously aware of a predictable relationship between their actions and the results thereof, and early hominids, chipping away to sharpen one stone with another, must have envisioned the potential utility for the hunt of the spearhead in the making. Why stop with human beings? Some great apes select and wield tools. And who is to say that the osprey, diving upon a shallow-swimming fish, has not chosen its prey and fixed the angle of its dive with a conscious eye to the effects of its decisions? Everything points to causality as a conatus, a virtually instinctual link between mind and matter. Yet it has eluded objective observation and description, and no philosopher to date has provided a completely workable analysis of it, nor even an entirely satisfactory definition.

Undefined, it remains interesting. The coexistence of reasonable yet differing views on the subject signifies the coexistence of reasonable yet differing worlds. And in fact a multiple cosmos awaits us in novels, each a "universe" with its own harmony arising from the character of the codes which inform it. The concept and the code of causality evolved over the period here under study (approximately the 1870s to the 1970s), and with them—perhaps because of them—evolved the structure of fiction.

Yet define we must, for the sake of minimal clarity. *Causality* is the name of the relationship between causes and their effects. (*Causation* designates the same thing, but it also admits of more particular application: one may speak of the causation of a specific event, as the "act of causing" it or as the complex of its causes.) But what is a cause? A primary difficulty in defining is the multiplicity and diversity of relationships subsumed in this most general of terms. The relationships we perceive between the gravitational force and "falling," between the presence of certain bacteria and "disease," and between a house fire and the flight of the occupants belong to different orders of reality and thought, their very distinctness militating against the choice of a common designation. Still, a most unscientific instinct persists in telling us they indeed have something in common.

Present-day philosophers still find the term meaningful enough to pursue debates about what *cause* signifies. But contemporary formulations, and my own definition for the purposes of this study, are best deferred, in favor of a rapid survey of selected historical philosophical opinion, which forms the context of current approaches.

Not surprisingly, a common factor in post-Enlightenment theories of causality is the required presence of a human observer. David Hume launched the "modern" arguments in *A Treatise of Human Nature* (1739), a book whose suspiciously anthropocentric title suggests the turn etiological analysis was to take. The first part of one of his two-part definitions (book I, part III, section XIV) affirms that we may define a cause to be

> . . . *an object precedent and contiguous to another, and where all the objects resembling the former are plac'd in a like relation of priority and contiguity to those objects, that resemble the latter.* . . .[1]

From this, and from the reasoning from which it emerged, we may judge that, for Hume, a cause must be (a) temporally prior to its effect, (b) spatially contiguous, in some way or other, to its effect, and (c) part of a class of similar pairs of events, in which the prior ones resemble each other and the subsequent ones also resemble one another. This definition astutely avoids the assumption of any discernible connection between cause and effect; we simply note that actual event A_1 is followed by actual event B_1 in contiguity, that a similar A_2 is followed by a similar B_2, and A_3 by B_3, until we begin to suspect that causation is at work. Then we may predict that, for any A_n, we will observe a following B_n in the vicinity. Thus, without denying the potential "reality" of causation, Hume has nonetheless situated it in the mind of an implied human observer, endowed with memory and the ability to learn from experience, capable of classifying events, of discerning which are similar enough, and similar in pertinent ways, for categorization as examples of causality. If a tree falls in the forest, in the absence of a human observer, are there any causes for it? One may suppose there certainly will have been, when a human being discovers its demise. "Upon the whole," says Hume, "necessity is something, that exists in the mind, not in objects" (*Treatise*, p. 165).

In the second segment of the definition quoted above, Hume adds "imagination" to memory as a human faculty capable of discerning causes. If we avoid plunging headlong into rivers without knowing how to swim, he indicates, it is not because we necessarily have previous experience with drowning. General experience—with solids and liquids, and with breathing—allows us to form a mental image of the outcome. In no case, however, is causation for Hume objectively observable, for it is not an entity (situated perhaps between A and B, where one would have to explain how it connects to A on the one hand and to B on the other): it is a mental classification of events. As for the possibility that some "power" or "energy" or "efficacity" is transmitted from A to B, that too escapes objective observation; indeed the use of such terms as synonyms of "cause," for Hume, is purely tautological.

Hume cautions that, in making causal judgments, one must take care to remove from consideration "all foreign and superfluous circumstances," although he fails to explain how we are to distinguish them. Furthermore, his formulation fails to filter out "sibling" effects, sequential effects of a common cause; his argument would allow one to reason, for example, that day causes night. But his principles remain influential, and certain of them are particularly useful for the study of fiction: that causation exists in the mind of an observer, and that it involves memory or imagination and classificatory judgment. For if causation exists in stories, it exists in the mind of the reader. Readers are the observers and final arbiters of causal relationships among narrated events. Even when a narrative text tells us that one event caused another, we are aware of the subjective, judgmental nature of the affirmation and may compare our notions of plausible causation to that of the voice of the text. While most fictional information must be taken on faith—the heroine's age, the color of her skirt—causal statements are all subject to doubt.

Kant never defined causality in the *Critique of Pure Reason* (1781, 1787), where the subject is little more than a detour on his road to other destinations, but his comments about our perception of causation in time are a source of critically useful principles. He sought to reestablish an "objective" link between cause and effect, but, because of his inherent idealism, his notion of objectivity actually posits a limited subjectivity, one unable to see sunny skies when it is raining, but able to draw the curtains and refuse to see anything meteorological at all. He describes our knowledge of phenomena in terms of a mental image or representation (*Vorstellung*): again the human "observer." He notes (first division, book II, chapter II, section 3, second analogy)[2] that these impressions occur in temporal succession, and that the order of succession is frequently determined (*bestimmt*). If the observer, however, selects the order, it is not determined. When we look at a house from top to bottom, no necessity causes the roof to preexist the foundation, for we might as well have observed the house from bottom to top or from side to side. But if we watch a boat drift down a river, we see it first upstream then further down; these mental images, according to Kant, could not have been received in the opposite order, and the change is therefore determined. In this sense, all our mental images derived from the reading of fiction are determined. But the Kantian distinction between "subjective" and "objective" succession presupposes perception of the distinction between present-future and past: what our *Vorstellung* tells us did in fact happen "objectively" is the only thing that could have happened. At the moment of mental image A (boat upstream), the future is indeterminate (p. 215), but when B occurs (boat downstream), it is the only possible outcome of A. Each present refers us to a correlative past from which it must, according to the "rule" that establishes its place in the succession, have sprung.

Obviously, this Kantian principle defines the reader's, as well as the observer's, present. What has been read in a given novel appears determined, while what remains to read appears indeterminate, whence the suspense, surprise, and so on we perceive as part of the reading experience. Readers know, of course, in fact that the story is determined all the way through, in the pages as yet unturned, but, at the watershed between "apparently determined" and "apparently indeterminate," the reader defines his or her separateness from the story and its narrator. When a narrative voice recounts a tale of events which supposedly occurred at some earlier time, it may be assumed that it knows the outcome when it delivers the first sentence: for the voice of the text, then, everything is determined. This dialectic establishes in large measure the reader's relationship of separateness with respect to the narrative voice: causal principles, once posited, work to determine the levels on which narratives exist, as textual evidence will reveal later on. On the other hand, if a narrator stands *in medias res* as she or he speaks, as in diary or epistolary novels, the relationship with the reader is profoundly altered. The future for the narrator remains indeterminate, just as for us, yet the unscanned pages lie immutable before us: to another consciousness, on a level beyond the narrator and us, causality seems to have played out its determining role. And the words stretch on toward the end, syntactically "determined" by their predecessors, often connected by (names for) action: the transitivity of linguistic narrative flashes across our minds, from the fluidity of the possible to the solidity of the "real," in Kantian time.

Causality is thus a quasi-instinctual perceptual grid that our minds, in reading as in living, may impose upon events, or mental representations thereof, for the purpose of explaining or perhaps predicting them. Nietzsche, therefore, attacks its validity as an intellectual tool, and it is with Nietzsche that the deconstructionists begin to take an interest in the history of etiological theory.[3] In the collection of fragments and notes published under the title *The Will to Power* (1883–88),[4] the philosopher maintains that there are no such things as causes and effects, that these terms designate a falsely perceived relationship, anthropocentric in origin, whereby we attribute intentionality to nature, seeing things as agents and patients. Furthermore, he sees our own perceptions, including pleasure and pain, as terminal phenomena, disconnected, atomistic, and causes of nothing. In this general context (if there can be context in an assemblage of fragments), one note[5] evokes a chronological inversion (*chronologische Umdrehung*), by which causes reach our consciousness after their effects, despite their presumed chronological precedence. Feeling a pain in my leg, I reach down and discover a pin in my chair (Jonathan Culler's example): the perception of the effect has caused me to seek and discover the cause. The deconstructive neatness of the example resides in the disconnecting of causal logic (before-after) for the purpose of reinstating it, reinvesting it with the power to operate in the reverse order (after-before). Having denied the existence of causality to begin with, Nietzsche seems less eager than Culler to revitalize it. He merely observes that some fragment of the "real" world of which we are conscious "is born" after an effect has impressed itself upon us and is thus projected as its "cause." He does suggest that casting about for causes is a memory-based habit, the construction of a fiction that is familiar to us: that of an interpretable and explainable world in which we may feel more secure. Could this habit—or a perceived need for it—be a reinstated cause, which has crept in despite Nietzsche's efforts? He concludes: "to be able to read off a text as a text without interposing an interpretation is the last-developed form of inner experience—perhaps one that is hardly possible—" (here the note breaks off).[6] Can it be that our linguistic habits, acquired in reading, tend to spread to the interpretation of "reality"?

The metaphor binding a sequence of sense impressions to the reading of a text cannot fail to interest us in other ways. Most obviously, we are seeking a heuristic device for the interpretation of texts—a bad habit, but a tempting one, a delicious forbidden fruit that it is "hardly possible" to refuse, a habit that causality may make it possible for us to indulge "under erasure." Then too, "cause" is a word, an element of texts, subject to the limitations of language. A "cause" is "that which produces an effect" (one of those remarkable definitions which owe their richness to the fact that they explain nothing), and nothing can therefore be called, truly or falsely, a "cause" until it has produced what we perceive as an "effect." While we may seek to predict what will be a cause ("If you drop that glass, it will break!") or propose a counterfactual ("If you had dropped that glass, it would have broken"), on the semantic level causes are radically simultaneous with their effects. And vice versa: the "pain" in the Culler example was an event, but it did not become an "effect" until its cause was perceived, unless we admit to the instinctual habit of seeing all events as caused. In any case, the semantic simultaneity, and the *chronologische Umdrehung*, define the reason why a narrative event, like the shooting of Madame de Rênal, creating causes out of what had been simply (antecedent) events, leads readers to reevaluate and restructure the readerly "past."

Finally, the word "cause," while masquerading often as the name of a particular relationship, in reality designates, as we have observed, a class of supposedly similar relationships. In an oft-quoted little essay, *On Truth and Falsehood in the Extramoral Sense* (1873),[7] Nietzsche uses language to subvert language, calling particular attention to the problematics of the general and particular in words. Language is, he says, a metaphor for our sense impressions, yet we make of it the repository of truth. In fact, although no two leaves are alike, we apply the word *leaf* to them all, conveniently forgetting the individual differences. Language thus leads us to believe that there is a fundamental *Urform* of *leaf*, of which all leaves are but inept copies. And so the leaves, which gave rise to the *leaf*, seem to us to be caused by it (*"das Blatt ist die Ursache der Blätter,"* p. 313). *Cause* could, of course, *mutatis mutandis*, be substituted for *leaf* in the example. Does the existence of the abstraction *cause* lead us to infer the myriad of specific causes we perceive about us? I will argue rather that the unwieldy abstraction itself fills a need. If the perception of causes serves, as Nietzsche suggests, to aid in satisfying our craving for an explainable and partly predictable world, the generality called "causality" provides the essential unifying factor: not only does the world appear explainable, but it provides explanations according to the same, universal law.

No claim will be made here that causal reasoning is valid (on the contrary, its hypothetical nature is what makes it interesting), nor that the "universal law" is true. Across the period we will be studying, roughly from Zola to Robbe-Grillet, suspicions about the "universal law" begin to pervade the consciousness not only of philosophers, but of writers and readers of fiction. All are left with a language whose every transitive verb implies causation, in a world in which causation has become suspect. How changing narrative structures managed to weaken and ultimately eliminate the causal stranglehold of language over fiction will be explored in part II. Some of the reasons for the means chosen spring, in France, from the poetic and philosophical revolt of the late nineteenth century, which deserves brief mention here.

An important inhibitor to general public acceptance of Nietzschean attacks on causality was the perception that science—notably the experimental sciences, but also Darwinian biology—was moving from triumph to triumph with causality as its foundation. Denial of the causal relationship as a false mental construct seemed to fly in the face of sound empirical data. But the revolt occurred when the scientific principle was expanded to explain and predict the human personality. Hippolyte Taine was both the flagstaff and the lightning rod of the expansion, writing, for example:

Que les faits soient physiques ou moraux, il n'importe, ils ont toujours des causes; il y en a pour l'ambition, pour le courage, pour la véracité, comme pour la digestion, pour le mouvement musculaire, pour la chaleur animale. Le vice et la vertu sont des produits comme le vitriol et le sucre, et toute donnée complexe naît de la rencontre d'autres données plus simples dont elle dépend.[8]

(No matter whether the facts are physical or mental, they always have causes; there are causes for ambition, for courage, for veracity, just as there are for digestion, muscular movement, and animal warmth. Vice and virtue are products, like vitriol and sugar, and every complex datum arises from the conjunction of simpler data on which it depends.)

The fact that Zola chose the "vitriol and sugar" part of the famous quotation as an epigraph for the second edition of *Thérèse Raquin* is indicative of the infusion of belief in the "universal law" in the general culture of the period. Taine's view that we are all the result of *la race*, *le milieu*, and *le moment*, both physically and psychologically products of environment and heredity,[9] was to be long influential and exemplifies the dominance of causal structures in the popular mentality.

Rimbaud, of course, objected, in his "lettre du Voyant"[10] (a letter to Paul Demeny dated May 15, 1871), in which he refers to Taine, that poets could avoid being part of the causal chain by disrupting the functioning of their senses, through "all the forms of love, of suffering, of madness," as well as "poisons"—doubtless alcohol and other narcotics. Environmental influences upon the mind must first pass through the senses; by untracking the sensory filter, Rimbaud declares, we attain that "monstrous" soul, in which the effects of external stimuli are no longer predictable.

The philosopher Henri Bergson, whose approach, though frustratingly intuitive, is often on the mark (it was he who, long before E. O. Wilson and the sociobiologists, described organisms as mechanisms invented by genes for the production of other genes),[11] saw no need for such drastic measures. Each individual from birth is already differentiated in heredity and/or environment from all others, with a unique sensory apparatus; no external cause can produce the same effect in two individuals: we are unpredictable (pp. 131, 499). Bergson's primary arguments against the mechanistic application of causal laws to the human mind may be summarized as follows: (1) The physical laws applicable to matter cannot be extended to the human consciousness, which is qualitatively different. (2) The human psyche is alive, dynamic, and spontaneous, not merely a measurable accretion of experience. (3) Language, which is essential to causal analysis, is inadequate to the description of states of consciousness, because words, at once too specific (my "jealousy" cannot be clearly dissociated from all the other emotions I feel concurrently) and too general ("my" jealousy is not the same as "yours"), are unsuited to the task. (4) Causal diagrams are inadequate to the description of human consciousness, because they suppose that human time is comparable to space; space, in a diagram, preexists in its entirety, while time is constantly becoming. (5) While it is possible to guess an individual's behavior in specific circumstances, it is impossible to predict it with certainty, for one cannot "know" another's psychic state: of the two ways to seek to know it (intellectually, by words or diagrams—see 3 and 4 above—and experientially, by having lived the other's life), neither is feasible. (6) Causal logic is flawed, even in predictions about inert matter, insofar as it tends toward a relationship of identity between past and present (*Essai sur les données immédiates de la conscience*, in *Oeuvres*; see especially pp. 93–145).

Bergson's distinction between mechanistic, quantifiable causality, valid for the physics of the period (which I will term "rectilinear"), and psychological causation, unquantifiable, undefinable, and unpredictable (which I will try to show as surfacing in "nonrectilinear" forms) was to evolve. For Bergson, it was obviously joyous liberation; later, the essential difference between mind and matter was to be perceived as alienating the human consciousness from knowledge of material reality. Imprisoned at first in the machinery of material causality, humankind is more inclined of late to see itself as prisoner in the lonely recesses of entirely separate consciousnesses.

Science, meanwhile, went its own way. By 1913, Bertrand Russell was already pointing out that, insofar as causality is the "thought or perception" of an observer and not a property of matter, it is of no scientific value.[12] Indeed, if experiments are replicable, that demonstrates the relative uniformity of nature, an inductive probability, rather than the existence of a "law" of cause and effect. He asserted that scientific observations and experiments made no use of causal concepts, that the relationships among phenomena are scientifically described in terms of differential equations, each reduced to its simplest terms, but without omitting any significant variable. Thus, while a particular occurrence may be a "function" of another variable or set of variables, it is improper to hold that such variables are its "cause." And so Russell called for the "extrusion" of the word *cause* from philosophical vocabulary.

The noun *function*, together with some of its mathematical underpinnings, made its way into critical vocabulary with the Russian formalists, as the name of a "variable" narrative unit. With some redefinition, it has become a mainstay of structuralist terminology, where it designates those units that exist in consecutive and logical correlation, a close approximation of what I will be calling "causality." Like Russell, however, the structuralists have as their valuable and fruitful aim the discovery and description of the properties of matter (i.e., of the properties of narrative, *sub specie realitatis*), and not the thought or perception of an observer. Thus Barthes and other structuralists, eschewing the term "causality" for excellent Nietzschean and Russellian reasons, must seek on theoretical principle to factor the reader out of their calculations. Yet, for practical purposes, there he or she remains: a unit is not an *énoncé* ("utterance") itself, but "what it means";[13] the connecting logic presupposes an observing and reasoning consciousness. An example from Barthes reveals the logic at work:

> . . . si, dans *Un coeur simple*, Flaubert nous apprend à un certain moment, apparemment sans y insister, que les filles du sous-préfet de Pont-L'Evêque possédaient un perroquet, c'est parce que ce perroquet va avoir ensuite une grande importance dans la vie de Félicité: l'énoncé de ce détail (quelle qu'en soit la forme linguistique) constitue donc une fonction, ou unité narrative. (P. 176)

> (. . . if, in *Un coeur simple*, Flaubert informs us at a given moment, apparently without stressing the point, that the daughters of the assistant administrator of Pont-L'Evêque owned a parrot, it is because that parrot is going to be, later on, of great importance in Félicité's life: the expression of this detail [whatever linguistic form it may take] thus constitutes a function, or narrative unit.)

The revelatory "it is because" involves a readerly hypothesis about Flaubert, which, although it doubtless comes close to certainty once the story is read, remains dubious on first reading for some time after the initial reference to the parrot.

I shall examine a similar case in greater detail later, with respect to Zola's *La Bête humaine* and the levels of narrative. I shall work consistently from concepts that incorporate an observing mentality, since one perforce is present, to see whether it might not be possible, by observing the ways in which narratives allow for readers' logic, to succeed after all in making a relatively objective statement or two about the properties of narrative per se.

Russell also criticizes the notion of "events," on which causal theories are based, as elusive. An *event* is traditionally defined as a change, but

Russell sees change as process, with no finite boundaries. Where does the cause end and the effect begin? If we set arbitrary boundaries, declaring that the cause begins here and ends there, it will have no identifying unity, since between here and there some progression, some change, will already have taken place. Besides, for Russell as for Nietzsche, if events can somehow be arbitrarily defined, no two will be alike, so that subsumption under the headings of *cause* and *effect* contains an inherent error. In response to Russell's first objection, this study will seek to remove change arbitrarily from those fictional events called *effects*, by simply selecting a point in the narrative and terming the state of affairs at that point an *effect*. Anything prior to that point in narrative time which fulfills the other criteria of causation may be called here a *cause*. As for the nature of those criteria and for Russell's second objection, I will call on two more recent philosophers for help.

Causal vocabulary has continued to serve, of course, despite Nietzsche and Russell, in both philosophical and everyday discourse, and attempts continue to be made to define its practical meaning. When an expert testifies that a short circuit caused a fire in a house, what does she or he mean? Certainly not that, in the absence of the short circuit, the house could not burn, nor that every short circuit in it would lead to conflagration. J. L. Mackie (1965) devised an analysis of causation that purported to explain the use of causal vocabulary in such specific instances.[14] A cause, he says, is an insufficient but necessary component of a condition which is itself unnecessary but sufficient for the production of the effect. In the example, the short circuit was not of itself sufficient to cause the fire: it had to occur in the presence of combustible material and in the absence of such precautions as a working system of fuses or an adequate sprinkler system. But it was a necessary part of the complex condition, since the other elements—nearby combustibles, inadequate fuses or sprinklers—could not of themselves have produced the blaze. The complex condition itself is unnecessary, since it need not have existed (if nothing else, the short circuit might not have occurred); when it did exist, however, it sufficed to produce the fire. Mackie terms this set of circumstances an "INUS condition," from the initials of the key words: insufficient, necessary, unnecessary, sufficient. This system, which includes a mechanism for screening out other minimally sufficient causes that were present in a given instance but which did not, in fact, come into play, approaches a realistic definition of what most people mean when they say, "X caused Y." Despite the generality of the term "cause," it is used with specific application (*this* house at *this* time), by a speaker whose identity and purpose for speaking are understood. This semantic approach includes quite properly the observer-reporter and evokes a kind of causal reporting more frequent in daily life and in fiction than the more general theories.

G. E. M. Anscombe, in a Cambridge lecture[15] that does not mention Nietzsche, draws a concept of causality even more directly from language. "Causality," she says, "consists in the derivativeness of an effect from its causes." Thus she seeks to separate causation from the notion of "laws," of necessity, and of universality. Even in human reproduction ("everyone will grant that physical parenthood is a causal relation"), she points to the derivation of the effect, by cellular fission, from the cause, rather than to a general principle based on repeated observation. For her, to say that B comes from A does not imply that every B-like thing comes from an A-like thing or set of circumstances, nor that, given B, there had to be an A for it to come from. In this way, she detaches causality from the Humean logic of comparison and brings it to rest among Nietzsche's leaves. Without denying that general laws can sometimes be formulated, she nonetheless discovers the apprehension of causation in the isolated example; individual causes would exist, one supposes, whether consistent principles could be uncovered or not. As for Hume's contention that causing itself is not objectively observable, she suggests that he has merely misdefined "observable." We are unable to perceive the "efficacy" of causation? "Nothing easier: is cutting, is drinking, is purring not 'efficacy'?" Causality as derivativeness is plainly discoverable by the senses. The senses may be mistaken, "false" causes assigned, but the (apparent) derivativeness of effect from cause remains obvious to the observer.

Anscombe hints that words are at the origin of the observer's capacity to observe:

> The truthful—though unhelpful—answer to the question: How did we come by our primary knowledge of causality? is that in learning to speak we learned the linguistic representation and application of a host of causal concepts. Very many of them were represented by transitive and other verbs of action used in reporting what is observed. Others— a good example is "infect"—form, not observation statements, but rather expressions of causal hypotheses.[16]

Her assertion that our concepts of causality have their source in language returns us, perhaps closer than she would like, to Humean comparison with previous experience. For many of us derive most of our previous experience from words, some of it indeed from novels. The appearance of derivativeness comes aided by comparison. But her reference to causal hypotheses is of capital importance. I would insist further, if the senses are capable of assigning "false" causes, that all causal statements are hypotheses, for their truth value is relative.

Whether language is the origin of our causal perceptions or whether our causal perceptions, stemming from more primitive needs, are at the origin of language (I prefer this latter stance), there can be no doubt that our natural codes are infused with causality, notably in those "transitive and other verbs of action" which express cause. Such verbs *are* in part the language (if they did not exist, a natural language would not be a "language" as we understand it to be), and they require observer/reporters (and narrators in fiction) to express causation whether they "perceive" it or not. "She drank my wine" declares the derivativeness of the result: "She caused my wine to be drunk (with herself as agent)." Causality inheres in language. The element of naïveté in such philosophical analyses as we have pursued from Hume onward lies in the expectation that causal statements are intended to be "true." With causality locked into our discourse, however, in nonphilosophical, nonscientific parlance, observers, speakers, listeners, writers, and readers all perform their functions with far greater flexibility, remaining, more or less, on the near side of certainty, in the realm of the hypothetical.

While laying the groundwork for what is to come, the foregoing dialectic has brought us to the point at which we can attempt a definition of the central concepts. My approach to the notion of "events" has already been expressed. As for causality in fiction, for the purposes of this study, it is *a readerly hypothesis about a relationship of derivativeness between two observed phenomena*. Some might have expected or preferred that I close the definition with a narrower phrase, such as "between two narrated events." But readers may obviously perceive causation on other levels than that of the "events" of a story, and I hope exploration of these levels too will be useful in constructing a general theory.

More specialized terms, such as *necessary*, *sufficient*, and *probable cause*, will generally be avoided here. Of the three, only *necessary cause* has an agreed-upon definition in the literature, and that is so restrictive as to make such causes rare indeed.[17] A *condition* is those circumstances or sets of circumstances that allow a state of affairs to come into existence. (The causes for making a statement in French may be many and varied, but ability to speak French will always be a condition of the utterance.) I will include conditions among causes, making the distinction explicit whenever logic requires it.

Causal reasoning serves two practical purposes: predicting and explaining. Ability to foresee the consequences of a given course of action helps us calculate and select our behavior and achieve desired ends or avoid pitfalls. Explanations—causes perceived, according to the Nietzschean reversal, after the effect—tend to make us feel secure in a familiar, ordered world, as Nietzsche himself points out, and they may fill our memory with data (Hume) on which to found future predictions. If we can find no explanation for an event, we will doubtless prefer to presume nonetheless that one exists, somewhere beyond our powers of perception or intellection, rather than to envisage the possibility of a causeless event, whose very existence would threaten not only our power to predict but human foresight in general. Even "miraculous" remissions of incurable diseases may be explained by scientists as resulting from such statistically vague "events" as the patient's "positive attitude" or "will to live."

Philosophers and physicists make careful distinctions between causal "laws" and statistical "probabilities." In everyday speech, the distinction is, quite rightly, more blurred. Hume himself provides a general treatment of probability (*Treatise*, pp. 124–55), and sees causality only as the endpoint of a "gradation" of probability. In our more relativistic world, that endpoint itself remains hypothetical.

Though scientifically difficult to verify, the whole notion of human motivation, of which we all make constant use, is essentially causal in nature. With the exceptions of psychomotor reflexes and of the autonomous nervous system, however, there are no necessary causes in human behavior. Still, we make frequent predictions on the basis of what we deem to be probable causes (i.e., on the basis of hypotheses) in our decisions about how to treat others, guessing how large a salary offer will be required to entice someone to come and work for us, deciding whether jealousy games will attract our lovers to return or alienate them forever, or simply judging how another will react to a suggestion. Most of us are wrong often enough to make us wary, but without a causal assumption, based on learning and other past experience, we would have no grounds whatever for choosing one line of conduct over another, all forms of behavior appearing to offer an equal chance of success in attainment of our goals. Ability to predict accurately from a causal assessment of probabilities may be a primary determinant in our success in business, courtship, childrearing, and other activities requiring us to base our actions on a prediction of their "effect" on others. It is also possible to assume that success is a matter of luck, randomly distributed. But that assumption would endow us with the frightening total freedom of the mad.

Why the causal concept is a useful device for textual analysis in fiction should now be apparent: it is a prime juncture between stories and people, between novels and readers, across most of the period here under discussion. Inherent in language, it inheres also in naïve human reactions to the environment, a comforting habit that can operate in reading as in other phases of life. Furthermore, causation, when it is imagined, appears as a temporal bond, connecting events in time; it also functions as an element of metonymy in certain fictional texts, thus marking a junction between the perceived linearity of human time and that of fiction, as well as between the grammar of stories and of language. Finally, the truth value of the causal concept has been placed in increasing doubt, as we have seen, across the period of this study. The response of textual strategies to this loss of faith evokes clearly the curious trail of the evolution of novel structure in France; application of the perceptual grid of causality uncovers that trail.

As a reader living at the end of the period in question, I see causation as a subjective pattern, as a model of some practical utility in the specific situations of everyday life, but meaningless as a scientific or philosophical generality. Earlier readers did not share this outlook, however, and the texts of their times reflect cultural codes that differ from ours. By revealing which texts accommodate it well or poorly, and why, the causal model helps describe the evolution of novel form between the 1870s and the 1970s. Causal statements are not, as I have pointed out, intended to be "true"; they are hypotheses. This study functions therefore as a hypothesis, with causation accepted "under erasure," until contemporary texts find ways at last, despite the ingrained strictures of language, to do it in.

In part I, I demonstrate how causality, as readerly hypothesis, functions on the standard levels of narrative. Chapters one and five present the principles of analysis, in relation to certain previous studies, and the conclusions. The intervening chapters are illustrative analyses of relatively "traditional" novels, whose texts allow causation to operate, with a few exceptions, in a straightforward and mechanistic way (the exceptions revealing the cracks already appearing in the causal edifice). The choice of such generally "rectilinear" examples simplifies the initial task. But it also provides for a diachronic comparison with the texts examined in part II. There, in a series of essays on more "modern" novels, I undertake to show through application of the same heuristic device how texts reveal increasing skepticism about causality, through new ways of facilitating, and especially of inhibiting, readers' causal inferences. Chapter ten includes a theoretical component on the role of causality in those *Vorstellungen* I am calling "mental representations," as they occur in characters and readers, in preparation for the general conclusion on the interaction of reader and text in the creative act.

In the search for "typical" causal strategies, my corpus has become highly—perhaps excessively—"canonical." It therefore reflects the heedless male-dominance bias of the period it treats and leaves unanalyzed the rich French-language literatures of Africa and the Antilles (where the dual narratee—colonizer/colonized—provides a differing reaction to the causal grid), and the important francophone texts of Canada. It also neglects the anticausal strategies of Céline, Bernanos, Duras, Queneau, and numerous others equally worthy of study. What it does provide is a minimal basis for comparison: with respect to it, future causal analyses can describe, explain, and extol fruitful etiological differences. This is, then, an introduction, in need of completion, if completeness is possible in a typological problem of this magnitude.

It is inevitable, as we approach the study of fictional causality, that someone will ask the metacausal question: why? Three of my purposes are straightforward; the fourth is more personal and diffuse.

First, these pages are intended to describe and illustrate a general theory of the operation (or nonoperation) of cause and effect in fiction. Second, through analysis of novels for the most part well established in the French canon, I seek to present a typology of standard causal structures, for future comparison with other literatures, and with other French texts. Little that is new can be said here about the "meaning" of the works in my oft-treated corpus, but the role causality plays in these texts as the armature of the plot, and sometimes too as theme, makes of them a worthy and interesting standard of comparison. Third, a description of the evolution of causal structures in French fiction from the mid-1870s to the mid-1970s provides some measure of the relationship between changing ideas, notably concerning the truth value of causal assertions, and the changing techniques for organizing stories.

My fourth incentive has to do with lines and spaces. So much has been accomplished through the study of literature as space, as area, that an introductory approach to an element of the linear nature of stories seemed enticing. Peter Brooks, Gerald Prince, and others [18] have broken important ground. But the paradigmatic axis, projecting the syntagmatic line onto a plane, was providing the primary basis for our understanding of prose fiction. Synecdochic comparisons of narrative units to the whole text in which they occur, as well as comparisons of narrative texts to a common matrix or model, were providing not only the finest insights into fiction as genre and into individual novels, but also creating our concept of what "understanding" is. A series as such seems to offer little to be understood: 1, 2, 3, 4, 5, 6, 7, 8, 9, 10, 11, 12, 13, 14, 15, 16. Beyond the potential discovery of a "law" making it possible to predict the next term, and aside from an apparent openness on both ends, what does a linear series hold out for discovery? A spatial figure, however, with its inherent comparisons, provides instant meaning:

1	2	3	4
5	6	7	8
9	10	11	12
13	14	15	16

Now there is a "whole," to serve as the sum of its "parts," and the understanding of internal comparabilities (e.g., $1:4::2:8::3:12::4:16$) leads to a meaningful abstraction: $16 = 4^2$. As Lucien Dällenbach's *Le Récit spéculaire* illustrates, perception of specularity is in itself understanding. [19]

Metaphor appears analyzable; metonymy does not. If nothing else, sympathy for the underdog moves me to point out that metaphoric expression itself is subject to the chronological linearity of language, and to attempt to show, in what follows, the importance of that fact. Spatial criticism often (not always) tends to describe books that have been read, thus annulling a critical distinction between reader and narrator in Kantian time, and forgetting that these books may differ in decisive ways from the same texts in the highly temporal act of being read. [20] Is it possible, in criticism, to adhere entirely to a metonymic viewpoint? Probably not. Even

Peter Brooks evokes, for comparison, a Freudian transference model. But if comparison reveals what is "significant" in prose fiction, a linear approach uncovers what is "consequential," and therefore fictionally "important." *Meaningfulness* includes both significance and consequentiality, and the second attribute is not unworthy of discussion. So I try to hew to the line. It is tempting, for example, in describing causality, to allow diagrams to proliferate, replete with significant arrows. I have resisted the temptation as unwholesome (for my purposes) spatialization. But my resistance has not been completely successful; in that and in other matters, comparison gains its revenge in my text. Its subject thus does not complete the polysemic shift to become a truly championed Cause. But even as we pursue causality in its very absence, perhaps another more fundamental notion of "understanding" will emerge for the reader as an unstated aim.

Notes

1. David Hume, *A Treatise of Human Nature* (Oxford: Clarendon Press, 1888), p. 172. Future references in the text are to this edition.
2. Immanuel Kant, *Kritik der reinen Vernunft* (Heidelberg: Georg Weiss, 1884), pp. 207–23. Future references in the text are to this edition.
3. See especially Jonathan Culler, *On Deconstruction* (Ithaca: Cornell University Press, 1982), pp. 86–88.
4. Friedrich Nietzsche, *Der Wille zur Macht*, in *Nachgelassene Werke*, 15 (Leipzig: E. G. Nauman, 1901). See also the Kaufmann-Hollingdale translation, *The Will to Power* (New York: Random House, 1967).
5. Nietzsche, pp. 270–72 (Kaufmann, pp. 265–66).
6. Kaufmann's translation, p. 266. In *Nachgelassene Werke*, 15, 272: "einen Text als Text ablesen können, ohne eine Interpretation dazwischen zu mengen, ist die spätiste Form der 'inneren Erfahrung,' vieleicht eine kaum mögliche."

7.   Friedrich Nietzsche, "Uber Warheit und Lüge im aussermoralischen Sinn," in *Werke in drei Bänden*, 3 (Munich: Carl Hanser Verlag, 1956), pp. 309–22. Future references in the text are to this edition.

8.   Hippolyte Taine, *Histoire de la littérature anglaise* (Paris: Hachette, 1873), 1, xv.

9.   Taine, 1, xxiii–iv.

10.   Arthur Rimbaud, *Oeuvres* (Paris: Presses Universitaires de France, 1950), pp. 303–7.

11.   Henri Bergson, *Oeuvres* (Paris: Presses Universitaires de France, 1959), p. 517. Further references in the text are to this edition.

12.   Bertrand Russell, "On the Nature of Cause," *Proceedings of the Aristotelian Society*, 13 (1912–1913); also in his *Mysticism and Logic* (New York: W. W. Norton, 1929), pp. 180–208.

13.   Roland Barthes, *L'Aventure sémiologique* (Paris: Editions du Seuil, 1985), p. 177. Further references in the text are to this edition. It contains an excellent historical summary of the notion of textual "functions," pp. 175–89.

14.   Example and analysis are from J. L. Mackie, "Causes and Conditions" in *Causation and Conditionals*, Ernest Sosa, ed. (London: Oxford University Press, 1975), pp. 15–38.

15.   G. E. M. Anscombe, "Causality and Determination" (1971), reprinted in *Causation and Conditionals*, Ernest Sosa, ed. (London: Oxford University Press, 1975), pp. 63–81.

16.   Anscombe, p. 68.

17.   A "necessary cause" is one for which three criteria apply: (1) if A obtains, then B always obtains; (2) in the absence of A, B never occurs; (3) at any time in the past at which A did not, in fact, obtain, if it had obtained, then B would have occurred.

18.   Peter Brooks, *Reading for the Plot* (New York: Alfred A. Knopf, 1984); Gerald Prince, *A Grammar of Stories* (The Hague: Mouton, 1973); see also chapter one, where it will begin to become apparent how much I owe to Wolfgang Iser, *The Act of Reading* (Baltimore: Johns Hopkins University Press, 1978), and to others.

19.   Lucien Dällenbach, *Le Récit spéculaire* (Paris: Editions du Seuil, 1977).

20.   Roland Barthes, *S/Z* (Paris: Editions du Seuil, 1970), pp. 22–23, is noteworthily conscious of the difference.

Part I
Rectilinear Causality in Narrative

I

Causality in Fiction

La similitude relie un terme métaphorique au terme auquel il se substitue. En conséquence, quand le chercheur construit un métalangage pour interpréter les tropes, il possède des moyens plus homogènes pour manier la métaphore, alors que la métonymie, fondée sur un principe différent, défie facilement l'interprétation. C'est pourquoi rien de comparable à la riche littérature écrite sur la métaphore ne peut être cité en ce qui concerne la théorie de la métonymie. Pour la même raison, si on a généralement aperçu les liens étroits qui unissent le romantisme à la métaphore, on a le plus souvent méconnu l'affinité profonde qui lie le réalisme à la métonymie.

(Similarity binds a metaphorical term to the term for which it is substituted. As a result, when the scholar constructs a metalanguage for interpretation of tropes, he has more homogeneous means for dealing with metaphor, whereas metonymy, based on a different principle, readily defies interpretation. That is why nothing comparable to the rich literature on metaphor can be cited with respect to metonymy. For the same reason, if the close bonds linking romanticism to metaphor have been widely perceived, the profound affinity connecting realism to metonymy has most often gone unrecognized.)

—ROMAN JAKOBSON

Modern references to the structural role of causality in fiction commence with E. M. Forster, who pointed out in the 1920s that, if a "story" is a narrative of events in temporal sequence, to build a "plot," one must emphasize causality. "The king died and then the queen died," he told us, is a story; "The king died and then the queen died of grief" is a plot. [1] But the concept of "plot" becomes increasingly undefinable the more closely one looks at the multilayered way in which causal relationships develop in readers' minds. Forster's simplistic example suggests that a story can gain a plot through the mere addition of words, a notion on which he himself would scarcely have staked his reputation. Indeed, he indicates in the same context that it is the reader's question "why?" (for a plot), rather than "and then?" (for a story), which characterizes the distinction. For "why?" is always a matter of inference, even in the presence of explicit explanations: are they to be believed or not? Still, given the vagueness of the term, on the rare occasions when I speak of "plot" here, it will be rather as a synonym for the more recent concept of *histoire*.

We all recall how Roland Barthes situated causal relationships in the empirical "proaïretic code" he uncovered in *S/Z*[2] (Aristotelian "proaïresis" being the "faculty of deliberating upon the outcome of a course of conduct," p. 25). He correctly saw them as branching, interconnecting relationships, forming the strongest armature of the readerly text and the basis for a kind of structural analysis. He also stresses in *S/Z* the importance of readers' past experience, for Humean comparison, in inferring the causal connections: the proaïretic is the "déjà-écrit," "déjà-lu," "déjà-vu," "déjà-fait" ("already-written, -read, -seen, -done"). But the Aristotelian stricture, limiting the code to psychological causes (of physical and/or psychological effects), tends to screen out physical causes; yet, as we shall see, from infectious diseases, to a broken drive rod, to a blazing sun on the beach, these can be prime determinants of the way events turn.

As the structuralist approach developed, following the principle of objective description we have noted, it sought to derive functional relationships rather than "causes." This critical stance has produced sound general theories about the connecting devices that hold narratives together. Starting from his famous linguistic, semantic model, A.-J. Greimas derives an impressive set of formulae for the interaction of characters.[3] His "modèles actantiels" ("actantial models"), devised to describe types of connections, tend to define characters ("actants," "patients," etc.) as functions of the narrative energy, mechanisms for the production or experience of actions. Perhaps constructed to avoid limiting the definition of characters to their deeds, Gerald Prince's grammar of stories is founded on the principle of connections between "events."[4] He develops the case for logical or definitive necessity, positing that stories are the caused reversal of an initial stative event, with the stated implication that narrative may take other forms, but that, without the caused reversal, the term "story" is inapplicable. (One person's story is, I suppose, as Forster might say, another's plot.) Prince's theory describes causation as a connective between narrative units, as a conjunctive feature reducible by transformation to the formulation: "as a result." But in his *Grammaire du Décaméron*, Tzvetan Todorov had already evoked a kind of pragmatic necessity for expressed causality, since, with the exception of narrative units which are related by repetition ("emphasis" or "inversion"), he finds all relations between units in these stories to be, in one way or another, causal.[5] Whereas for Prince the expression of cause is conjunctive in nature and thus optional (even though the negative option may not yield stories), for Todorov it is fundamentally related to the transitivity of narrative, to the ongoing modification which is the story, and hence to the function of verbs. The relationship of this critical position to Anscombe's philosophical argument is self evident: it underlies much of what follows in this study.

Claude Bremond marks, I think, an important advance in *Logique du récit*,[6] by defining causation as a relationship of implication, thus beginning to imply, at the same time, readers and their inferences, their hypotheses. While, like Greimas, he focuses on the relationships of characters to actions, he highlights characters' choices, thus neatly balancing actions as definers of characters against character traits as definers of action. But it was Todorov who came to see the relationship of character to action and the question of which defines the other as a causal problem: do characters produce actions, or vice versa?[7] Grasping what I have called the "radical simultaneity" of the perceived cause-effect relationship, he wonders whether the directionality of the causal connection is not, perhaps deconstructively, bivalent. I shall attempt a "reconstruction" in response to that, but not before the whole analytical apparatus is in place, at the end of this volume.

Underlying the structuralist positions is the question of whether causation is expressed or implied in fiction. Obviously, the causal idea reaches readers in both ways; the distinction is indeed constitutive of the narrative levels we shall consider presently. But one major study, which is not about causation at all, describes an approach to fiction that opens the way to the discovery of causation, not as an objective function to be discovered in the text, but as a readerly hypothesis. This study is Wolfgang Iser's *The Act of Reading*.[8] It describes how readers "constitute" the text, connect narrative units in groups or *Gestalten*, and fill the gaps, where necessary, in the narrative logic. The gaps themselves are absences, objectively present in texts, which call forth the reader's participation in the esthetic act. Iser's insights will be seen to have clearly conditioned my concept of reading.

When Nietzsche speaks, as we have seen, of the ability to read off a text as text, without interposing an interpretation, one is inclined to ask what sort of text this could be, and especially what kind of reading. For, if a text remains text, it may perhaps be "read off" (that is, "pronounced," as one can learn to sing a foreign-language song, by imitating a recorded version of it, with no idea of the sense expressed by the lyrics), but it can hardly be said to have been "read." For to read is to combine fragments, an activity necessarily subtended by interpretation.

The notion of the word as a unit of speech has long been taken by *writers* (quite rightly) for granted, by virtue of words' permutability and substitutability for one another, in divers contexts. Yet *readers* can scarcely perform their task at the level of the word: reading is, in large measure, an interlexical activity. Traditional grammatical parlance holds that adjectives "modify" the nouns they accompany, and the metaphor needs to be taken seriously, for they can indeed transform or recreate a mental image. As Greimas demonstrates, in blending the lexical data in a given context to form a mental picture, the reader obliterates the spaces between words.[9]

In *Allegories of Reading*, Paul de Man affirms:

> There can be no text without grammar: the logic of grammar generates texts only in the absence of referential meaning, but every text generates a referent that subverts the grammatical principle to which it owed its constitution.[10]

This distinction, part of a larger set of parallels de Man develops, separates writing neatly from reading. The writer, before the blank page, resides in the pre-text: grammar is the law which will constitute her or his discourse; the reader comes into existence only in the post-text and is, in envisioning the referent, a party to the subversion of grammar. Reading unites, in ways often highly individual to the particular reader, what grammar separates.

The word "green," surrounded by spaces, may evoke images ranging from chartreuse to ultramarine. But invent a banal sentence and limitations intrude: "He had no choice but to send green troops against the armored battalion." "Green" is totally meaningful, and therefore meaningless, until "troops" strikes the eye, determining the mental selection of a branch of signifieds springing from "unripe": "immature," "inexperienced," "untested." Thus, the space between "green" and "troops" becomes an absent absence on the semantic level.[11] Likewise, the distance separating "He" from its supposed antecedent disappears in context, and the meaning of "He" is further determined by the verbal components of the sentence, of which it is the subject. The "no . . . but" structure is an abstraction, suggesting selection of one unit within a set, all others being rejected: it requires union with "choice . . . to send" in order to evoke an imaginary "sense." The definite article before "armored battalion" indicates that the sense of that term has been partially predetermined in the context, and "send . . . troops against" suggests the possibility, if not the necessity, of further bellicose developments in succeeding sentences. Like most sentences with transitive verbs, this one designates a change and therefore affirms causation.

As soon as causality enters the picture, we are in the presence of a hypothesis, and readers will wish to know, as a condition of belief, to whom the text attributes it. The reading is not complete unless the reader knows who, according to the text, is making the inference that "He had no choice but . . . ," and on what grounds. Is it some inferable "author" or narrator, or is it the "He" of the sentence? Such information, of course, further unites the quoted words to their verbal surroundings. If the text hints that its writer (in the tradition of Wayne Booth's "implied author") has reached the conclusion, thus valorizing "His" decision, to what extent do we trust him or her? This query makes of the total text a context, for our judgment will surely depend on our knowledge of everything the text attributes to this "writer," as well as on the reasoning elicited in this instance, if any. On the other hand, if "He" arrived at the conclusion given, we will read the sentence in another manner, as a figure ("free indirect style"), and perhaps wonder whether the absence of options is not mere rationalization. While the antecedent of "He" and its context may have provided us data upon which to base our determination, some readers may react empathetically ("What would I have done in his situation?"), and others ideologically ("How does the military mind work?"). Then the context becomes an extratext of indeterminate but surely enormous proportions, limited only by the experience and psychological propensities of each reader.

Despite certain simplistic uses that have been made of his algorithm for meaning (signifier/signified), Saussure was well aware of the importance of the syntagmatic axis in the production of meaning.[12] For the notion of "meaning" with respect to a sentence or other syntagm occupies a fundamentally different realm from that of the "meaning" of a word. Words are understood by definitions, lists of denotations and connotations, so that "understanding" a word is a function of synonymity (as "bachelor" equals "unmarried man" in Jakobson's famous example),[13] which implies the mental substitution of "equivalent" terms. Understanding a syntagm, while it also involves substitution of mental images and concepts for terms, requires extensive combinatory activity, often ranging far afield within the text and into the reader's individual experience. This association of nonequivalent terms is, of course, metonymic in character: since the labor of combination must, in the final analysis, extend to the entire text (more essentially to the *memory thereof*), and to the relevant extratext of experience, the "meaning" of complete texts, the largest of syntagma, derives as well from metonymy. Even metaphors, which function essentially by substitution (comparison), are contingent upon metonymy, as elements of expressed syntagma, for their meaning:[14] Eluard's oft-analyzed "blue earth" metaphor would not achieve its celebrated effect, of course, if "bleue comme" ("blue like/as") did not signal a metonymic ellipsis: "comme une orange [est bleue]" ("as an orange [is blue]").

Now whenever the reader's combinatory activity is causal in nature, it takes the form of an inference (or hypothesis—with respect to fiction I use the terms interchangeably). And if all causes are hypothetical, all hypotheses are causal, at least in the first degree: "because of A, I infer B." A, in this paradigm, is an example of those special cases of causation termed "conditions." The prime cause of my inference is of course my desire to draw it; A is that condition which validates the hypothesis in my eyes. Since without such validation I should refuse, despite desire, to infer, the condition is itself a causal element. If $\Rightarrow$ means "is a necessary condition of," and if R means "reader," a reader's hypothesis can be expressed like this: $A \Rightarrow R(B)$. Most hypotheses of interest for this study are also causal in the second degree, for they concern supposed cause-and-effect relationships in stories. They may be stated, "because of C, I infer that A causes B." If $\rightarrow$ means "causes," one may write: $C \Rightarrow R(A \rightarrow B)$, or, for inferred conditions, $C \Rightarrow R(A \Rightarrow B)$. But where shall we go to look for C, that necessary condition that encourages inferences by tending to validate them? Is it to be found in the timeline of the narrative, where A and B reside, or in the timeline of the reader's own existence? Essentially, C is a point of juncture, situated at once in fiction and in life; as derivativeness, it belongs to the timeline of A and B, and as perception of derivativeness, based upon comparisons with readers' previous experience, with fiction and with life, it arises in the timeline of readers' existence. It is at such intersections of human experience and texts that reading, as such, takes place. Still higher degrees of causal inference are possible, although we shall not have need for them until the end of our analyses, when we face the question of imagined "authors'" inferred hypotheses about readers' potential causal inferences. If X stands for a hypothetical "author," one might write, for example, $D \Rightarrow X[C \Rightarrow R(A \rightarrow B)]$. But since such an "author" is entirely the product of dispositions within the text itself, our knowledge of X and D is limited to the data of A and B, and to the textual components of C.

Because notions of "authorship" are enforced upon us by our heuristic device of causation in texts, it is time for a disclaimer. First, our term in no sense refers to a real social or legal persona. It is the name for those dispositions within a text which provide a sense of purpose or intention; it seems to me no more bizarre to speak of an inferred author's intentions than to speak of the intentions of the text (I do both). Second, the inferred author, or the narrator (we shall distinguish between them shortly), as a product of readerly inference, can have only inferred intentions. Still, the inference is necessary and implied by texts: as with our example about sending green troops into battle, it is often useful for the readers to know who is speaking, and to infer why, as a condition of grasping the import of certain utterances. Finally, by definition, no hypothesis, including those about intentions and "sources" of utterances, is "true." Our "inferred authors" and narrators are devices, selected "under erasure," for describing the ways in which readers and many texts interact. As literature changes and interaction assumes new modalities, the device will "self-destruct."

At the more basic level of the sentence, it is often syntax that furnishes the conditions for inference. When the narrator affirms, in Camus's *La Peste*,[15] "Les bagarres aux portes, pendant lesquelles les gendarmes avaient dû faire usage de leurs armes, créèrent une sourde agitation" ("The riots at the gates, during which the police had had to use their weapons, created an undercurrent of agitation"), he institutes a cause ("riots"); he states, as Anscombe might say, its "efficacy" ("created"); and he names its effect ("undercurrent of agitation"). Standard syntax in both French and English alots, of course, temporal priority to the subject, so that subject stands in temporal relation to predicate as cause does to effect. The Nietzschean reversal is just as applicable: it is only when we reach the verb that we can think back and redefine the earlier noun as "subject." In simple observation statements like that of the main clause, the only hypothesis springs from our knowledge of life and of the narrator: whether we will infer that the affirmation is correct. For, like all statements of cause, it expresses after all an opinion. In the subordinate clause, the narrator chooses to highlight causation—and therefore the judgmental character of his inference—by the use of the verb "avaient dû" ("had had to"): the linguistic option, "firent usage de leurs armes" ("used their weapons") exists and would require no inference on his part. The narrator is electing to judge that circumstances made violent repression necessary and inviting readers by that choice to judge him: we may or may not believe that other police behavior might have been equally or more appropriate to the desired ends. On the whole, the encouragement to infer that the statement is true appears particularly strong, since the syntax reflects a classic INUS condition. The "riots" were necessary for the creation of the "undercurrent of agitation," but themselves were insufficient to produce it; the subordinate clause adduces the additional information for the larger condition, unnecessary (the riots might not have occurred, or the police might not have fired), but sufficient to produce the effect. Thus one might almost begin to suspect that the syntactic structures that create the metonymic associations were invented as vehicles for the linguistic transmission of causality, as much of the metalanguage of grammar suggests: "object," "subordinate," "conditional," etc.[16]

So far, the relationship of language to reality appears, with respect to causality, disturbingly unproblematical: syntax requires writers to imply causation and encourages readers to infer it. (It is to be expected that, in an age in which causality itself is viewed as suspect, there will be attempts to subvert its expression, as we shall see.) Metaphor may appear frequently in narrative, but it comes as a gratuitous enlightenment, exterior to the series of events which make up this story. Metonymy, on the other hand, is an integral part of individual syntagma and a constant connection between them. That which is gratuitous, of course, calls attention to itself by its presence; that which is necessary is evoked by its absence. We think (if I may be permitted to exaggerate for the sake of illustration) of tear gas only when it is present in our immediate environment, and of oxygen only when it is absent. Metaphors are striking in narration in that they are present when no need for them exists. Since they appear to be the product of a choice, they imply an intention beyond the initial decision to "tell a tale." The intentions of a story teller are highly valorized: it is through them that we know her or him. Indeed, it is only with the optional elements of discourse that an author (implied) or a story teller standing before us (real), can communicate with us; for the rest, linguistic conventions are speaking.

For the expression of cause and effect, two areas of optionality exist, two zones of "difference" from the norm (from the reader's standpoint), or of "différance" (from the writer's position). One is the area of absence, when causality is valorized by its abnormal disappearance. The causal chain breaks (by indetermination or underdetermination), weakens (through implausibility or relegation to a peripheral role), or is subverted (by means of paradox and contradiction). The other zone of difference is overdetermination. In addition to metonymic association, an impressively large vocabulary exists, in French as in other Western languages, to explain how and why events occur. Use of this vocabulary appears as a matter of choice, and it provides information about causation over and beyond syntactic norms. Examination of this second area of optionality should eventually lead us back to the first.

The specialized vocabulary of causation in French includes a metalanguage of causality (*cause, causer*) and a group of explicitly causal verbs, such as *laisser* and *faire* (plus infinitive), and frequently *devoir*. A number of prepositions, from *pour* (to express either intent or result) to the unobtrusive use of *à* ("A l'entendre bavarder, déjà je m'ennuyais") and of *de* ("Il la gâtait de mille soins") can explain purpose, result, or agency. As in English, French participles and adjectives can have causal force ("Ainsi coiffée, elle attirait tous les regards" ["Her hair thus arranged, she attracted all eyes"]). Nouns themselves, as Anscombe points out,[17] are often expressive of cause: if we learn that "l'incendie rageait" ("the fire was raging"), and later discover that objects have been burned, we will know why. Causal conjunctions (*parce que, car, d'autant plus que*, etc.) obviously introduce explanations. And, in addition to such terms, the mere juxtaposition of certain propositions can suggest, by parataxis, that a cause-and-effect relationship exists between them. I shall exemplify the functioning of this vocabulary in greater detail in the next chapter, with respect to specific texts, but basic inferences may be drawn at once from its existence.

As an optional mode of expression, this vocabulary is by nature judgmental. It implies not only a speaker, but one who is providing explanations of events, which, since they are perforce subjective, we may accept or reject. But at the same time it is informing us about the narrator. Such vocabulary reveals how (and if) narrators explain their worlds, and that revelation contains much of what we call "narratorial identity." It is based on two postulates, which are a part of the narrative pact we make with the novels we read (at least the traditional ones), the basis of which is the "willing suspension of disbelief."

The first postulate is that the narrator *has* a world. The exercise of causal judgment implies the experience of the "realities" to be judged. The narrator of a tale, intradiegetic or no, is perceived by the traditional reader, not as the inventor of the story (even if, like Scheherezade, she or he claims to be), but as its encoder and interpreter. Behind the narrative voice lies another entity, which has presented the events to the narrator's consciousness directly and without interpretation. The choice to provide causal explanation suggests a belief that it is needed, and the "need" implies the existence of unexplained data. These data are the narrator's "world," and efforts to explain it point to (1) the notion that the story's events "occurred" prior to their narration, (2) the principle that the events are foreign to the narrator, exterior to the narrator's mind, and difficult, in his or her opinion, to comprehend without explanation, and (3) the presence of an inferable author, inventor, or source of information, who or which provides the raw data to the narrator.

The second postulate is this: if an explanation is given, it is not the only possible one. Its very presence implies an absence. "Le discours manifeste ne serait en fin de compte," Foucault points out, "que la présence répressive de ce qu'il ne dit pas; et ce non-dit serait un creux qui mine de l'intérieur tout ce qui se dit"[18] ("The manifest discourse is doubtless, in the last analysis, only the repressive presence of what it does not say, and this unsaid seems a cavity, undermining from within all that is said"). Foucault's remark has far wider implications, but it expresses the basis of potential skepticism on the reader's part with respect to narrators' causal judgments. The word "potential" needs perhaps some underscoring: readers need not question such judgments, but merely remain aware of their freedom to do so, for that "cavity" marks their basic separateness from the narrative voice.

It is the notions of "narrator" and "inferred author" (since our stance is rigorously with the reader rather than the author, our concern with reading rather than with "poetics," this term appears more apt than Wayne Booth's "implied author")[19] that produce the levels of narrative around which we will group all our arguments. These levels are a standard in textual analysis, although they do not derive from the venerable tradition in which Wayne Booth's work is a landmark. Gérard Genette's definition of them is most interesting:

Je propose . . . de nommer *histoire* le signifié ou contenu narratif (même si ce contenu se trouve être, en l'occurrence, d'une faible intensité dramatique ou teneur événementielle), *récit* proprement dit le signifiant, énoncé, discours ou texte narratif lui-même, et *narration* l'acte narratif producteur et, par extension, l'ensemble de la situation réelle ou fictive dans laquelle il prend place.[20]

(I propose . . . to call *"histoire"* the signified or narrative content [even if this content happens to be, in a given instance, relatively uneventful or lacking in dramatic intensity], to name *"récit"* properly so called the signifier, utterance, discourse, or narrative text itself, and to term *"narration"* the productive narrative act, and, by extension, the totality of the real or fictive situation in which it takes its place.)

Despite Genette's reference, in speaking of *narration*, to an "act" with possible relationship to a "real" situation (and despite his evocation of a narrative content which sounds more like a referent than a signified), it is surely unlikely, in light of the context, that he is alluding here to a real and causative authorial presence. The "alliance" I am developing here between the Boothian tradition (with more recent echoes in Seymour Chatman's work)[21] and the principles of textual analysis is thus not a representation of the views of either, but a hypothetical device for uncovering relationships between readers and texts. Here are its basic assumptions.

The *récit* will be for us the domain of the narrator: the words he or she chooses to tell the story and their ordering on the page. The *histoire* belongs to the inferred author; it is the raw data, the series of events which he or she provides, as "content" for the narrator's pen. In general, one might say that there are no causal connections in any *histoire*, since events are not causally related unless someone—a narrator or a reader—perceives them to be. Still, verbatim conversations, interior monologues, characters' explicit thoughts, etc., are "facts" of the *histoire*, which the narrator can "quote," but not interpret in so doing. In such elements of the *histoire*, characters may evoke causation or explain their motivations. In this way, causation can enter the *histoire*, although readers retain, as always, their freedom to accept or reject, for cause, characters' causal explanations. The *narration*, as the productive act per se, is the realm of the author. Again, the "author" is not a persona but rather those elements of a supposed authorial thought process or intention which can be inferred from the existence and nature of texts themselves. Thus, the "author" is just as inferred as the "inferred author"; in rare instances, if I must mark the different kinds of inference involved, I shall call the "author" (of the *narration*) the "indexic author," for the text is a semiological index of her or him, just as smoke is of fire. All these inferences point to the presence of causation; indeed, just as (in my terminology) the *histoire*, supposedly preexisting, purports to be one of the conditions of its *récit*, so the *narration* (in my sense) is inferred as a cause of them both: the author invents the inferred author, creator of the story's content, and the narrator, with choice of words and syntax, as well. A few examples should suffice to clarify the distinctions.[22]

Detective fiction perhaps exemplifies the distinction between *récit* and *histoire* most clearly, for its form arises from the interplay of these levels. When the sleuth as narrator presents at last the explanation of the crime, perfect accord is supposed to exist between all the known data provided by the inferred author and the detective's *récit* of the reconstructed crime. Because we have willingly suspended disbelief, we cannot question the data, but narrative remains potentially suspect, since different verbal chains can express various causal bonds linking the same "facts." Thus detective stories will frequently introduce a confession from the accused, who will assure us that the investigator has described the causal links correctly. San-Antonio's hero-narrator is not averse to the use of violence to unite the causal strands of the two levels:

> —Regarde-moi, insisté-je en lui filant une beigne, c'est pas ça, dis?
> —Si, souffle le truand. . . .
> Je le chope par les revers. Je le tiens plaqué contre moi et, mon nez touchant le sien, je lui crache:
> —Ose dire que ça n'est pas ça?
> Il a peur, ses dents font un bruit de noix trimbalées dans un sac . . .
> —Oui, avoue-t-il . . . C'est bien ça . . .
> J'ai le trait de génie.[23]

> ("Look me in the eye," I insist, swatting him across the chops. "That's the way it was, right?"
> "Yeah," whispers the crook. . . .
> I grab him by the lapels; holding him smack up against me, nose to nose, I spit out the words:
> "I dare you to tell me that's not how it was!"

He's scared; his teeth are making noises like unshelled walnuts
bouncing around in a bag.
    "Yeah," he admits, "that's how it was all right . . ."
    I'm a natural genius.)

The reported conversation is a part of the *histoire*, fictive "fact" from the
inferred author, which the narrator, if he is to uphold in traditional fashion
his part of the narrative pact, cannot change. But it serves to confirm
("that's how it was all right") the causal explanation of the hero-sleuth-
narrator: "Tu as cramponné le magot et tu t'es apprêté à filer, ne voulant pas
te mouiller . . . Et puis tu as pris peur. . . . Alors, sans penser plus loin, tu
l'as balancé par la fenêtre," etc. ("You copped the wad and were all set to
beat it, since you didn't want to get in any deeper . . . And then you got
scared. . . . So, without another thought, you tossed it out the window,"
etc.) This explanation, given as part of the conversation, belongs in that
sense to the *histoire* as well. But as a verbal reconstruction of earlier events, it
constitutes a kind of *récit* itself, embedded in the longer *récit* which is the
text of the novel. Indeed, it enters that *récit* in the expression "trait de
génie," which summarizes it. Yet the narrator's comic arrogance and pro-
pensity for violence (would the "crook" dare contradict him, even if he were
wrong?) leave him ironically suspect. These elements constitute a condition
for reader inference that the confession is perhaps a lie, caused by fear. (The
story contains conditions for inferring that the confession is true, too; the
question can be resolved only on the level of the *narration*, after a more
detailed analysis.) Thus the reader's inference about causal relationships in
the *histoire*—Violence $\Rightarrow$ R (Violence $\rightarrow$ Confession)—can contradict the
narrator's version in the *récit*: Confession $\Rightarrow$ Narrator (Explanation =
Truth).
    Authors have long been conscious of the distinction between *récit* and
histoire,[24] and numerous kinds of encouragement are to be found in texts for
readers to perceive the separation. The narrator in Stendhal's *Le Rouge et le
Noir*, for example, often distinguishes himself from the story he is telling by
commenting upon it. He may express the opinion that "Julien avait raison
de s'applaudir de son courage"[25] ("Julien was right to congratulate himself
on his courage"); he may even compare Julien's provincial reactions in the
histoire to those of an imaginary young Parisian, imagined by the narrator in
the *récit* as a sort of "potential" hero in an alternative novel, that could be—
but was not—written (p. 78). He selects epigraphs for many chapters that

comment on the action of the *histoire*. Perhaps the most famous of these epigraphs comments on the *narration* itself (and the *narration* upon it): "Un roman: c'est un miroir qu'on promène le long d'un chemin," (p. 82); "A novel: it's a mirror trundled along a road."

Sometimes, narrators even criticize inferred authors (the *récit* may attack the *histoire*); Gide's narrators are not averse to marking such distinctions, although generally on esthetic rather than causal grounds.[26] In the famous central chapter of *Les Faux-monnayeurs* however (part II, chapter 7), the inferred author supplants the narrator, to admit the fictionality of his enterprise ("S'il m'arrive jamais d'inventer encore une histoire, . . ." [p. 284]; "If it ever happens to me to invent another story . . ."), and to call its causal basis into question. He suggests that, at this point, the future events of his *histoire* are as indeterminate for him as for the reader, but he seems to foresee that little Boris is doomed. Indeed, he pretends that he, as inventor of events, is limited by a conception of causality:

> Je crains qu'en confiant le petit Boris aux Azaïs, Edouard ne commette une imprudence. Comment l'en empêcher? Chaque être agit selon sa loi, et celle d'Edouard le porte à expérimenter sans cesse. (P. 280)

> (I fear that Edouard, in entrusting little Boris to the Azaïses, is acting imprudently. How to prevent him? Each being behaves according to its law, and Edouard's law impels him to ceaseless experimentation.)

Thus, the inferred author abandons his "inferred" status. His inventiveness remains unfettered, yet he seems to accept the constraints of a supposed causal verisimilitude which subtend the proposition that each being acts in accordance with its own law. This proposition, which affirms the causal predictability of characters, is however immediately subverted by the observation that Edouard's "law" is to experiment continually with something new: he is predictably unpredictable. But the purpose of experimentation is the discovery of causal laws and thus the revalorization of causal determinism: Boris's fate. By taking center stage, the (formerly) inferred author points up the inability of his narrator or narrators to reveal how the novel is balancing between determinism and absurdity: he accuses the weakness of the *récit*.

While freedom to judge the narrator's assessments is inherent in the novel reader's stance, passing judgment on the *histoire* is only occasionally permissible within the traditional narrative pact. To cast doubt on the veracity of the inferred author is to refuse to suspend disbelief, to challenge fictional "reality" itself. Still, an uncaused event in fiction may lead us to stand aside from its inventor, not merely by interpreting the data, but by adopting a skeptical position toward them. Uncaused events are those for which not only does the narrator provide no definitive and convincing explanation, but for which our life experience provides none either. They fall within the other area of optionality: the weakness or break in the causal chain.

Bernard, in *Les Faux-monnayeurs*, meets an angel in the Luxembourg Gardens, accompanies him to a political rally, talks to him, wrestles with him (pp. 438–44). Except for the fact other characters see Bernard but fail to see his angelic companion, the "angel" is no less a reality in the *histoire* than "Bernard." No hint of a credible explanation, founded in life experience, is provided (so much for the inferred author's causal fetters!), no suggestion that Bernard is, for example, hallucinating, or fantasizing about a lover. Although the metaphorical sense of the episode is readily apparent in context—the allusion to Jacob's struggle with the angel in *Genesis* is obvious—the appearance of a real angel in a novel otherwise devoid of the supernatural fits into no causal chain either in the *récit* or in the *histoire*. Since the narrative voice has no hesitation in commenting on the plausibility of events, it is difficult to believe in simple narrative reticence, in mere omission of some verb such as *s'imaginer* (to imagine) in the statement: "il vit s'approcher de lui . . . un ange" ("he saw approaching him . . . an angel"). With a causal void on the level of the *récit*, we can now move to the level of the *histoire*, but there no contextual event can have given rise to an angel. We are thus pushed back to our third level, that of *narration*, for an answer to the question: why? And our question is, "Why did the author include this episode in the novel?" Textual analysts would doubtless prefer to ask, "How do I read the angel in this text?" but our question implies more—the notion of textual elements indicative of intention or purpose which can guide our reading. We might ask: "What signs of intentionality are present in the text to inhibit or encourage specific readings of the angel?"; our "author" question is shorthand for that. Having thus advanced to the level of *narration* because of what is absent on the other levels, we are now aware of metacausality, the perception of which can transform the reading process into a questioning of our relationship to fiction in general.

It should now be apparent that a connection exists between the two types of causal expression we have observed (metonymic linking and over-determination through special causal vocabulary) on the one hand and the two most basic levels of narrative (*histoire* and *récit*) on the other. All narrative discourse belongs to the narrator. But an observation statement narrating an event, in which the subject causes the predicate (as in the main clause of our example from Camus), places the reader somewhat closer to the inferred author, to the raw data of the *histoire*. The use of special causal vocabulary, by valorizing the judgmental role of the narrator, situates us clearly in the *récit*. From this arises a peculiar temporal ambiguity in the reader's position with respect to narrative. The fictional events appear to be occurring as we read them, in a kind of sequential present, regardless of verb tenses. Yet the narrator can normally assess the causes only of events which have already occurred, so that events thus assessed seem "past." In this sense, reading an *histoire* is creating it "now"; reading a *récit* is learning why and how it happened in the past. We read by uniting fragments, by obliterating spaces, on both levels at once, thus seeking, at times unsuccessfully, to obliterate another gap: between past and present, between completed and incomplete.

When any of the gaps to which we have referred remains unbridgeable, when the spaces obstinately intrude between the words or events, narrativity becomes problematical, and therefore interesting. Analysis of causation in fiction provides a relatively precise way of discovering the gaps, for, as I have indicated, it is the breaks in the causal chain, rather than the chain itself, which attract attention. Subsequent chapters will seek to uncover such points of rupture in specific texts and to trace the evolution of their function in modern narrative.

Notes

1. E. M. Forster, *Aspects of the Novel* (New York: Harcourt, Brace, 1927), p. 130.
2. Roland Barthes, *S/Z* (Paris: Editions du Seuil, 1970), pp. 209–10. Further references in the text are to this edition.
3. A. J. Greimas, *Sémantique structurale* (Paris: Larousse, 1966).
4. Gerald Prince, *A Grammar of Stories* (The Hague: Mouton, 1973). See especially pp. 24–25.
5. Tzvetan Todorov, *Grammaire du Décaméron* (The Hague: Mouton, 1969), pp. 55–58. Todorov categorizes causal relationships by function: modification, desire, motivation, result, punishment, and hypothesis. On the relation of narrative causality to verbs, see pp. 34–35, 38.
6. Claude Bremond, *Logique du récit* (Paris: Editions du Seuil, 1973).
7. Tzvetan Todorov, *Poétique de la prose* (Paris: Editions du Seuil, 1971), pp. 78–82.
8. Wolfgang Iser, *The Act of Reading* (Baltimore: Johns Hopkins University Press, 1978).
9. Greimas, pp. 42–54.
10. Paul de Man, *Allegories of Reading* (New Haven: Yale University Press, 1979), p. 269.
11. Philip Hobsbaum, in *A Theory of Communication* (London: Macmillan, 1970), p. 209, points out the "misconception" that the word is the unit of language. (The same work, identical in content, pagination, and format except for the recto and verso of the title page, has appeared under the title *Theory of Criticism* [Bloomington: Indiana University Press, 1970].)
12. See Robert Godel, *Les Sources manuscrites du cours de linguistique générale* (Geneva, Paris: Droz, Minard, 1957), pp. 84–92.
13. Roman Jakobson, *Essais de linguistique générale*, tr. Nicolas Ruwet (Paris: Editions de Minuit, 1963), p. 52.
14. See Gérard Genette, "Métonymie chez Proust," in his *Figures III* (Paris: Editions du Seuil, 1972), pp. 42–55.
15. Albert Camus, *La Peste* (Paris: Gallimard, 1947), p. 128.
16. For the relationship bewteen syntax and Greimas's actantial models, see his *Sémantique structurale*, pp. 129–34, 172–91.
17. G. E. M. Anscombe, "Causality and Determination," in *Causation and Conditionals*, Ernest Sosa, ed. (London: Oxford University Press, 1975), p. 69.
18. Michel Foucault, *L'Archéologie du savoir* (Paris: Gallimard, 1969), p. 36.
19. Wayne C. Booth, *The Rhetoric of Fiction* (Chicago: University of Chicago Press, 1961), pp. 67–86 and passim.
20. Gérard Genette, *Figures III*, p. 72.
21. Seymour Chatman, *Story and Discourse* (Ithaca: Cornell University Press, 1978); see for example the diagram of narrative structure on p. 267.
22. It is obviously the hypothesis that causality exists which impels me to uncover a "responsible" source for each level, though Genette posits no such sources. Still, his observations that the *récit* as discourse must be proffered "by someone" (*Figures III*, p. 74) and that

narration is an "act" hint at a causal bias in his text; story content might, it seems to me, be just as necessarily invented "by someone."

23. San-Antonio, *Ça tourne au vinaigre* (Paris: Fleuve Noir, 1956), p. 217.

24. In a letter to Louise Colet (1852), Flaubert points out, for example, that in his first *Education sentimentale* he presents crucial causes and effects, while failing to trace in words the connections between them. Thus his *histoire* would be complete, but his *récit* would be deficient in causal explanation. Gustave Flaubert, *Correspondance* (Paris: Gallimard, Pléiade, 1980), 2, 30.

25. Stendhal, *Le Rouge et le Noir* (Geneva: Cercle du Bibliophile, 1971), p. 92. Further references in the text are to this edition.

26. In *Les Caves du Vatican* (Paris: Gallimard, 1922), p. 68, the narrator objects to the sensationalism of a character's action, calling it a "fait divers" ("news item"); in *Les Faux-monnayeurs* (Paris: Gallimard, 1925), p. 166, the narrator criticizes the author for inserting a "grotesque" event in the *histoire*; etc. Future references to *Les Faux-monnayeurs* in the text are to this edition.

2

Causal Options in the
Récit: Gide

"When I use a word," Humpty Dumpty said . . . , "it means just what I choose it to mean—neither more nor less."

"The question is," said Alice, "whether you *can* make words mean so many different things."

"The question is," said Humpty Dumpty, "which is to be master—that's all."

Alice was too much puzzled to say anything; so after a minute Humpty Dumpty began again. "They've a temper, some of them—particularly verbs: they're the proudest—adjectives you can do anything with, but not verbs—however, *I* can manage the whole lot of them! Impenetrability! That's what *I* say!"

—LEWIS CARROLL

From the perspective of Taine and the determinists,[1] authors of parables, like compilers of laboratory reports, must believe in the replicability of the cause-effect relationship; moralists and scientists both describe a procedure and indicate the results obtained; both suppose that, under similar conditions, the same operation produces virtually identical results. According to this mechanistic outlook, our ability to learn from others' experience depends upon our belief that similar deeds have similar consequences: causal replicability is thus a moral as well as a scientific notion.

That André Gide was aware of this dubious double role of rectilinear causality is evident in the parallel verve with which he mocks, in *Les Caves du Vatican*, Anthime's early confidence in the scientific method and his later faith in papal infallibility and in the ethical doctrines of the Church. Gide's 1914 satire stigmatizes, of course, not the principle of causation but, as he made clear,[2] the naïve belief in obvious, mechanistic causes and in the predictability of human behavior which lay at the base of some social sciences and of literature with ethical pretensions. Yet Gide was himself an author of moral tales, notably of *L'Immoraliste*, in which the causal chain seems to lead so directly from the beginning to the end that Pierre Laurens could offer this succinct analysis of the work shortly after its appearance in 1902: "Je suis malade, tant pis pour moi. Je suis guéri, tant pis pour elle!"[3] ("I'm sick: too bad for me. I'm cured: too bad for her!"). More recent critics agree: "Marceline must 'decrease' so that Michel may 'increase'"[4] and "le principal personnage de *L'Immoraliste* ne pouvait recouvrer sa santé qu'au prix de celle de sa femme"[5] ("*L'Immoraliste*'s main character could regain his health only at the expense of his wife's"). How then did Gide move from the confident affirmation of causality as a didactic device in *L'Immoraliste* to ridicule by exaggeration of this "ragoût de logique" ("logical potpourri"), also for didactic purposes, in *Les Caves*? A comparison of the causal vocabulary and relationships in *L'Immoraliste* and in the companion work, *La Porte étroite* (completed 1908; published 1909), indicates the central position occupied by perceived causation in Gide's thought, as well as his equivocal attitude toward it.

Comparisons will also shed light on the relationship of reader to narrator. Both tales are told by intradiegetic narrators; indeed each is the central figure in his own *récit*. The double reference of the narrative "je" (I who speak/I who acted)[6] already marks a sharp distinction between reader and narrator, for, while we remain in direct communication with "I who speak," we are as far removed from his acting alter ego as from any other character: "I who acted" has his actions mediated and explained by the *récit*. "I who acted" belongs to the narrative past, and his actions to the inferred author; "I who speak" is the encoder and mediator of these actions in a narrative present. Encoding involves reporting of the "raw data" of the *histoire*, in which causation appears immediate, passing directly from subject to predicate. This is the sort of ubiquitous narrative causality to which Todorov refers in his *Grammaire du Décaméron*. Mediation includes the explanations, the causal judgments passed by the narrator upon the events of the *histoire*. This expression of causality is optional and resides in the use of explicit causal vocabulary in the *récit*, overdetermining the generalized causality inherent in the recounting of any *histoire*. As both levels of expressed causation exist in both Gidean texts herein examined (as in virtually all narrative fiction), filtered through the double "je," possibilities for contradiction, or at least for suspicion, arise. That is to say, the reader may doubt, on the basis of the *histoire*, the causal explanations of the *récit*.

It will be a simple matter to keep the *post-hoc-propter-hoc* fallacy in proper perspective, for the fundamental question, on the level of the *récit*, is not whether A caused B, but whether the narrator says or implies that it did.[7] Causal vocabulary results from the perception, attributed to a narrator, of a causal relationship, independent of the objective existence of any causation. Indeed, studies have shown that in real life subjects frequently make erroneous assertions of causation, either because they are mistaken in their perceptions (e.g., primitive tribes who do not associate copulation and procreation), or because language itself encourages affirmations of causation even when none is perceived. Thus subjects will speak of a point of light "bumping," "pushing aside," or "pulling along" another point of light on a screen, even when they are aware that the laws of motion are not operable in such a situation,[8] so that the very existence of causal vocabulary seems to call forth a causal description of events. Again, it is the transitivity of verbs, the "causal" relationship of subject to predicate associated with the *histoire*, that can make us express causality in spite of ourselves.

A survey of causal vocabulary from sample pages of *L'Immoraliste* and *La Porte étroite* is described in appendix A. It reveals both the remarkable ubiquitousness of causal expression in language and some fundamental specific differences in technique between Michel and Jérôme as narrators.

First, the general remarks. Any reference to causal vocabulary calls to mind the standard metalanguage: *cause, to cause, because (of)*. But such terms are relatively rare; if we think a bit harder, we may realize that conjunctions such as *for*, *since*, and *as* often express causation, as do *so that*, *so as to*, etc. Adverbs of logical conclusion also come readily to mind: *thus*, *so*, and so forth. But it is with verbs that we note the tremendous expansion of the causal lexicon, for all transitive verbs that designate a modification affirm causality. In addition, there are a number of relatively common special verbs of etiological significance: *to allow*, *to permit*, and *to make* (plus infinitive or adjective: to make them do it; to make them happy). Causal verbs account for about half the expressed causation in our sample, and neither narrator can do much to eliminate them from his style.

But causation is also lurking in prepositions, adjectives, and present participles. Among the prepositions, one might think of *by* (agency) and *to* (motivation: she rose to speak). Yet cause can also be implied by *with* (overcome with joy), *from* (suffering from catarrh), *according to* (we fasted, according to family custom), or even *of* (died of grief) in English, and French prepositions, quite frequent in the sample, are at least equally capable of simple, naïve, almost invisible attribution of cause. As for participles and adjectives, they commonly are substituted for *because* plus clause in English (she tore a tendon lifting weights; discontent with my lot, I took to gambling) and for *parce que* plus clause in French, as the sample reveals.

Furthermore, whether we realize it or not, we express causation in certain expressions of degree (usually based upon *so . . . that*: so moved was he that he began to cry) which indicate that attainment of a vague threshold was a necessary condition of a triggered effect. With similar subtlety, causal expressions can be masked as spatial (e.g., in my office, no one shouts) or temporal (when I saw him, I blanched).

Finally, while narrators can impute causes explicitly with expressions such as *to blame it on* or *to put it down to*, they can also imply them by the mere juxtaposition of two logically related events, leaving out all causal vocabulary (parataxis). At times, *and* (*et*) may link such events (e.g., he tripped and fell), but causation remains implied. A special subcategory of causal parataxis operates in all reported conversations: even though there is seldom a lexical indication that one character's words come as the result of the preceding words or gesture of another, without a sign to the contrary it is obviously implied causality that forms the transitivity of reported dialogue. In his analysis of *Little Red Riding Hood*, Gerald Prince appears ambivalent on the matter; he notes a causal connective between the mother's command and Little Red Riding Hood's departure, as well as between two elements of the Wolf's dialogue with the grandmother,[9] but his transformational rules turn up no causal relationship between the Wolf's tap on the door and the grandmother's "Who is there?" Nor do they reveal one between elements of the famous dialogue of the Wolf and Red Riding Hood, such as "Grandmother, you have such big teeth!" and "It's to eat you!" Still, considering that answers presuppose questions, and that accusations, reflections, opinions (and knocks on doors) are encouragements, if not implied commands, to respond, readers are justified in finding a relationship of implication between elements of a dialogue. Since reported dialogue is, however, essentially an encoding of the *histoire* with little noticeable mediation by the narrator, this sort of parataxis provides implied causation coming from the inferred author, rather than from the narrator.

This rather tedious general survey has demonstrated, I hope, that language has resources for etiological expression far beyond those usually considered, and that all of them need to be taken into account in causal analysis of *récits*. When we do so for *L'Immoraliste* and *La Porte étroite*, striking differences begin to appear between the texts and between the two narrators, Michel and Jérôme.

The distinction is not to be found in the transitive verbs of modification (e.g., *avait aggravé* in "Mon deuil n'avait pas assombri, mais comme aggravé notre amour," [p. 515]; "My mourning had not darkened our love, but rendered it, as it were, more serious"), for language obliges both narrators to employ them, and they do so with nearly equal frequency. But when there is a choice, Michel expresses cause more frequently than Jérôme in those ways which are naïve, direct and straightforward. He selects causal *faire* ("to make" plus infinitive) more frequently, and causation surfaces far more often in his prepositions. This is particularly noteworthy with causal *de* (for which there is no consistent English equivalent; it is often translated *of*, *with*, or *from*), a simple and unobtrusive locution connecting effects to their causes almost as if the latter possessed the former. Since a certain effort is required to avoid use of this common connective, it is all the more significant that, in the sample for *La Porte étroite*, where Jérôme's prose predominates, only eight occurrences of causal *de* are from his pen, while 15 come from Alissa (letters and diary) and two from Abel. Michel, in the sample from "his" novel, uses the locution 42 times; Jérôme is obviously more wary of simple causal connectives than he—more even than Alissa. Michel also uses adjectives and participles in a causal sense more frequently than Jérôme, and he chooses many more causal nouns for the straightforward naming of motivations (*intention*, *résolution*, *sentiment*, *élan*, *influence*, *désir*), physical forces, and states of being which produce an effect. He employs the obvious ritual vocabulary of logical conclusion more often as well, and, perhaps less straightforwardly, he outdoes Jérôme in implying causation through standard parataxis. In general, then, Michel's tale is a series of events causally linked by their narrator.

But Jérôme surpasses Michel in four categories of causal expression. First, he uses a few more causal conjunctions than his counterpart (his numerical advantage here stems primarily from his more frequent use of *car*, which serves to introduce explanations after the fact). Then too, he predominates in his selection of more subtle causal expressions: those of degree (the vague causal "threshold") and those which mask causation as a merely temporal relationship. These techniques express causality while concealing it. Finally, far more conversational parataxis appears in the sample for *La Porte étroite*; the fact that Jérôme often quotes conversations verbatim underscores the importance for him of reporting (rather than interpreting) events. Jérôme-as-narrator is less a mediating presence in his tale than Michel in his, and when Jérôme does provide causal mediation he proffers it in the least apparent ways.

This comparison leads to an obvious conclusion. *L'Immoraliste* is an interpretive summary of events, mediated by Michel. It expresses causality more frequently than *La Porte étroite*, according to our sample, often choosing, when a choice exists, direct and naïve terms, as though cause and effect were elements of a single reality. *La Porte étroite* reports a series of events, but Jérôme, and to some extent Alissa as well, is less able or willing to infer causal relations among them. Here, we find a greater number of less forthright causal expressions—those especially of temporality—as if the narrator were consciously eluding the *post-hoc-propter-hoc* peril. The sample suggests that things happen more frequently across the subject-predicate relationship than in *L'Immoraliste* and that more verbatim replies are cited (conversational parataxis), so that causation subsists in the *histoire*, where it is the reader who must infer it, while fewer explanations of causality are provided on the level of the *récit*.

Michel, it must be remembered, is telling his story to intradiegetic narratees, friends to whom he has called out for help. It would seemingly be in his interest to bring them to understand his perception of the consequential nature of events in his life. Unless one believes that "one thing led to another," Michel's cruelty toward Marceline appears gratuitous and therefore all the more blameworthy. Furthermore, since Michel's oral tale has been enclosed in a letter, it must have been transcribed by someone (one of the narratees?), who could have (unwittingly?) selected certain causal terms. But for whom is Jérôme writing? For the general public? If he, like Michel, feels some guilt about the outcome, it would be important that the causes of that result remain hidden. Michel says, in essence, "Understand the causes of my reprehensible acts"; Jérôme might well be saying, "I caused nothing and am therefore not reprehensible." The relationship between narrator and narratee is thus in part defined by the use of causal vocabulary.

The subtle reduction in the special terminology of causal expression in *La Porte étroite* is often combined with the clustering of explanations around a particular event, so that the reader may know all the immediate causes of an action, as the narrator sees them, without being able to connect it to any other important action or to a causal chain.[10] The result is a partial loss of transitivity in the 1909 work, with a corresponding increase in Barthes's *scriptible*. At least three readings of the *histoire* of *La Porte étroite* seem pertinent to the data, and, with some exaggeration, may be summarized in this manner: (1) Alissa's puritanical, ascetic tendencies gradually destroy all hope of the earthly happiness which Jérôme seeks to offer her with his love;[11] (2) Jérôme—insensitive if not secretly sadistic—drives Alissa to her death by offering physical love on the one hand while constantly suggesting, on the other, that for Alissa to accept it would be a betrayal of religious principle and a debasement of herself;[12] (3) both Jérôme and Alissa entertain a Cornelian notion of honor or merit and institute if not a sadistic at least a "Cidistic" rivalry between them to determine which can become the more worthy of the other by exhibiting a greater capacity to sacrifice their earthly relationship,[13] a little game Alissa wins hands down—by dying. The existence of a plurality of readings would seem to leave us without a positive ethical clue: if, as Gide suggested,[14] this is an ironical and critical work like *L'Immoraliste*, what sort of conduct is criticized?

The fact that Gide stressed the similarity of these two texts, even calling them "twin" works,[15] that he seems to have taken pains to construct them in parallel, invites a structuralist reading: perhaps if taken together the works affirm something they cannot declare singly. If the timelines of the two *récits* are juxtaposed, the principal common features become apparent, revealing in their very similarity the nature of the essential differences. Each narrator chooses his father's death as a starting point; each presents three crises capable of influencing the course of his life; and each provides a thrice-repeated testing event, three similar occurrences which allow us to judge the progress of the changes taking place in the characters. In both stories, these features occur in the same order (father's death, first crisis, first test, second crisis, second test, third test, third crisis), and with nearly equivalent spacing along both timelines. Comparison and contrast of these features reveal the role of causal links in determining the function of specific narrative sequences.

In Michel's story, the narrator marks causal connections between major events. For this reason, his father's death constitutes a true beginning: obedience to his father's deathbed wish leads him to marry Marceline and thus gives rise to the central moral question of the tale; an inheritance from his father brings Michel La Morinière and other possessions, which will serve as touchstones to his attitude toward property and liberty throughout the story. On the other hand, although Jérôme indicates three times that his *histoire* begins with his father's demise (pp. 495, 497), this death has little direct bearing on subsequent events. Jérôme appears to suggest two reasons for seeing it as a beginning. First, he alludes to his new awareness, at this date, that he and Alissa were no longer children, with a hint that "perhaps" the sight of his mother's grief might have precociously awakened his sexuality. Here, we may either score one point for those who see in Jérôme a sadist, or we may question the explanation on grounds of our own experience, on the belief for example that biological processes and not periods of mourning determine the onset of puberty. The use of the dubitative "peut-être" ("perhaps"), not unusual in Jérôme's style, undermines the assertion of causation and encourages our questioning. In the second place, Jérôme points to his father's death as a beginning because it allows Lucile to demonstrate her character by failing to remain in mourning, yet this is an obvious artifice: Lucile will show far greater resources for illustrating her individuality. Thus, Jérôme's explanations—ever so cautiously expressed and patently incomplete—begin to subvert our confidence in the causal bond between events; while the death of Michel's father starts a true chain reaction, Jérôme's loss remains a vaguely associated early memory without recognizable consequences.

Both *histoires* show further similarity in the presentation of three crises. The first appears to determine the basic direction of the tales, since both narrators make "resolutions" about the course of their conduct immediately thereafter. The second seems to be a turning point, occurring near the midpoint of the texts and marked as similar by the proximity of Christmas in both narratives. The third is ostensibly the tragic outcome: a woman's death. But if these crises are indeed what they seem in *L'Immoraliste*, they are something quite different in *La Porte étroite*, because of breaks in the causal chain of the *récit*.

Michel's initial crisis is carefully prepared: his weak constitution—further enfeebled by precocious adoption of a sedentary life, debilitated again by mourning for his father, the excitement of a wedding, and the fatigue of the honeymoon trip, and finally assailed by the chill of the African night—is an obvious receptacle for that "initial stative event" which is the presence of the bacillus in his lungs. On the verge of death, Michel faces his first crucial moment, and the results are stated as explicitly as the causes: on the one hand, desire to get well leads to self-discipline in diet and exercise, tending to fortify the body, while on the other, preoccupation with his own corporality brings Michel to discover the "old man" within him.

But such precise causes and effects do not surround Lucile Bucolin's flight, the initial crisis evoked by Jérôme. We are not even told why Lucile leaves hearth and home. Jérôme's portrayal of her as evilly sensual depends in part on our acceptance of the righteousness of his point of view. When, for example, she tickled him under his blouse, to his great embarrassment, was she wantonly arousing an adolescent, or did she believe she was playing with a cute little boy in a sailor suit? The narrator's vagueness about dates makes it difficult to guess. She received a lieutenant in her room, without her husband's knowledge according to Alissa, but still in the presence of her two younger children, a procedure seldom recommended for those seeking to preserve secrecy. [16] She suffered from apparently neurotic "crises," which Jérôme's mother believed to be feigned (p. 501), although the reason for play-acting is difficult to discover; they are hardly a "cover" for a love affair, since they seem to require the presence of her husband, not his absence. Perhaps they (and even the lieutenant's playful visits) are intended to break what might have been for her the monotony of her Bucolin existence, although objective certainty is impossible. That she eventually leaves home is, of course, a fictional reality, but the reasons are surprisingly obscure. When Jérôme asks if she had left "with someone," Miss Ashburton replies: "Mon enfant, tu demanderas cela à ta mère; moi je ne peux rien te répondre" (p. 504); "Ask your mother, child; *I* can't give you any answer." The first clause smacks of the traditional evasion for a child, but the second is ambiguous: indeed it does seem unlikely that she could provide information on this subject on the mere basis of the telegram from Le Havre. Since Jérôme makes it a point never to ask his mother, we cannot know. Departure with a lover is plausible, but so is flight to escape the insidious boredom of Le Havre and Fongueusemare, or even to avoid recrimination, now that the secret is out (p. 504) of the possibly unadulterous but surely suspicious rendezvous. Considering the ease with which we could have been informed of Lucile's purposes and ultimate fate—two or three well-placed words would have left no doubts—one begins to suspect that there is conscious suppression of causal connectives. Scarcely clearer is the effect of the desertion on the protagonists, for Jérôme seldom mentions Lucile in what follows. Alissa appears conscious of her father's suffering, and she seems to fear that her own nature is contaminated with her mother's sensuality (pp. 585–86). Still, causation is not explicit. Nor is it suggested (indeed there is a hint to the contrary) that such a fear would of itself suffice to make Alissa refuse Jérôme's repeated proposal of marriage.

These crises lead directly, in both works, to the formulation of resolutions by the narrators. Michel declares, "I had made resolutions" (p. 384, "j'avais pris des résolutions"), and we are told precisely what they are: deep breathing, exercise, proper diet. After the account of the "strait gate" sermon, Jérôme too uses the word "résolutions," surrounded by a cluster of causal vocabulary of extraordinary density:

> J'étais parvenu vers la fin du sermon à un tel état de tension morale que, sitôt le culte fini, je m'enfuis sans chercher à voir ma cousine— par fierté, voulant déjà mettre mes résolutions (car j'en avais pris) à l'épreuve, et pensant la mieux mériter en m'éloignant d'elle [aus]- sitôt. (P. 506)

> (I had reached such a state of moral tension toward the end of the sermon that, as soon as the service was over, I fled without seeking to see my cousin—out of pride, already desirous of putting my resolutions [for I had made some] to the test, and believing I became more worthy of her by distancing myself from her at once.)

Seldom have so many reasons explained so little. The parenthetical "car," for example, calls our attention to the resolutions, but gives such a literal-minded cause as to be virtually redundant. All the causes alleged (threshold of moral tension, resolutions, pride, desire for a test of strength, belief that immediate separation is a means to worthiness) tend to explain the individual act of leaving the church without a word to Alissa, but they leave us in the dark as to the nature of the continuing resolutions. We are thus impelled to determine the nature of these vows inductively; we may note perhaps that long separations characterize the relationship of these lovers, and that poor verbal communication is typical of their moments together. We may suppose as a result that Jérôme has resolved to deserve Alissa more by communicating with her less. Whether such a reading is accurate or not, the essential notion is that we must read *La Porte étroite* inductively on this question, while we can follow Michel's conduct deductively, watching his theory become its application. Michel provides satisfactory explanations of direct causation, while causes are so diffuse in Jérôme's *récit* as to drive the reader to attempt his own causal analysis of the *histoire*. Jérôme's clustered causal vocabulary, "explaining" the immediate at the expense of the long term, subverts our belief in his perception and reporting of the causal relationship: where causal terms abound and yet provide no answers to the fundamental questions, we can entertain doubts about their worth.

Further on, both works evoke a Christmastime crisis. Marceline loses her baby, with phlebitic complications leading to cardiac and pulmonary embolisms (pp. 437–39). This major turn of events is carefully prepared, with credible medical data linking each illness to the preceding one. The source of the initial fever is unexplained, like the source of Michel's tuberculosis; the prescription of quinine for it might suggest a late-appearing malaria, perhaps contracted in North Africa, an interesting idea symbolically, but quite inductive. Still, from the fever on, the causal chain is clearly marked, as Marceline becomes, for her husband, "une chose abîmée"—"damaged goods." In *La Porte étroite*, Juliette's traumatic engagement to Teissières, beside Aunt Plantier's Christmas tree, is well explained in terms of immediate causes (Abel adduces them for us, pp. 537, 539), but major questions remain. Has Jérôme, knowingly or unwittingly, encouraged Juliette's love for him? Why does he make no attempt to prevent the engagement when Alissa begs him to, even though he says he would have "given his life" to ease Alissa's anguish at this moment? Even if, to explain such things, we attribute to Jérôme a blind and bungling nature, there is no easy way to connect this incident to what follows. Its consequences seem to melt away; Juliette's sacrificial marriage becomes a normal and rather happy one; Alissa, freed at last to marry Jérôme, continues to refuse just as before, so that the story of Juliette appears as an episode, with roots and branches barely touching the central, Jérôme-Alissa relationship. Connections may be induced (did Juliette's capacity for self-sacrifice spur Alissa on to greater abnegation?), but the explicit causal links, of the sort we find in *L'Immoraliste*, are absent.[17]

The same contrast is apparent in the death that ends each story. The succession of carefully interconnected maladies that weaken Marceline, and Michel's all too well-considered conduct that brings her to her grave, are clearly set forth in Michel's narrative, with more than sufficient causal vocabulary to justify the word "crime" (p. 471). The cause of Alissa's death, however, must be inferred, and the wealth of evidence provided makes inference difficult rather than easy. We have Jérôme's declaration that, when he last saw her, less than a month before her death, she was alarmingly pale and thin (p. 579). We have Juliette's opinion that Alissa, without being precisely ill, was simply dying away. We have medical opinion, from

Dr. A… in Le Havre, that there was nothing seriously wrong with her, and, from Alissa's Parisian doctor, that she needed an operation (p. 593). We also have Alissa's conduct (flight to Paris carefully incognito, unwillingness to see the doctor there, ruse to delay the operation) and her symptoms (consciousness that death was near, vomiting, weakness). Is this death from a broken heart? Novels evoking such things seldom list vomiting as a symptom, and operations are rarely prescribed. Can it be death from self-abnegation, including perhaps starvation? That might not be inconsistent with Alissa's secretive flight from Le Havre, where she was known, but the prescribed operation scarcely fits that diagnosis. Why not cancer?[18] That disease fits all our information rather well, except for poor Dr. A…'s opinion. If we allow ourselves some skepticism about provincial doctors of the period, cancer, with Alissa seeking to avoid treatment and thus collaborating (for reasons of self-abnegation, or out of despair?) in her own death, fits everything, except her age—and the rest of the book. If Alissa is one of those rare individuals to be stricken with cancer in their early twenties, at a time when cancer was virtually incurable, it makes little sense, whether she avoids treatment or not, to suggest she died of excessive asceticism, or that Jérôme killed her. Her death, if from cancer, is simply absurd, without direct causal connection to any other element of the work. The narrator of *Le Rouge et le noir* states no cause for Madame de Rênal's death either, at the close of his *récit*, but readers can readily intuit one from the *histoire*. Where inductive analysis of the *histoire* leads to nothing but further disconnections, we are clearly in a different sort of fictional world.

Finally, in both Gidean tales, the narrator provides a repeated event (the first occurrence falling before the Christmas crisis) which serves as a test of progression, much as a chemist might test the progress of a complex chemical reaction at intermediate stages, to ascertain whether the expected transformations are taking place. In *L'Immoraliste*, the tests are purely anecdotal and as much exterior to the causal chain as litmus paper is to a chemical solution. Three times (pp. 404, 445, 462)[19] unruly drivers appear, testing the progress of Michel's growing "immoralism" by the protagonist's reaction to them (first: violent rage; second: curiosity; third: complicity). The test for progress in *La Porte étroite* is Jérôme's repeated proposal of marriage to Alissa, which recurs in the timeline with a rhythm analogous to Michel's unruly drivers (pp. 521, 563, 578). No anecdote this, for Jérôme is asking a question that has become uppermost in readers' minds. With the weakening of the linear causal chain, repetition, rather than causality, begins to carry the narrative. Reversal, of course, does not occur: Alissa's answer is always "no." Jérôme makes no progress toward the altar, if indeed that was where he sought to go.

The presence in the narrative of Alissa's point of view can give us few additional certainties. One can scarcely imagine a less rectilinear mode for the presentation of her version of events than the few selected letters we are allowed to read, than the fragmentary entries of her partially destroyed journal—and she is nearly as cautious as Jérôme with causal terms. Indeed, in this ill-joined world, there would be some impertinence in asking why Lucile flees, or from what Alissa dies, in invoking thus expectations which are exterior to the story, were it not for *L'Immoraliste*, which, between analogous structural building blocks, supplies the mortar[20] and fulfills the expectations. Comparative reading shows a weakening of causal connections from *L'Immoraliste* to *La Porte étroite*, with resultant opening of the second work to multiple interpretations and a corresponding reduction of useful didactic content.

At the very heart of his tale, Michel provides us with a paradigm of it, in his summary of his first Parisian lecture (p. 424). Replete with causal connectives, this passage explains how Culture, a spontaneous product of human life, in order to perpetuate itself becomes restrictive and thus destructive of life. Likewise, Michel's personal liberation—rising spontaneously from his instinctive being—when it is transformed into a course of conduct with rules necessary to keep it intact, becomes destructive of life and of the vital nature from which it springs: "l'ardu, c'est savoir être libre," (p. 372); "the hard part is managing to live free." The implication is that, if anyone seeks liberty, as Michel does, it will be impossible to maintain it, for the price of maintenance is loss of liberty. The possibility of such a paradigm and of its moral implications rests firmly on the underlying causal links. As Michel's lecture was didactic, so is his tale.

Obviously, one might suggest as well that Alissa's perseverance in pursuit of virtue contains in similar fashion the seeds of its own destruction, for the quest for moral perfection removes us unvirtuously ever farther from our ordinary fellow mortals. Thus perseverance in a single direction might be the moral evil denounced in both stories. Yet, in *La Porte étroite*, perseverance loses its essential aspect: continuity. Is it pursuit of virtue, flight from sensuality, a contest with Jérôme, or now one, now another? The second work seems, in its mode of narration, to sacrifice didactic certainty to the beauty and interest of a less predictable world. Because of this very unpredictability, Jérôme and Alissa appear somehow sadly freer to be them-selves, to evade responsibility for each other's earthly happiness. Certainly the didactic and critical sense of the two works taken together includes the notion that real freedom, unfortunately, springs less from the rebellious gesture than from one's outlook, from a world view in which events have no simple, deterministic, causal relationships. And herein lies the irony of our two texts: it is *L'Immoraliste* that provides the strait gate, through which readers must pass in the single file of general exegetic agreement, while *La Porte étroite* opens the spacious road of multiple interpretations. Indeed, as the paucity of replicable causation tends to destroy its potential for moral instruction, the 1909 work becomes the truly "immoralistic" one.

Causal expression, in its presence or its absence, is the basic metonymic structure of these stories, as of nearly all narrative fiction, essential not only to the intelligence of the themes, but also to the reader's manipulation of the story. The optional expression of causation sets the narrator apart from the inferred author. It is a touchstone by which the reader determines the narrator's credibility—a trait far more important than narrator "person-ality" (neither Michel nor Jérôme is especially likable or admirable) in establishing the reader's involvement with the narrator. It provides a system of links and gaps, which readers use in the mental (re)creation of the narrative. The links may be plausible or implausible, strong (providing desired explanation) or weak (offering unneeded or useless explanations). When weak links are numerous, readers may suspect the narrator of sub-verting causality to his own ends, of creating a "cover up." Gaps in the causal chain send readers back to the inferred author, to seek to infer causes for themselves from the basic "facts" of the *histoire*, just as unsatisfactory links do. In either case, the reader will try to fill the gaps or strengthen the links, creating as she or he does so a personal mental *récit*, in competition with that of the narrator. As biological cells have exterior receptors for bonding with other organisms, so the gaps in the chain of causality bond the reader to the tale.[21]

One might suspect as well that causality and its expression could change from decade to decade, that causal analysis might yield diachronic results of interest. Gide seems to be balancing on a tightrope between a world of clear causes and effects and a more modern, more absurd, world, in which credible explanations are harder to come by. On the one hand he gives us the causally plausible *Immoraliste*, and much later the equally direct causality of *Thésée* (1944); on the other, with *La Porte étroite*, we find the ambiguous *Faux-monnayeurs*, and the all too explicit *Caves du Vatican*, where simplistic causality is ironically reinstated, only to self destruct.[22] A look backward to a simpler time of more naïve faith in causation, before Nietzsche's message had begun to sink in, may illuminate the pre-Gidean world and provide contrast with the post-Gidean outlook. We return, then, to the "scientific" causation of Emile Zola (to which the word "naïve" is not always applicable!), before observing more recent texts.

Notes

This chapter is a revised version of an article of mine which appeared under the title "Gidean Causality: *L'Immoraliste* and *La Porte étroite*," in *Symposium*, 31, 1 (Spring 1977), 43–58. Reprinted with permission of the Helen Dwight Reid Educational Foundation. Published by Heldref Publications, 4000 Albemarle St., N.W., Washington, D.C. 20016. Copyright © 1977.

1. See the Introduction, above.

2. André Gide, "Faits divers," *Nouvelle Revue Française*, 30 (1er juin 1928), 841–42.

3. Reported by Gide in his *Journal 1889–1939* (Paris: Gallimard, Pléiade, 1951), p. 134.

4. John C. Davies, *Gide: L'Immoraliste and La Porte étroite* (London: Edward Arnold, 1968), p. 56.

5. Jean-Jacques Thierry, in André Gide, *Romans, récits et soties, oeuvres lyriques* (Paris: Gallimard, Pléiade, 1958), p. 1515. Subsequent parenthetical references in the text are to this volume.

6. On the symbolic and indexic qualities, in Peircian terms, of the first-person pronoun, see Roman Jakobson, *Essais de linguistique générale*, tr. Nicolas Ruwet (Paris: Editions de Minuit, 1963), pp. 178–80.

7. On the *post-hoc-propter-hoc* problem in narrative analysis and on the relationship of implication, see Claude Bremond, *Logique du récit* (Paris: Editions du Seuil, 1973), pp. 122–25.

8. Albert Michotte *et al.*, *Causalité, permanence et réalité phénoménales* (Louvain: Publications Universitaires, 1962), pp. 16, 19. Michotte concludes that the notion of physical causality is a human structural organization, an "impression" of the general unity of two distinct movements, p. 116.

9. Gerald Prince, *A Grammar of Stories* (The Hague: Mouton, 1973), pp. 84–95.

10. On clustering, see Prince, pp. 48–49.

11. Justin O'Brien, *Portrait of André Gide* (New York: Alfred A. Knopf, 1953), pp. 216–20, bases an interpretation of this sort on Gide's own statements about the work; see also Harold March, *Gide and the Hound of Heaven* (Philadelphia: University of Pennsylvania Press, 1952), pp. 152–57; Germaine Brée, *Gide* (New Brunswick: Rutgers University Press, 1963), pp. 159–62; Davies, *op. cit.*, pp. 30–31. Elaine Concalon's Greimasian reading tends in the same direction, but it requires us to intuit a God as *Destinateur* in the work, and victory of Alissa, freed to devote herself to virtue, over Jérôme, whose life is "entirely destroyed," *Modern Language Notes*, 90, 4 (May 1975), 590–96.

12. A subtle and convincing reading, which concludes that "Jérôme kills Alissa as surely as Michel kills Marceline," is that of Loring D. Knecht, "A New Reading of Gide's *La Porte étroite*," *PMLA*, 82, 7 (December 1967), 640–48.

13. Gide has referred to the error of "gratuitous Cornelianism" which this work illustrates: Paul Claudel and André Gide, *Correspondance, 1899–1926* (Paris: Gallimard, 1949), pp. 103–4.

14. Gide, *Journal*, pp. 428–29.

15. Gide, *Journal*, pp. 365–66.

16. The lieutenant is absent from the more autobiographical version of the same scene in *Si le grain ne meurt* . . . : André Gide, *Oeuvres complètes*, 10 (Paris: Gallimard, 1936), 162–63.

17. Gide seems to be aware of it, for he explained to Claudel that he indeed wished Alissa's drama to unfold without exterior constraints, but that Lucile's "fault" and the Juliette plot were necessary to provide some humanizing motivation: *Correspondance*, p. 104.

18. Although my conclusions are based solely on the text, it is possible that Gide drew Alissa's solitary death from his experience with Anna Shackleton's, following her tumor operation: see Gide, *Oeuvres complètes*, 10, 278.

19. Davies, p. 34, notes the testing function, but cites only the first and third occurrences. See also Henri Maillet, *L'Immoraliste d'André Gide* (Paris: Hachette, 1972), pp. 43–47.

20. Gide uses similar metaphors (*Journal*, pp. 276, 387) in reference to Jérôme's prose, which he calls the *mastic* or *rejointement* for the passages by Alissa. He finds this mortar limp ("flasque") and not without *préciosité*.

21. On the relationship of the reader to gaps and indeterminacies in fictional texts, see Wolfgang Iser, *The Act of Reading* (Baltimore: Johns Hopkins University Press, 1978), pp. 47–48, 168–75.

22. John McClelland, "The Lexicon of *Les Caves du Vatican*," *PMLA*, 89, 2 (March 1974), 261.

3

Causal Options in
Histoire and *Narration*:
Zola's *L'Assommoir*

On voit également que cette description du discours s'oppose à l'histoire de la pensée. Là encore, on ne peut reconstituer un système de pensée qu'à partir d'un ensemble défini de discours. Mais cet ensemble est traité de telle manière qu'on essaie de retrouver par-delà les énoncés eux-mêmes l'intention du sujet parlant, son activité consciente, ce qu'il a voulu dire, ou encore le jeu inconscient qui s'est fait jour malgré lui dans ce qu'il a dit ou dans la presque imperceptible cassure de ses paroles manifestes. . . .

(It is also apparent that this description of discourse works against the history of thought. There again, a system of thought can be reconstituted only on the basis of a defined total body of discourse. But that body is so treated that we try to rediscover, behind the utterances themselves, the intention of the speaking subject, his conscious activity, what he meant to say, or also the subconscious interplay that came to light in spite of him in what he said or in the almost imperceptible crack in his actual words. . . .)

—MICHEL FOUCAULT

If Gide is capable of having his narrators muddy the causal waters by selective use of specific vocabulary, surely Zola, with his penchant for impartial narrators ("le romancier n'est plus qu'un greffier qui se défend de juger et de conclure"—"nowadays the novelist is merely a scribe, who refuses to judge and to conclude")[1] and for mechanistic determinism ("Un même déterminisme doit régir la pierre des chemins et la cerveau de l'homme"—"One same determinism must govern the stone in the road and the brain of man"),[2] will give us a measure of how clear and direct causal chains can be. One senses that rigorous causal laws are at work in his novels, as R.-M. Albérès declares in his introduction to the *Oeuvres complètes* edition of *L'Assommoir*; he finds that our greatest pleasure in rereading *L'Assommoir* is in entering a literary world with its own laws, and he adds:

La loi naturelle y est dure, la loi sociale y est cruelle, la psychologie y est conditionnée et laisse peu de place à la liberté ou même à la responsabilité. Mais ce n'est pas un monde sans lois. Ce monde est atroce, non pas un monde absurde. Zola est l'anti-Gide. . . .[3]

(In this world natural law is hard, social law is cruel, psychology is conditioned, leaving little room for freedom or even for responsibility. But it is not a lawless world. It is an atrocious world, but not an absurd world. Zola is the anti-Gide. . . .)

The atrociously lawful world of *L'Assommoir*, and its language, will serve well as our points of departure in search of pre-Gidean causal contrasts. And perhaps *La Bête humaine*, in which certain events appear to determine others with a rigor like that of the railroad tracks leading trains from Le Havre to Paris, is one of the best examples in all Zola of causal exigency: a trip down its ineluctible rails will provide, in chapter four, another, quite different view of Zola's deterministic landscape.

Yet neither work is wholly deterministic. If the extradiegetic narrators are relatively objective in their causal judgments (and even there one may find room for argument), the inferred authors leave gaps and weaknesses in the causal chains of the *histoires* themselves, especially in *L'Assommoir*, through which critical questions can arise. Students of naturalism have long been pointing out that there are (at least) two Zolas—one "scientific," a believer in deterministic causality, and the other mythic, if not mystic.[4] A glance, for example, at *La Faute de l'abbé Mouret*, in which myth absolutely overwhelms *mimesis*, is all it takes to find the eternal behind the linearly temporal. It lurks as well behind the "cracks" in the causal strands of *L'Assommoir*. And, while its plot is bonded by physical causation, *La Bête humaine* raises cogent, rational doubts about our ability to observe causes. The differences we will uncover with respect to Gide are therefore less likely to reveal bipolar opposition (presence/absence of causation) than differences of degree, differences of kind, and differences of the position of the reader in relation to both *histoire* and *récit*.

The narrator of *L'Assommoir* (written in 1875–76, first published in serial form in 1876–77) exhibits bourgeois prejudices, notably with regard to the supposed improvidence and laziness of the poor, which critics have not hesitated to attribute to Zola himself.[5] Yet the narrator is not Zola, not only for the obvious ontological reasons, but for linguistic ones: he lapses (or rises), with disconcerting frequency, into the vernacular of the working class.[6] He also slips with ease into free indirect discourse and out of it, so that it can be difficult to judge whether the language of the underclass is defining him or some character on the scene. Gervaise is planning her saint's-day banquet:

> Cette année-là, un mois à l'avance, on causa de la fête. On cherchait des plats, s'en léchait les lèvres. Toute la boutique avait une sacrée envie de nocer. Il fallait une rigolade à la mort, quelque chose de pas ordinaire et de réussi. (P. 750)

> (That year, for a month in advance, they talked about the feast. They looked for recipes and licked their chops over them. The whole shop was damn well ready for a high old time. They needed to laugh till their sides split—not your ordinary party, but one that really came off.)

The narrator speaks, but he just might be rendering in her words the thoughts of some laundress in the shop. Later on, the narrator describes the party:

> Et le vin donc, mes enfants! ça coulait de la table comme l'eau coule à la Seine. Un vrai ruisseau, lorsqu'il a plu et que la terre a soif. Coupeau versait de haut, pour voir le jet rouge écumer; et quand un litre était vide, il faisait la blague de retourner le goulet et de le presser, du geste familier aux femmes qui traient les vaches. Encore une négresse qui avait la gueule cassée! (P. 767)

> (And what about the wine, kids!—flowing on the table like water in the Seine. A real stream, after a rain, when the land is thirsty. Coupeau poured from high up, to watch the red jet foam, and when a liter was empty, he clowned around, holding the bottle upside down and squeezing the neck, like a milkmaid squeezing a cow's teat. One more dead Indian!)

The potentially thirsty earth sounds like a narrator's image, but the rest seems to echo the thoughts of some half-inebriated guest. On the one hand the indeterminacy of the narrative voice, and on the other its identification with the laboring class it describes, tend to create some doubt as to the reliability of the causal data it provides. Without calling into question the narrator's desire for objectivity, one may entertain questions about his ability to understand the forces at work. If he is identified, by his language, as a member of the working class, he may be limited to a working-class viewpoint. This notion in no way contradicts his apparent addiction to bourgeois stereotypes of the poor, for the novel also suggests that members of the underclass have readily accepted certain middle-class attitudes, as we shall see. The integration of the narrator into the class he describes tends to reinforce the idea that the poor have assimilated a low opinion of themselves; it also makes the narrator more nearly intradiegetic, like Gide's. And, as with Gide,[7] when readers can begin to suspect that their interpretation of events might not coincide with the narrator's, the inferred author and the *histoire* gain increased influence over the nature of the interpretation.

Appendix B is intended to facilitate further general comparison with Gide on the level of the *récit*. Most obviously, with respect to the percentage of occurrences of causal expressions, the two samples look remarkably alike; linguistic similarities far outweigh the differences. Zola's narrator does appear proportionately less wary in the use of causal conjunctions. Furthermore, he and (other) speaking characters mask causality in temporal terms even more than do Gide's. Coupeau brings Lantier home to Gervaise, for example, and little Etienne recognizes his long-lost father: "quand il aperçut Lantier, il resta tremblant et gêné," (p. 783); "when he caught sight of Lantier, he stood there trembling and embarrassed." Clearly the sight of Lantier is the cause of the trembling and embarrassment. But this construction may be less an effort to obscure causality than to reproduce the patterns of everyday speech, in a novel in which the working-class idiom predominates. In that sense, the "when" is to be read literally, and the reader is presumed to catch the causal undertones, almost as if by parataxis. Indeed, the relatively frequent use of parataxis in *L'Assommoir* suggests a kind of causal innuendo not uncommon in ordinary oral communication. Perhaps the most striking difference, though, between the Gide and Zola samples lies in the percentage of verbs used to express causation. The narrator of *L'Assommoir* contrives to use relatively fewer "verbs of transitivity," in which the subject affects a change in the predicate through an action, as well as fewer special verbs of causation. This is not without importance, for it seems attributable to his penchant for "describing" actions instead of "narrating" them (see the quotation from the banquet scene, above), relying heavily on the imperfect tense, expressing tendencies rather than precise effects. Even passages of detailed narration (and they are far from rare) tend to exist somewhat in isolation, without narrative links between them. The relatively elevated percentage for conversational parataxis in the *Assommoir* sample (actually, it is only slightly higher than the percentage for *La*

Porte étroite, although noticeably greater than for the Gide sample as a whole) may stem from the same phenomenon: we read individual scenes in detail, with verbatim reports of conversation, although narrative connections between scenes may be reduced or eliminated.

Behind this sort of fragmentation in the *récit*, the *histoire* follows a simple curve, as it traces the rise of Gervaise Macquart (from urban poor, to labor, to skilled labor, to the lower fringes of the *petite bourgeoisie*, as she marries and acquires her own laundry business), and her decline (downward again to urban poor, to slow starvation, begging and soliciting, to death apparently from hunger and exposure). If Gervaise's pitiable end is to be seen as the result of the working of inexorable laws, we should be able to trace the chain of causes and effects leading to her downfall. R.-M. Albérès makes much of the initial event (Gervaise's abandonment by Lantier) as a mark of her predestination, of her ill-starred inner destiny ("fatalité intérieure," p. 592). In what follows, then, we will examine the nature and expression of causation in this initial event; next, we will analyse the expressed and the inferable causal factors in Gervaise's downward slide, and finally we will note the remarkable reversal that links the initial events (through Gervaise's humiliation of Virginie) to our heroine's final degradation (humiliation by Virginie). Causation is far more markedly in operation here than in *La Porte étroite*, but it is at times less mechanical in nature than one might suspect.

1. *The initial event*. The proximate causes of Lantier's departure are manifest: his bad character, financial difficulties, and the absence of a marriage contract to bind him to Gervaise. We have ample evidence of his unsavory traits at the outset: he spends the night with Adèle, leaving Gervaise to worry at home; when he returns, he upbraids her just as brutally for her loving remarks as for her sarcasm, chiding her as well for her supposed failure to keep her person and their dingy lodging clean; he forces his "wife" to pawn some of her belongings, pocketing the cash himself to hire the carriage that will transport his own possessions as he abandons Gervaise for Adèle. The financial difficulties are apparent in the ugly confrontation over the pawning of Gervaise's clothes: this is obviously not the first dispute on the subject. Adèle has a steady income (from a factory job as a "burnisher"), possibly augmented by prostitution; since Lantier appears both selfish and unwilling to work, life with Adèle could be tempting for financial reasons. But how do such causes predestine Gervaise?

Lantier's departure leaves Gervaise penniless with Claude and Etienne to raise, but she will manage remarkably well, finding work as a laundress, earning promotions, marrying Coupeau, who has a steady income as a roofer, and finally starting her own—initially successful—laundry business: being free of Lantier seems, if anything, beneficial. Yet Albérès notes, of the initial incident, that something or other tells us that she is doomed ("Un je-ne-sais-quoi nous avertit qu'elle est perdue," p. 592). One might look for it in the fatal stupidity or weakness which caused her to move in with Lantier in the first place. But she has been with him some nine years (Claude is eight), and, if the relationship were inevitably destructive, the destruction ought to have occurred before this. Furthermore, Lantier had rescued her from her abusive father in the provinces and had brought her to Paris as soon as he could afford to, sharing with her his meager inheritance. She accuses him of having squandered it (pp. 606, 612), but he reminds her, "Tu as croqué le magot avec moi" ("you shot the wad with me"), and she admits to having enjoyed theater, dinners, cabs, and good clothes upon their arrival in Paris. Now the money is gone, and she will have to work in any case; Lantier's departure leaves her with three mouths to feed instead of four.

The evidence presented concerning initial causes is of two sorts: narrated scenes and conversations, including Gervaise's confidences to Mme Boche. In neither case is causation unequivocally noted: the reader must seek to determine the facts by inference (does Lantier leave in part because Gervaise is really dirty, or is his insult gratuitous cruelty?), or take the word of Gervaise, a fallible character with manifest self-interest in the way she describes the situation to a friend. Gervaise herself is obviously surprised and uncomprehending when told that Lantier has moved out (p. 616); if she fails to perceive her abandonment as probable or inevitable, the reader is scarcely a more privileged judge of the forces at work.

In at least one instance, narrator and conversation are in disagreement about cause. Gervaise weeps when she learns that Lantier has abandoned her. Mme Boche sees the tears as possibly shed for a lost love: "Est-il possible de se faire tant de mal pour un homme! . . . Vous l'aimez donc toujours, hein? ma pauvre chérie" (pp. 616–17); "How can you go through such agony over a man! . . . So you still love him, huh? poor dear." If the "donc" denotes a conclusion based on evidence, the "hein?" suggests a hint of doubt. The narrator sounds more confident of his opinion:

> Le souvenir de sa course au mont-de-piété, en précisant un fait de la matinée, lui avait arraché les sanglots qui s'étranglaient dans sa gorge. Cette course-là, c'était une abomination, la grosse douleur dans son désespoir. (P. 616)

(The memory of her trip to the pawn shop, bringing to mind one of that morning's specific events, had torn loose the sobs that were choking in her throat. That errand was an abomination, the greatest pain in her despair.)

Humiliation might well be, in context, a more accurate statement of the cause of the tears (Gervaise herself had just spoken of it) than love. Yet the fact that Gervaise will later take her lover back suggests that Mme Boche may not be totally in error. In this work, such little ambiguities abound, little gaps through which the reader enters the work.

If we are to see Gervaise as predestined in this initial event to a life of suffering, our belief will have to spring not entirely from the text but from our own experience. We may believe, for example, that Paris is no place for a poor, uneducated country girl, that it is the "Sin-City" atmosphere of the metropolis that led the couple astray, destroying an otherwise happy union, or that the experience of sudden "wealth," followed by a return to poverty, is destructive of character. The narrator says nothing about what *fatalité* caused the separation after nine years of union; the inferred author simply thrusts Lantier and Gervaise onto the scene in parallel to thousands of other provincials arriving in Paris with a little money in their pockets, or rather, in parallel to prevailing beliefs about what happens to such *déracinés*— the "uprooted" country folk. If we are on our own in search of general causes, we will not retain the freedom to interpret we found in *La Porte étroite*; for there is a myth of underclass Paris at work in the text, and more personal myths as well, that will gradually limit our freedom of interpretation. But at this point already, Albérès's "something or other," his "je-ne-sais-quoi," is not in the text, but in reader interaction with the text.

2. *The "inevitable" decline.* The narrator seems to recognize the beginning of the fall in a scene (p. 710) which occurs while the laundry is still prosperous; great heaps of dirty petticoats and blouses cover the floor, while Gervaise's crew of laundresses work away at ironing on a large table. Coupeau returns home in an inebriated state, and, lurching forward to embrace his wife, falls face down in the soiled clothes. Gervaise helps her husband to rise, offering her cheek to be kissed, but he seizes her breasts, under the amused eyes of her workers, then kisses her passionately on the lips, as she abandons herself to his ardor. The narrator observes:

. . . le gros baiser qu'ils échangèrent à pleine bouche, au milieu des saletés du métier, était comme une première chute, dans le lent avachissement de leur vie.

(. . . the big, full-mouth kiss they exchanged, in the midst of the filth of her trade, was like a first fall, in the gradually increasing slovenliness of their life.)

Like many French nouns ending in *-ment*, "avachissement," with its connotations of debilitation, softening, loss of moral fiber, is the name of a result, but it also appears to be the immediate cause of Gervaise's fatal decline: a general lowering of the standards of quality in the laundry's work (leading to a loss of clientèle and the eventual collapse of the enterprise), disappearance of self-discipline in Gervaise (splurging, nonpayment of debts, self-gratification, inability to resist Lantier's advances when he returns), and loss of pride (increased willingness to accept degradation and humiliation without a fight, a growing desire to die). Thus the stylistically enhanced significance of "avachissement," here used as a name of both a cause and an effect, seems to make of it a causal link between the first third of the novel and the decline that follows.

But the early chapters hardly suggest the onset of any moral decay within Gervaise. She rises by hard and conscientious labor from the straits in which Lantier leaves her. She resists Coupeau's initial propositions and agrees to live with him only after marriage. In marrying him, she selects a hard-working, relatively well-paid skilled laborer, dependable and opposed to the use of alcohol; his income plus hers will provide an almost comfortable living for them and her two children. Residing now in a slightly more prosperous *quartier*, she wins the respect of her neighbor, Mme Goujet, and the tender admiration-from-afar of Mme Goujet's son; these friendships lead to a loan for the establishment of her own laundry: by conscientious application of middle-class principles, Gervaise, now herself an employer, enters the middle class. Her rise is marked by energy, self-respect, self-confidence, discipline, and reasonable ambition. The birth of Nana seems to consecrate the bourgeois family ideal; profligacy, degeneracy, "avachissement," seem alien to the text's vocabulary.

Reference to the drunken kiss as a "first" fall, evoking thus a primal cause-without-a-cause, would seem to confirm the sharp causal rupture between rise and decline. But the term "chute," operating as it does here as both vehicle (Coupeau's physical tumble in the dirty linen) and tenor (the Coupeaus' moral degeneration) of a metaphor, reaches out to other images of falling in the text. This strategem shifts the transitivity of the narrative from the purely syntagmatic realm of the causal link and engages it in a symbolic paradigm: one might say that readers, having been fed a bite of the metaphoric apple, are driven from the garden of metonymic innocence. At any rate, the cultural myths again come into play; readers may be expected to conjure up visions of the biblical Fall, in which overweening pride and concupiscence lead to expulsion from Eden. Suddenly all "downward" transformations, changes from "good" to "bad," from joy to despair, from prosperity to poverty, may be included in the paradigm. As descriptive of the plot structure, "chute" takes on the coloration of a metalanguage, announcing prophetically the ever dwindling fortunes of the heroine, so that as misfortunes befall they appear prepared for, preplanned: their causes desert the fictional reality in which Gervaise lives to take up residence in the predispositions of the inferred author. Gervaise will "fall" because our story teller planned it that way, and the nature of the "fall" will be moral, emotional, social, and economic, because misfortune in these areas is culturally viewed as a downward movement which, once begun, can seldom be arrested by the victim.

As a lexical item, the expression "première chute" ("*first* fall") is an element of the *récit*. It reveals on that level that the narrator is privy, as we might expect, to what lies ahead for Gervaise. But it also points to an intent for us readers to know the future as well, and to be predisposed to think of it as a "fall." Thus a connection is made here too on the level of the *histoire*, between the tumble in the dirty linen and the subsequent degradations, all "sibling" effects of a common cause: "avachissement." But what is more remarkable is that, in their metaphorical connotations, the words evoke the novel's structuring, a mythic intent on the part of the "author" to portray a moral fault and its consequences, and to reveal them as akin to the original sin and its aftermath. At this juncture, we are seeking the cause of this "fall" in the *narration* itself, in the "author's" plan for the work. Making an *histoire* conform to the structure of a preexisting myth is a way of reflecting what Genette's definition calls the "real or fictive situation" in which the narrative "act" functions—a means of representing the *narration*. If, in the *récit*, this incident appears as an unprepared beginning, in the *narration* it has a "cause," which is an inferable intent, borne out by the remainder of the novel.

But this "première chute" is neither the first nor the principal "fall" in the *histoire*: it contains an obvious allusion to Coupeau's earlier tumble from a rooftop, which appears superficially to be a partial cause of his subsequent moral decline. That physical fall, however, has itself no necessary cause; it is, on the literal level, an accident. Coupeau is soldering a bonnet to a rooftop stovepipe, while Gervaise and little Nana wait for him on the sidewalk below:

> Il souda, il cria à Gervaise:
> "Voilà, c'est fini . . . Je descends."
> Le tuyau auquel il devait adapter le chapiteau se trouvait au milieu du toit. Gervaise, tranquillisée, continuait à sourire en suivant ses mouvements. Nana, amusée tout d'un coup par la vue de son père, tapait dans ses mains. Elle s'était assise sur le trottoir pour mieux voir là-haut.
> "Papa! Papa! criait-elle de toute sa force; papa! Regarde donc!"
> Le zingueur voulut se pencher, mais son pied glissa. Alors, brusquement, bêtement, comme un chat dont les pattes s'embrouillent, il roula, il descendit la pente légère de la toiture, sans pouvoir se rattraper.
> "Nom de Dieu!" dit-il d'une voix étouffée.
> Et il tomba. Son corps décrivit une courbe molle, tourna deux fois sur lui-même, vint s'écraser au milieu de la rue avec le coup sourd d'un paquet de linge jeté de haut. (P. 688)

> (He soldered, then called out to Gervaise:
> "There, it's done . . . I'll be right down."
> The stovepipe to which he was to fit the bonnet was in the middle of the roof. Gervaise, her mind at ease now, kept smiling as she followed his movements. Nana, suddenly amused at seeing her father, was clapping her hands. She had sat down on the sidewalk to get a better look up at the roof.
> "Daddy! Daddy!" she was shouting at the top of her lungs; "Daddy! Look!"
> The roofer started to lean out, but his foot slipped. Then suddenly, stupidly, like a cat with its feet entangled, he rolled down the slightly sloping roof, without managing to get a handhold.
> "God damn it!" he said in a stifled voice.
> And he fell. His body described a gentle curve, turned over twice upon itself, and smashed down in the middle of the street with the dull thud of a laundry bundle tossed from a height.)

Analysis of the expressions of causality in this text reveals that known causes are related to Gervaise and Nana. Gervaise is "tranquillisée" by Coupeau's words, by his position in the middle of the roof, as Nana is "amusée" by the sight of her father perched high above; we even know for what purpose Nana has sat down. Her cry is obviously caused by her amusement, although the text fails to make this connection explicit (parataxis), as we break away from the causal chain. Coupeau's decision to lean forward appears to be the result of his daughter's appeal to "look" at her (parataxis again), so that the child's cry itself becomes an implied cause of the fall. Still, the action of leaning out is not of itself a sufficient cause; to demonstrate that, the inferred author has carefully provided an earlier incident, when Coupeau leans quite safely toward the edge of the same roof to chat with Mme Boche below (p. 686). But this time, Coupeau's foot slips for no expressed reason, and if that error is surprising in an experienced roofer, it is perhaps no more surprising than the choice of simile: doubtless no animal is less likely to get its feet entangled than a cat—the inferred author is exercising his options to make unusual things happen. Coupeau's roll down the roof is situated temporally rather than causally ("Alors" rather than "Donc"), and his inability to catch hold of a chimney pipe or even a ridge in the roofing, while stated, is unexplained. The reason for his oath is abundantly clear (parataxis), but his fall through the air is connected to the tumble on the roof only by "Et": the events are narrated in detail, as if they had been permanently inscribed on the retina of some horrified onlooker, but the causal sequence remains unexpressed. This technique tends to reify the event for the reader, like an action seen in reality or on film. But it does not fully "textualize" the scene, nor mediate it as an interpreted whole; the event merely happened, whence its "accidental" quality. The sound of Coupeau's body striking the pavement like a bundle of laundry tends to resituate the event in the mind of Gervaise, the laundress. Is it Zola's narrator who chose to reify the incident for us, or have we been watching through Gervaise's eyes all along? This additional level of indeterminacy separates the fall still further from any underlying causal chain.

If the narrartor (or Gervaise?) gives us no cause for the slip, we begin to look once more to the inferred author, to other events in the *histoire*. At the point where the explained worlds (Gervaise and her daughter) meet the unexplained, in Nana's call to her father, contributory responsibility for the fall appears to rest on Nana's tiny shoulders. Why? Why indeed is little

Nana even brought to the scene? It is her first visit to a work site, and only the second for superstitious Gervaise. Nana will, in the course of this volume, evolve into a nasty brat and a rather vicious adolescent; she will have her own novel, *Nana*, in which to expose her adult depravity. Her innocent cry, "Regarde donc!" as a contributing cause of Coupeau's misfortune, seems, on the level of the *histoire*, an initial repetition, a sign of the magical evil already present in the little girl, the "mark of the beast," which will make of her a constant source of suffering for others. This reading is partially predetermined by Gervaise's expressed intuition, almost an occult "precognition" (pp. 686–88), that her presence or Nana's at a work site would provoke a fall. The inferred author seems to be preparing us for the action, hinting, if not at magical, at least at nonphysical causes for the accident. Beyond the existential realities, "son pied glissa. . . . Et il tomba," we have a hint of the uncanny, and a suggestion of Nana's evil nature which will later, with no apparent cause, come to the surface. Since Coupeau is subsequently at a loss to explain his misstep (pointing out particularly that he had not drunk a drop of alcohol before ascending the roof, p. 693), the mythic and magic underpinnings hold the story line together far more effectively than observed cause and effect. Repetition and reader comparison (of Nana's evil deeds, of recurrences of the Fall motif) become, at this crucial juncture, the mortar of the story, replacing metonymic linkage.

As for the result of Coupeau's four-story plunge to the street below, it involves a remarkable and unnecessary double implausibility. First, unbelievable as it may seem, Coupeau not only survives but recovers completely from his temporary injuries, returning for a time successfully to his work. Second, although mentally and physically fit for work, he lapses into idleness and alcoholism. These implausibilities are all the more amazing since a change in a single "event" of the *histoire* would have removed them both. Suppose the fall had left Coupeau partially incapacitated—a "bad back," a twisted hand, or a simple psychological fear of heights—and the miracle cure is obviated on the one hand, while on the other enforced idleness and self-doubt provide solid explanations for the newfound drinking habit. If the inferred author chooses to put a "link" in his chain that fits poorly at both its ends, when metonymically adaptable links were readily available, he calls attention to metaphoric structure at the expense of the metonymic: it is easier to see the symbolic parallelism between the physical fall and the subsequent moral tumble than to trace precise causal relationships from one to the other. By exercise of an option, the inferred author is determining a metaphoric reading.

So Coupeau is cured; Gervaise cares for him at home, where her love works its miracle and, incidentally, begins the "avachissement" which will lead to the "first fall" we observed earlier. The causal chain is more apparent on this level, although less obvious than it might have been, and it has two branches.

On the one hand, Gervaise and Nana had come to the work site to meet the roofer in order to inspect together a storefront suitable for a laundry. Even after the accident, thanks to the Goujet loan, she goes ahead with her project. Having her own business produces in her an optimistic faith in future prosperity, although her husband is still convalescing. There is perhaps a certain hubris in going into debt to found a business in a rented shop with no other income to fall back upon. Like Coupeau on the rooftop (reader comparison again), Gervaise feels falsely at ease in a precarious position and thus may be riding for a fall. If so, the inferred author's choice of events might be an attempt to "prove," as a law, that overconfidence leads to disaster.

On the other hand, by spoiling her injured husband at home and providing him with extra cash when he goes out, Gervaise appears to destroy in Coupeau all desire to work. In a sudden about-face, the virtual teetotaler begins drinking with the boys at the Assommoir, and his long slide into alcoholic stupor originates. While Gervaise's vague *gâteries* seem to be the primary cause, it is also possible that the inferred author presupposes in the roofer an alcoholic heredity. Coupeau's father had suffered an accident after drinking; for this reason, perhaps, Coupeau has shunned alcohol. His fall and the opportunity to drink are thus possibly all that is needed to cast him over the hereditary precipice. But neither the characters of *L'Assommoir* nor the narrator himself, whose language tends to identify him with the underclass, has the education necessary to explain the physiology of alcoholism from the "raw data" provided by the inferred author.[8] We shall see the symptoms, the effects, including description in almost clinical detail of *delirium tremens*, but the causes are not adduced for us.

As for Gervaise, it is indolence rather than alcohol that overcomes her. And carelessness in her work is soon accompanied by moral slovenliness. When Lantier returns during the saint's-day feast, and the besotted and spineless Coupeau ends up inviting the still jobless hatter to move in with them, there is another mouth for Gervaise to feed, in addition to Coupeau's mother, now also living with them. Although the text points to this as a cause for their weakened finances, it must be noted that the children are soon off working as apprentices, so that the additional expense to feed Lantier would scarcely be disastrous.

However, Gervaise quickly begins sleeping with Lantier again, on nights when Coupeau is too drunk to fulfill her needs, and the neighborhood is at once abuzz with rumors that tarnish the little laundry's image. The narrative voice stresses Gervaise's laxity:

> Au milieu de cette indignation publique, Gervaise vivait tranquille, lasse et un peu endormie. Dans les commencements, elle s'était trouvée bien coupable, bien sale, et elle avait eu un dégoût d'elle-même. Quand elle sortait de la chambre de Lantier, elle se lavait les mains. . . . Elle aurait voulu changer de peau en changeant d'homme. Mais, lentement, elle s'accoutumait. C'était trop fatigant de se débarbouiller chaque fois. Ses paresses l'amollissaient, son besoin d'être heureuse lui faisait tirer tout le bonheur possible de ses embête-ments. . . . N'est-ce pas? pourvu que son mari et son amant fussent contents, que la maison marchât son petit train-train régulier, qu'on rigolât du matin au soir, tous gras, tous satisfaits de la vie et se la coulant douce, il n'y avait pas de quoi se plaindre. (Pp. 814–15)

(In the midst of this public indignation, Gervaise lived on, tranquil, relaxed, and somewhat sleepy. In the beginning, she had considered herself very guilty, very dirty, and she had been disgusted with herself. Whenever she left Lantier's bedroom, she washed her hands. . . . She would have liked to change her skin when she changed men. But, slowly, she got used to it. It was too much of a bother to wash up every time. Her laziness was making her soft, and her need to be happy made her extract all the happiness she could from her little miseries. . . . So long as her husband and her lover were happy—right?—so long as the household merrily followed its little daily routine, so long as they laughed from morning till night, all fat, satisfied with life and taking it easy, there was nothing to complain about.)

The evolution here described is from moral conduct to immoral conduct with guilt, to the same behavior without guilt. The major expressed causes for the disappearance of guilt are habit, laziness, and "her need to be happy," all of which produce in Gervaise a kind of sleepy lassitude, of indifference to public opinion, so long as the laundress knows her men are happy. So the immediate causes are clear, and, in the following paragraph, Gervaise advances three more basic causes to explain her conduct: (1) when one has a filthy, drunken husband, one looks for "cleanliness" elsewhere; (2) since Lantier was her first and true "husband," "natural law" authorizes her conduct; and (3) everyone in the neighborhood is engaged in some sort of sexual irregularity. These may be mere excuses, but if Gervaise believes them, they can structure a sound causal chain of the sort one might expect to find in the works of a determinist. Once readers accept the initial *avachissement*, the downward slide becomes indeed inevitable.

Yet the first two reasons for the moral collapse contain mythic elements. The cleanliness-purity theme is ubiquitous in Zola, and, in the later novels, such as *Le Docteur Pascal*, males can play the role of purifiers and redeemers of women, who, in the *Rougon-Macquart* novels, are often naturally impure.[9] The return to Lantier can thus be read as a misguided search for salvation. And in turning to her first lover, she turns to her "true" husband. In an astute analysis of this phenomenon in Zola, Jean Borie evokes imprinting:

> La défloraison n'est pas pour Zola épisode futile et sans lendemain. Elle est, au contraire, prise d'amour pour l'éternité; elle a valeur de mythe et trouve sa place dans cette anthropologie imaginaire que nous essayons de définir. Lorsqu'elle "se donne" pour la première fois, la femme absorbe, et garde en elle à jamais, sous forme d'empreinte, la virilité de l'homme qui l'a pénétrée.[10]

(For Zola, deflowering is not a futile, inconsequential episode. It is, on the contrary, capture by love for eternity; it is endowed with mythic value and has its place in the imaginary anthropology we are trying to define. When she "gives herself" for the first time, a woman absorbs and keeps within her forever, in the form of an imprint, the virility of the man who penetrated her.)

These two reasons taken together suggest that an "imaginary anthropology" functions indeed as the root cause of the *avachissement*.

For the third excuse, Gervaise proposes a primary cause as well: "Oui, oui," she says sarcastically, "quelque chose de propre que l'homme et la femme, dans ce coin de Paris, où l'on est les uns sur les autres, à cause de la misère" (p. 816); "Oh, sure; men and women lead real clean lives, in this corner of Paris, where we live on top of each other on account of poverty." Here we rejoin the myth of working-class Paris: poverty causes overcrowded living conditions, which lead inevitably to sexual promiscuity. Uttered in defense of her conduct by a character with an ax to grind, none of the three reasons is an objective observation of causation in the story line. Readers will decide for themselves what to believe. But in the absence of privileged explanations from the narrator, and in view of the relative plausibility of these reasons as statements of the way Gervaise's mind works, acceptance of Gervaise's causal logic is tempting. If readers acquiesce, Zola's inferred author will have inserted both mythic and ideological causes at the origin of the mechanistic chain.[11]

To explain how *avachissement* leads to ultimate destruction, the novel sets a final psychological cause in place: the joyous side of self-destruction, a kind of financial and physical death wish. As customers begin to fall away, as debts mount up while Coupeau and Lantier eat (and drink) Gervaise out of house and home, the narrator explains that "she was virtually inebriated by a rage for indebtedness; she drove herself dizzy, chose the most expensive items, gave free rein to her appetites, now that she couldn't pay" (p. 794; "elle était comme grisée par la fureur de la dette; elle s'étourdissait, choisissait les choses les plus chères, se lâchait dans sa gourmandise, depuis qu'elle ne payait plus"). This clear declaration about the psychology of credit might function as a "law." Indeed, when nearly all is lost, Gervaise returns to the pawn shop, and the narrator affirms: "she was in the grip of pawn-shop mania and would have shorn her head if she could have gotten a loan on her hair" (p. 821; "elle était prise de la rage du clou, elle se serait tondu la tête si on avait voulu lui prêter sur ses cheveux"). "La rage du clou" has the ring of a ready-made expression—pawn-shop mania—as if the desire to transform all stable, physical possessions into liquid assets, to feed upon and drink up one's own physical reality, were a well-known and catalogued disease. Like Rimbaud's greatcoat, which, through excessive wear, was "becoming ideal," so Gervaise's substance is joyously transformed into an abstraction: *avachissement* becomes self-manducation, until she eagerly asks the neighborhood undertaker to carry her away before she is dead (p. 929). Gilles Deleuze perceives the death wish as underlying all instinctual behavior in Zola, the absent cause, the void at the center of being:

> . . . c'était déjà cela, la découverte de Zola: comment les *"gros appétits"* gravitent autour de l'instinct de mort, comment ils fourmillent par une fêlure qui est celle de l'instinct de mort, . . . comment il constitue à lui seul la grande hérédité, la fêlure.[12]

(. . . and this was already Zola's big discovery: how the *"major ap-petites"* gravitate around the death instinct, how they swarm through the crack which is the death instinct, . . . how it alone constitutes the principal hereditary factor, the crack.)

The joy of self-destruction finds perhaps its clearest objective correlative in the Assommoir bar. Here foregathers the gang with the colorful nick-names—Mes-Bottes, Bibi-la-Grillade, Bec-Salé, also called Boit-sans-Soif, Cadet-Cassis (Coupeau)—false names covering true identities like joy covering pain, lightheartedness concealing the fear of mortality. The horror-masked-by-gaiety of drinking is a kind of absent cause in the novel.

Absent, that is, until Gervaise, when she too at last begins to drink, unmasks the horrible underside of the cozy tavern, in a famous passage:

Elle se tourna, elle aperçut l'alembic, la machine à soûler, fonction-nant sous le vitrage de l'étroite cour, avec la trépidation de sa cuisine d'enfer. Le soir, les cuivres étaient plus mornes, allumés seulement sur leur rondeur d'une large étoile rouge; et l'ombre de l'appareil, contre la muraille du fond, dessinait des abominations, des figures avec des queues, des monstres ouvrant leurs mâchoires comme pour avaler le monde. (P. 867)

(She turned and caught sight of the still, the stupor machine, shudder-ing under the glass roof of the narrow courtyard with the vibration of its hellish cookery. At night, the copper parts were darker, lighted only on their rounded bellies with a large red star; and the shadow the machine cast on the back wall conjured up abominable pictures, figures with tails, monsters opening their jaws as if to swallow the world.)

With its causal *à*, the expression "machine à soûler" links drunkenness to a very mechanical, predictable cause. Although the text says nothing of it, readers may be aware that behind the machine lie the greed of the brandy merchants and perhaps the political motivations of the ruling class; in front of it, the universal death-thirst, activated among the masses by poverty. But, since the machine itself assumes in Gervaise's mind the gigantic proportions of Hell itself, whose purpose is to "swallow the world," the sociological causes for the existence of the machine seem subsumed in it, so that the evil of society, whatever the reader perceives that to be, appears to function like a machine, predetermined by some occult, demonic force. We have seen the Fall, and it has taken us straight to Hell. The linguistic transformation of definable sociological ills into Satanic forces leaves the reader free to invent plausible sociological causes, while at the same time that invention is determined and limited by the infernal metaphor. Zola's inferred author, abetted by a narrator with limited insight, leaves gaps and indeterminacies in the causal chain on the diegetic level, but he binds the story together on the exegetic plane through metaphor and symbol. Primary causes remain unexplained, but they are replaced by magic (Coupeau's fall from the roof as prefiguration; mythic anthropology at the origin of *avachissement*) or demonic powers (the maleficent force in Nana and the brandy maker's hellish still).

As if to stress the superhuman force of the demons at work in the narrative, the inferred author gives both to Gervaise and to Coupeau the means to avoid their slide to oblivion. Two incidents provide escape hatches; although they fail to crawl through them, the possibility to do so was presented, so that the downfall is inevitable only if mystical or deep psychological forces made it impossible for them to see and profit from their opportunities.

After Coupeau's convalescence, he takes a roofing job well south of Paris, in Etampes:

> . . . et là il fit près de trois mois, sans se soûler, guéri un moment par l'air de la campagne. . . . A son retour, il était frais comme une rose, et il apportait quatre cents francs, avec lesquels ils payèrent les deux termes arriérés de la boutique . . . ainsi que d'autres petites dettes du quartier. . . . (P. 844)

> (. . . and there he put in nearly three months, without getting drunk, cured for a time by the country air. . . . When he got back, he was fresh as a daisy, and he brought home four hundred francs, with which they made the two back payments on the shop . . . and settled other little debts in the neighborhood. . . .)

This favorable sign should have sent the couple scurrying to live in the provinces, where the healthful conditions and a modicum of available work would have kept them afloat, far from the Parisian demons.

Perhaps more surprising is Gervaise's failure to accept the offer of young Goujet, to whom she is visibly attracted. Coupeau is drinking, Lantier is back, and the laundry business is poor. Goujet, a skilled, industrious, and prosperous smith, one day gathers his courage and asks Gervaise to run off with him (pp. 798–99). He could get a job in Belgium, and they could make a new start together. Her refusal, essentially on moral grounds, seems to run counter to the *avachissement* which has her in its grip:

> "Ce serait très mal . . . Je suis mariée, n'est-ce pas? J'ai des enfants. . . . nous aurions des remords, nous ne goûterions pas de plaisir. . . . Quand on reste honnête, dans notre position, on est joliment récompensé. . . ." (P. 799)

> ("It would be a very evil thing to do . . . I'm a married woman, you know. I have children. . . . we'd feel remorse; we'd get no pleasure. . . . When you stay honorable, in our position, you're very well rewarded. . . .")

The last sentence is surely not ironic in Gervaise's mind, but one can question the deep-seated sincerity of her moral judgments. Perhaps she is being "moral" to save Goujet from going down with her: "I'm very fond of you too," she says, "too fond to let you do stupid things. And this would be a stupid thing, of course . . ." ("Moi aussi, j'éprouve de l'amitié pour vous, j'en éprouve trop pour vous laisser commettre des bêtises. Et ce seraient des bêtises, bien sûr . . ."). Perhaps she is simply too *avachie* to envisage such a radical change in her life. It might be that a (supernaturally inspired?) passion for Lantier is holding her back, or even that she has truly been taken in by the moral preachments which the rich use to keep the poor in their place. The indeterminacy of cause, here again arising from the fact that an interested character gives the only explanation, leaves thus yet another gap in the causal chain of the novel. Given a glimpse of a happier life, both Coupeau and Gervaise elect to remain in their ruinous situation. Readers are left to seek the reasons in demonic forces, or in their psychological correlative, *la fêlure*.

Instead of the freedom to interpret we found behind the gaps in the *récit* of Gide's *La Porte étroite*, we discover here a mythic substratum with its own metonymy. The problem is to determine whether this mythic causal chain is a referent of the tale, a part of its *histoire*, or whether it expresses an intent of the *narration*. If Gervaise, despite her initial gumption and her later opportunities, is foredoomed, is it because of social ills and a psychological flaw, present in the *histoire*, or because of an intent in the *narration* to illustrate a theory of supernatural causation and to work through a modern esthetic of the tragic? Readers may reach differing conclusions, but the major reversal in the text points to the importance of the intent of *narration*.

3. *The chiasmic reversal*. In the rise and fall of Gervaise Macquart, the conjunction of mythic and esthetic causation is nowhere more obvious than in the reversal inherent in her relationship to Virginie, the sister of her rival for Lantier, Adèle. The first time we see them together, in a public laundry, they engage in a brutal physical combat from which Gervaise emerges triumphant. Virginie is mysteriously present when little Claude and Etienne arrive to inform their mother of Lantier's departure, and Mme Boche guesses at the reason: "Elle rit de vous voir pleurer, cette sans-coeur, là-bas. . . . Elle a emballé les deux autres et elle est venue ici leur raconter la tête que vous feriez," (p. 617); "She's getting a laugh out of seeing you cry, that heartless beast over there. . . . She got the two of them going, and now she's here so she can tell them all about the expression on your face." If Mme Boche is right, Virginie, who shares the one-room flat where Adèle receives Lantier, would thus act as a major contributing cause of the initial event, having inspired the Lantier-Adèle affair. But the transitivity that runs through "a emballé," as a part of a character's speech, comes from the inferred author; the speech itself is an "event" which could be situated in its own causal chain. If readers perceive Virginie as the primal urge, the evil force that gets the narrative moving, it is the inferred author, rather than the narrator, who has instigated the interpretation.

The fight begins when Gervaise perceives Virginie's taunting stare:

> Quand elle aperçut devant elle Virginie, au milieu de trois ou quatre femmes, parlant bas, la dévisageant, elle fut prise d'une colère folle. Les bras en avant, cherchant par terre, tournant sur elle-même, dans un tremblement de tous ses membres, elle marcha quelques pas, rencontra un seau plein, le saisit à deux mains, le vida à toute volée.
>
> "Chameau, va!" cria la grande Virginie. (P. 617)

> (When she caught sight of Virginie standing in front of her in the midst of three or four other women, speaking in low tones, staring at her, a wild rage took hold of her. Stretching out her arms, feeling around on the ground, turning in circles, trembling from head to toe, she took a few steps, came upon a full bucket, picked it up with both hands, and hurled its contents with all her might.
>
> "You stupid ass!" cried big Virginie.)

In an almost Gidean way, the expression of causality begins by hiding behind a temporal mask ("Quand" for "Parce que") and lurking in participles ("parlant bas, la dévisageant"). The passive voice ("fut prise") avoids an opportunity for direct attribution of cause. The narrativity flows through the inevitable causal verbs, of course, but parataxis intervenes between the thrown water (we will learn only later that it struck Virginie's feet) and the result: Virginie's insult. The links are there, but this is scarcely the style of a narrator seeking to express the workings of natural laws through obvious causal chains. Violent actions abound in the fight, which is described in lurid detail—clawing, drenching, ripping away of clothing—but the psychological forces that engender them remain unnamed. Superficially, they are obvious, but upon encountering the reversal, the reader will need to return to this passage and infer some unexpressed relationships.

Why does Gervaise win? Struck on the arm with a laundry paddle, she summons an unnamed force: her strength is suddenly multiplied "ten fold." Stripping her opponent, she succeeds at last in applying the paddle, repeatedly and vigorously, to Virginie's bare buttocks, humiliating her in her sex itself. The reader can infer the combination of hatred, pain, and frustrated sexual desire that underlies this violence, caused (supposedly, mysteriously) by Virginie's instigation of Lantier's departure and by her subsequent taunts. In the light of the later reversal, Gervaise's brutality here will appear to be the sadistic half of a sadomasochistic rite, of which the masochistic portion will be played out, with startling symmetry, near the end of the novel.

Gervaise's degrading service in Virginie's fine-food grocery and sweet-shop at the close of the work constitutes the obvious reversal. Virginie has acquired the very storefront in which Gervaise ran her unsuccessful laundry; she has taken Lantier along with the shop; and she has reduced Gervaise to scrubbing floors in the transformed store. It is tempting to seek a causal chain between the two humiliations. Quite probably, Virginie is still harboring a grudge when she encounters Gervaise, apparently by chance, in a stairway, many years after the fight, although that is never stated as fact and can only be inferred in light of subsequent events. Gervaise at first expects to be struck across the face with the mackerel her old enemy is carrying:

Mais non. Virginie eut un mince sourire. Alors la blanchisseuse, dont le panier bouchait l'escalier, voulut se montrer polie.

"Je te demande pardon, dit-elle.

—Vous êtes toute pardonnée", répondit la grande brune.

Et elles restèrent au milieu des marches, elles causèrent, raccommodées du coup, sans avoir risqué une seule allusion au passé. (P. 736)

(But no. Virginie gave a meager smile. Then the laundress, whose basket was blocking the stairway, determined to be polite.

"I beg your pardon," she said.

"And pardoned you are," the big brunette replied.

And there they stood, in the middle of the stairs, chatting, friends again on the spot, without having risked a single allusion to the past.)

No indication of ill will from Virginie, no explanation of Gervaise's sudden decision to be polite. This is a critical juncture, and mysterious forces are at work: suddenly and without explanation, the two women are fast friends.

A frequent visitor to the laundry, Virginie apparently contrives to whet its proprietress's appetite for Lantier by talking of him often. Shortly thereafter, when Lantier reenters Gervaise's life, readers may wonder if he did so on Virginie's urging. It is difficult to infer that Virginie is plotting from the outset to take over Gervaise's storefront, since the laundry's failure is at this juncture far from a foregone conclusion, and since it is Lantier himself who, later on, encourages the brunette to take this action (p. 826). Yet unmentioned forces seem to be conspiring, from the meeting in the stairwell onward, to bring about the reversal of fortunes. The purchase of the lease to the shop is dependent, for example, on an "inheritance" which Virginie had fortuitously received from an aunt, and which is revealed only late in the tale (p. 826). No law of nature decrees that schemers inherit the wherewithal to accomplish their machinations: less natural powers are seemingly at work.

And so it appears particularly noteworthy that Gervaise and the narrator are in remarkable agreement about the fact that Virginie's acquisition of the shop and her subsequent humiliation of the former laundress therein constitute a "vengeance." When the brunette seeks, through Lantier, to acquire the store, Gervaise's hostile reaction is reported in free indirect style:

Non, non, jamais! Elle avait toujour douté du coeur de Virginie: si Virginie ambitionnait la boutique, c'était pour l'humilier. Elle l'aurait cédée peut-être à la première femme dans la rue, mais pas à cette grande hypocrite qui attendait certainement depuis des années de lui voir faire le saut. Oh! ça expliquait tout. Elle comprenait à présent pourquoi les étincelles jaunes s'allumaient dans les yeux de chat de cette margot. Oui, Virginie gardait sur la conscience la fessée du lavoir, elle mijotait sa rancune dans la cendre. (P. 827)

(No, no, never! She had always doubted Virginie's affection: if Virginie had her eye on the shop, it was just to humiliate her. Maybe she would have let it go to the first woman in the street, but not to that big hypocrite who had surely been waiting around for years to watch her go off the cliff. Oh, that explained everything! Now she understood why the yellow sparks were glinting in that chatterbox's catlike eyes. Yes, Virginie had never forgotten the paddling in the laundry, simmering her grudge over the coals.)

Much later, when circumstances have reduced Gervaise to scrubbing floors in what had been "her" shop, while Lantier and the new proprietress look on, the narrator describes the scene:

Et tous les deux, le chapelier et l'épicière, se carraient davantage, comme sur un trône, tandis que Gervaise se traînait à leurs pieds, dans la boue noire. Virginie devait jouir, car ses yeux de chat s'éclairèrent un instant d'étincelles jaunes, et elle regarda Lantier d'un sourire mince. Enfin ça la vengeait de l'ancienne fessée du lavoir, qu'elle avait toujours gardée sur la conscience! (P. 890)

(And both of them, the hatter and the proprietress of the sweet-shop, struck a still more pompous pose, as if on a throne, while Gervaise dragged herself around at their feet, in the black slop. Virginie must have been getting a thrill, for her catlike eyes gleamed for an instant with yellow sparks, and she looked at Lantier with a meager smile. This at last avenged her of the old paddling in the laundry, which she had never forgotten!)

Both passages explicitly declare the existence of a causal relationship between the paddling in the laundry and Gervaise's humiliation. But both also put in question the competence of the speaker to make such a judgment. In the first text, "elle avait toujours douté du coeur de Virginie" is surely one of those lies we tell ourselves to cover the shame of being taken by surprise: Gervaise, who "comprenait *à present*," appears to have been completely taken in and to have uncovered the causal connection after the fact. In the second text, the narrator, although potentially omniscient, admits his uncertainty about Virginie's emotions ("*devait* jouir") and his need to judge on the basis of exterior signs. The causal connection of a preplanned vengeance appears virtually certain, but its certainty resides less in the affirmations than in those remarkable exterior signs and in the astounding conjunction, across 63 pages of text, between the vocabulary of Gervaise and of the narrator.

The verb "jouir," used as it is without complement in the second passage, is invested with quasi-orgasmic connotations. The exterior signs of this "thrill" are given as the "yellow sparks" in Virginie's eyes and her "meager smile." The presence of the yellow sparks in the earlier passage marks the beginning of this sexual victory, which culminates in Virginie's seduction of Lantier, in a time anterior to the attempt to acquire the shop. The "meager smile" sends us all the way back to the meeting on the stairs (p. 736): repeated vocabulary unites the passages, preparing the reversal far more clearly and effectively than obvious causation.

But the lexical coincidence ("yeux de chat," "étincelles jaunes," "garder sur la conscience," "fessée du lavoir") does more than unify the second Virginie segment as a prepared vengeance. The narrator's corroboration of Gervaise's hindsight tends to validate it, of course, to make us believe in a planned connection between the two humiliations. But the choice of identical words functions also to unite the two speakers, Gervaise—the creature of the inferred author—and the narrator. For Gervaise—her sudden strength, her later weakness, her long-term love for Lantier, her belated hatreds—all are the work of the inferred author. When her language coincides with the narrator's, inferred author and narrator unite; the narrative at that point conjoins them: from a causal viewpoint, both are "the author," or at least all the movements and decisions in the text which we can read as "authorial presence."

This is another way of saying that the vengeance, the reversal, occurs on the level of the *narration*. By itself (and despite Zola's affirmations in *Le Roman expérimental* about subservience to the laws of nature), the notion that a novel is what its "author" makes it is, in causal systems, a truism. But "authors"—whether you define them as individual human wills or pervading sociocultural megatexts—can provide in the discourse credible causes for their events or leave literal causation implausible or indeterminate. The *récit* of *L'Assommoir* does the latter, leaving the reader to seek explanations on other levels.

It is thus possible, for example, to read the two Virginie segments as "testing events," of the sort we observed in Gide, measuring Gervaise's power as she is rising and her weakness as she falls. Or, structurally, we may infer in the text an esthetic desire for symmetry. Or the reversal, in the repeated evocation of Virginie's feline eyes momentarily alive with yellow glints, can revive the symbolical, like the repeated "fall." Virginie has the traits of a sorceress who, with evil eye, can change the lives of others.[13] As Satan's minion, she could be the dynamic behind all that happens, giving the novel a unified and tragic structure. Gervaise's initial flaw: sexuality, living with Lantier. Her punishment: abandonment. Her cardinal sin: rejecting the punishment, fighting against fate (the conquest of Virginie, rising in the social hierarchy). Whence the Fall: *avachissement*. The diabolic order of the world is restored: Virginie is re-enthroned, and Gervaise, converted and assenting to her fate, is hounded willingly to her death. In the absence of the Freudian vocabulary of sadomasochism, unavailable to this text, such supernatural correlatives construct a mythic chain of causation to obliterate the gaps in the mechanistic one.

But our purpose is neither to propose nor to defend a single "coherent" reading of the text. It is not the doughnut but the hole, so to speak, that has been our focus, and the ways in which breaks and weaknesses in the causal chain bring the reader into contact, no longer with the *récit*, but with *histoire* and *narration*. For the text seems to expect that a causally coherent reading will be sought. It provides causally linked metonymic structures, either at the level of *histoire* or *narration*, and it offers gaps in the literal *récit*, thus inviting the reader's creative participation in "constructing" the novel. If one believes that the Satanic forces mentioned have as their referents "real" psychological or social tendencies demonstrably present in Gervaise's and Coupeau's world, then causal linking functions in the *histoire*; if they are read as "occult" references, symbolic of novel structure, the metonymic linking is in the *narration*. Causation may be read either at the level of "story" or of "production-of-story." Table 3.1 lists some of the primary options, by level, at key points where the gaps make them evident.

The conjoining of fragments that is reading reflects symmetrically the fragmentation that is writing. One can scarcely assume on the part of a traditional writer an "intent" to fragment, for fragmentation is inherent in language (*récit*) and in "events" (*histoire*) arbitrarily perceived as such. But when major changes in character—from energy and ambition to *avachissement*—are not explicitly explained (Michel's conversations with Ménalque in *L'Immoraliste* suggest more clearly the reasons for Michel's "downward slide"), when unnecessary implausibilities, like Coupeau's complete recovery from a four-story fall, invade the causal chain, the reader can infer, with respect to reality-referential texts, that narrative options are being exercised

Table 3.1

EFFECT	EXPLANATION, BY LEVEL (explicit in *récit;* possible inferences for *histoire* and *narration*)
1. Lantier's departure	*Récit:* Not fully explained. *Histoire:* Virginie's evil machinations? *Narration:* Textual manipulation to prepare reversal?
2. Coupeau's fall	*Récit:* Unexplained. *Histoire:* Nana's evil nature? *Narration:* Textual manipulation for creation of symbol?
3. Coupeau's miraculous recovery	*Récit:* Implausible. *Histoire:* Gervaise's love conquers Fate? *Narration:* Textual manipulation to reveal mythic substratum of Coupeau's decline?
4. Coupeau's inability to profit from cure	*Récit:* Questionable. *Histoire:* Satanic (psychological?) forces? *Narration:* Textual manipulation for tragic structure?
5. Gervaise's *avachissement*	*Récit:* Poverty, overcrowding, imprinting for first lover, need for pleasure. *Histoire:* Satanic (psychological?) forces? Death wish? *Narration:* "Hubris" for tragic structure?
6. Virginie's triumph	*Récit:* Fortuitous inheritance; Gervaise's capitulation as laundry fails. *Histoire:* Virginie's evil "magic"? *Narration:* Textual manipulation to achieve reversal?
7. Gervaise's ruin and death	*Récit: Avachissement,* starvation, exposure. *Histoire:* Gervaise's death wish? *Narration:* Textual manipulation to complete tragedy?

for extradiegetic reasons. Using causal logic, readers can then seek to infer, from their effects, the reasons for the choices made.

Since causation functions across many pages in *L'Assommoir* (the "first fall" is a distant precursor of Gervaise's fate, and the chiasmic reversal near the end imposes the rereading-as-cause of the initial Virginie segment), a constant dynamic appears, in retrospect, to have inhabited the story from one end to the other. The mythic dimension of the novel, springing from symbols and repetitions, also implies a permanent dynamic, an inevitable flow of causal forces. Reading metaphorically is a relatively static experience, viewing a highway from a high, hovering helicopter. Reading metonymically is seeing the same highway from a motorcycle at seventy miles per hour (one good crack in the pavement can be fatal). Readers tend where possible, I think, to take the helicopter. Thus *L'Assommoir* attains its "anti-Gidean" appearance of constant, inevitable causality. It is only an appearance, but when there are gaps in which we can employ our creativity, *L'Assommoir* limits more stringently, with symbols, the kinds of connections we can make than does, for example, *La Porte étroite*. As Michel Serres points out of the whole Rougon-Macquart family tree: "Le mythe . . . rend connexes des variétés locales déchirées. Il noue des carrefours. . . . Il enjambe une faille. Il coud les lèvres des crevasses. Fait du haillon une tunique."[14] ("Myth . . . brings broken-off local varieties into connection. It binds crossroads together. . . . It straddles a fault line. It sews up the lips of crevasses. Makes the tattered rag a tunic.")

Notes

1.   Emile Zola, *Le Roman expérimental*, in his *Oeuvres complètes*, 10 (Paris: Cercle du Livre Précieux, 1968), 1240.

2.   Zola, *Le Roman expérimental*, p. 1182.

3.   In Zola, *Oeuvres complètes*, 3 (Paris: Cercle du Livre Précieux, 1967), 596–97. Page references to *L'Assommoir* in the text are to this edition.

4.   See, for example, J. H. Matthews, *Les Deux Zola* (Geneva, Paris: Droz, Minard, 1967); Roger Ripoll, *Réalité et mythe chez Zola* (Paris: Honoré Champion, 1981); and Jean Borie, *Zola et les mythes, ou de la nausée au salut* (Paris: Editions du Seuil, 1971).

5.   Ripoll, pp. 585–86, 597–99.

6.   Matthews, pp. 36–38.

7.   Especially in *La Porte étroite*; see chapter two, above.

8.   Matthews points out, p. 38, that Zola's characters are capable of expressing ideas that would seem to surpass their capacity, but that does not occur here.

9.   See Chantal Bertrand-Jennings, *L'Eros et la femme chez Zola* (Paris: Klincksieck, 1977), especially pp. 109–15.

10.   See Jean Borie, p. 59. Borie points out that in Zola a woman's children are all, regardless of paternity, exterior manifestations of this imprint. That theory might explain why Nana is cast more nearly in the mold of Lantier than in that of her biological father, Coupeau. The origins and obvious erroneousness of these and similar nineteenth-century male-dominance myths are treated by Hilde Olrik, "La Théorie de l'imprégnation," *Nineteenth-Century French Studies*, 15, 1 & 2 (Fall-Winter 1986–1987), 128–40, with specific reference to Zola.

11.   Of the three principal mythic causes, "male imprinting" and "underclass Paris" are charged with obvious ideological overtones. Belonging to a different "culture," the "Fall from Eden" myth, despite its Judeo-Christian origins, will not appear ideological until the myth of the underclass unites with it in the final Satanic imagery.

12.   In Zola, *Oeuvres complètes*, 6 (Paris: Cercle du Livre Précieux, 1967), 16.

13.   On the anthropology of the evil eye superstition and its role in vengeance, see Tobin Siebers, *The Mirror of Medusa* (Berkeley: University of California Press, 1983), pp. 27–56. Consult Siebers's example of yellow glints in the evil eye in Théophile Gautier, *Jettatura*, in his *Romans et contes* (Paris: Charpentier, 1923), p. 142.

14.   Michel Serres, *Feux et signaux de brume: Zola* (Paris: Bernard Grasset, 1975), p. 49.

4

Causal Chains and
Textualization: Zola's
La Bête humaine

C'est pourquoi, hors le feu, j'ai tenu à *la Bête humaine*: construite sur un jeu ouvert, elle compte parmi les oeuvres qui rompent cet état cyclique et font éclater la clôture. Jeu de hasard et feu aléatoire, état nouveau de la systématique.

(That is why, short of putting my hand in the fire, I have clung to *La Bête humaine*: constructed on an open game, it is one of the works which break that cyclical state and burst the bonds of closure. Game of chance and aleatory fire: a new state of systematics.)

—MICHEL SERRES

Beginning, as it were, with a "gap," *La Bête humaine*[1] (written 1888–90, published serially in 1889–90) illustrates Zola's "other side," with a most tightly linked causal system. Its protagonist, Jacques Lantier, is supposedly the second son of Gervaise and her good-for-nothing hatter, although, in *L'Assommoir*, there is no son between Claude and Etienne.[2] After that initial inconsistency, the novel constructs a number of tightly woven and interconnected causal chains that tie each event to the next explicitly—across occasional implausibilities, the role of which we will explore—with all the rigor of a laboratory experiment. Zola's concept of the "experimental novel" involves, of course, a major sophism or two, of which he was doubtless aware at the time of publication of *Le Roman expérimental*, if only through the critique of his friend Céard.[3] Zola writes, for example, in his theoretical essay, after quoting Claude Bernard on controlled experimentation:

Eh bien! en revenant au roman, nous voyons également que le romancier est fait d'un observateur et d'un expérimentateur. L'observateur chez lui donne les faits tels qu'il les a observés, pose le point de départ, établit le terrain solide sur lequel vont marcher les personnages et se développer les phénomènes. Puis l'expérimentateur paraît et institue l'expérience, je veux dire fait mouvoir les personnages dans une histoire particulière, pour y montrer que la succession des faits y sera telle que l'exige le déterminisme des phénomènes mis à l'étude.[4]

(Well then, returning to the novel, we note that the novelist too is made up of an observer and an experimenter. The observer in him gives the facts as he has observed them, fixes the point of departure, and establishes the solid ground on which the characters will move and the phenomena develop. Then the experimenter appears and launches the experiment; I mean, he makes the characters move in a particular story, to demonstrate therein that the succession of facts will occur just as the determinism of the phenomena under study requires.)

And he adds, in reference to the experimental novelist: "He has set out from a position of doubt in order to reach absolute knowledge; he will not cease doubting until the mechanism of passion, taken apart and put back together by him, functions according to the laws established by nature." ("Il est parti du doute pour arriver à la connaissance absolue; il ne cessera de douter que lorsque le méchanisme de la passion, démontée et remontée par lui, fonctionne selon les lois fixées par la nature.")[5]

The obvious logical problems posed by these declarations and others like them are a trifle embarrassing. First, while experimental science has among its goals the defining of those constant relationships that we call "laws of nature," and which allow us to predict and control events, a definition of "the laws established by nature" and of the "determinism" of phenomena is a precondition of the novelist's "experiment," not its conclusion, for the obvious conformity of novelistic phenomena to these laws is its aim. "Absolute knowledge" must therefore precede the absolute knowledge which is the writer's demonstration: not only the existence but the knowledge of "causal laws" is a foregone conclusion. Second, these sentences express an abiding faith in the constancy of causal relationships. A remarkable number of unchangeables conjoin in these texts, from the "solid ground" on which the characters walk, the environment that will interact with their heredity (as if a natural environment would really "hold still" long enough for a replicable sociological experiment), to the "determinism" of the phenomena themselves, to the "mechanism" of passion, so that even the moving parts of the experiment ("marcher," "se développer") achieve a kind of stasis, like that of immutable scientific truth. Third, of course, if it is the experimenter in the novelist who "makes the characters move," it is not the laws of nature that do so.

Critics have long questioned the ability of historical texts to represent the reality of history. Fredric Jameson has perhaps pushed the argument a step further; his formulation holds:

> . . . that history is *not* a text, not a narrative, master or otherwise, but that, as an absent cause, it is inaccessible to us except in textual form, and that our approach to it and to the Real itself necessarily passes through its prior textualization, its narrativization in the political unconscious.[6]

It would be hard to find a more succinct statement of the problem: phenomenon and text do not belong to the same species, as it were, so that a gap exists between any real event and the account thereof ("absent cause," and the neologisms in "-ization" indicating transformation); the words "text" and "narrative" evoke a grammatical linking of semantic elements, while their negation suggests the absence of any such clear linkage among real phenomena; knowledge is associated with "text" and not with the real ("inaccessible to us"), so that observation itself, as conceived by Zola in *Le Roman expérimental*, may seem a doubtful enterprise. Jameson's formulation further implies that, whether textualization takes the form of a history book, a novel, or simply a mental construct, the apparent laws of nature are actually a reflection of the rules of grammar. Here we may join with Valéry in stating that no possible formal or technical distinction can be drawn between written history and written mimetic fiction, and in adding that the "admirable causality" of which some historians (and novelists) seek to persuade us depends essentially on the talents of the writer and on the reader's critical resistance.[7]

La Bête humaine is a laboratory of textualization. Zola's "observer" plays *grosso modo* the role of our "narrator": his "experimenter," that of our "inferred author." Their interaction can tell us little about the "laws" that govern the physical and psychological world in which we live, but it can reveal with striking precision what happens to the idea of causality when it is expressed. The very quantity of tight causal chains (in which A causes B, which causes C, etc.) permits comparison of several kinds of causal logic and of causal problems, so that the concepts of "known" and "expressed" causality are put in doubt on rational grounds. Indeed, Zola's conclusion here seems to approach Jameson's.

The text raises questions about the role of an observer-explainer-narrator when the implausible, despite all, happens. It points to the structural and formal role causal chains assume in narrative, and to the dual nature they thus acquire as representatives of the "real" and as fictional functions, exemplifying a theatrical ambiguity akin to that of the real actor or real prop in a fictional play. The novel shows random, aleatory events intervening to influence the course of causation, so that reported causality loses its function as a predictor. Indeed prediction is at times easier here on the level of *narration* than on the level of the *histoire*: causation functions as a predictor for the text better than it does as a predictor for the events the text recounts.

Zola's sketch-notes for the preparation of this novel suggest that construction of the causal chains posed serious difficulties for him.[8] His first problem was to invent two interconnected murders. Then he expressed a desire to work into that fabric the notion of murder by heredity—a homicidal maniac whose genes would predispose him to kill. He wished to include a description of the judicial system at work, and a portrayal of life on the railroad ("l'administration du chemin de fer, le poème d'une grande ligne, avec le milieu de la compagnie"—"the railroad administration, the poetry of a main line, with the social atmosphere of the company"), all without distracting interest from the central notion, the hereditary killer. "Le besoin de tuer et de tuer une femme," he notes. "Mais comme cela s'arrange mal avec le reste, comme cela est difficile à s'arranger!"[9] ("The need to kill, and to kill a woman. But how poorly that jibes with the rest, how hard that is to jibe!"). These difficulties led perhaps to the emphasis on causality in the work, to the discovery of the complexities of causal systems, in which the same apparent cause can produce, in several instances, several different results. Zola's approach to the problems led him as well to the construction of an inside-out detective story, in which we see the crimes from the standpoint of the perpetrators, only to discover at last the logical reasons why the detective, in possession of all the physical evidence, must nonetheless reconstruct the causal chains all wrong. Denizet's erroneous reconstruction of the crimes provides the clearest definition in the work of the distinction between real and textualized causation.

When readers set out to trace a causal chain, they must begin with a state of affairs they select as a final effect. One may write that A causes B causes C causes D, but, since no logic leads ineluctably from A to D, one will have to begin with D and work backward to construct the chain.

Denizet, like us, faces this difficulty; as Nietzsche pointed out, in this sense the effect precedes the cause. The corollary holds that authors must work in the same way: to construct a causally coherent sequence, one must plan from effect to cause in antichronological order. Then, for mimetic value, since life seems to evolve from cause to effect without such preplanning, the narrator must "perceive" and relate the events in reverse (i.e., chronological) order. [10] The ambiguity of "to relate" ("to narrate" and "to connect") was never more evident: events can only be related backward, so that they can subsequently be related forward. [11]

Furthermore, in an uncontrolled, open system, it is usually reductive to speak of A as the cause of B. Observation of reality suggests a multitude of interrelated conditions, INUS or not, that allow for and produce B. Criminal justice traditionally proposes three conditions for willed human actions: means, motive, and opportunity. (This system is also reductive: what constitutes means for one person does not for another, does not for the same person at another time. And, since the three must coexist at the moment of the action, timing is a factor; while means and motive may or may not persist, opportunity is usually presumed to be momentary, although that is not always so.) If we assume these three conditions as cause, each condition may be the result of an action itself having three (or more) conditions, so that reasoning backward from "effect" to "cause" should produce, not a chain, but a branching tree, in whose foliage an observer would soon be lost. As narrator, his situation would be hopeless, for language is not suited to tracing simultaneous, sinuous interconnections, as twigs move to branches to trunk: there is perhaps no better demonstration of these limits of causal narration than Michel Butor's *Degrés*. In addition to the distinction created by the fact that logical order is antichronological, textualization of cause and effect requires simplification. To construct a causal chain, rather than a causal "tree," one must eliminate all but the most important conditions of an event. The narrator of *La Bête humaine* performs such reductive judgments about what is important, which brings him at last, theoretically at least, into conflict with the author: how hard indeed all that is to "jibe"! To examine Zola's "deconstruction" of causal logic, we shall observe its workings in the following examples: the special case of the Misard chain; a typical linear chain (Flore); chains constructed in parallel, by character (Lantier, Séverine, Roubaud), and by primary conditions (love triangles); and finally the Denizet reconstruction.

1. *The Misard chain.* Phasie's inheritance is the initial stative event, and her decision to hide the money somewhere in the house or yard, rather than to share it with Misard, her sniveling, little second husband, sets the chain in motion. His attempt at extortion, slowly poisoning Phasie by secret means, turns the action back upon itself to form a remarkably "circular" or "reciprocal" chain between two secrets: old Phasie growing ever sicker, seeking the source of the poison in her diet, and old Misard, frantically searching every cranny of the house to find a thousand francs. But fear and greed are only the initial motive force: it soon becomes a classic test of wills, in which the obstinacy of one partner feeds the stubbornness of the other, until desire to "win" completely replaces the money as the system's dynamic. The pair is bonded in a life-and-death struggle fueled by a petty but almost superhuman determination.

The transitivity of the chain flows back and forth, from Phasie to Misard, from Misard to Phasie, in a closed causal system. None of this energy can escape directly to drive the central plots of the novel. What then is the function of this chain in the economy of the story? First, as a special case of causation, it points, in contrast to the more open, linear chains, to the existence of different kinds of causal relationships, thus designating causality as a theme of the novel. Second, as an example of pair bonding through exchange, it reflects by similarity other relationships based on exchange—the central Séverine-Lantier bonding, for example. Passion can feed upon passion as determination upon determination.

Third, without providing direct energy to other causal chains, the Misard system stands in *tangential* relationship to the major lines of narrative force. Living at la Croix-de-Maufras, the Misards are located right on the main-line railroad tracks between Paris and Le Havre, on which Misard works as a signalman, while Phasie's daughter Flore is a crossing guard. Indeed, as we are learning of the circular chain through Phasie's explanation to Jacques of her hideous marital situation, the narrator often interrupts her tale (pp. 49–53) with descriptions of Misard and Flore performing their duties just outside the window. The circularity of the two opposing obstinacies that define the *ménage* is juxtaposed to the linearity of the tracks and of the trains that thunder straight down them. Insofar as the trains themselves may be taken as symbolic for the causal forces, social and political, driving the anonymous masses ("flots de foule," p. 52) of French society toward war (p. 297), the circular and the linear can be taken as models for the tangential relationship of personal to social realities. At the end of her account of Misard's murderous cruelty, Phasie unites her conception of human bestiality with the marvelous invention of the steam-powered locomotive: "Oh, it's a fine invention, there's no denying. We're going fast, getting smarter. . . . But savage beasts are still savage beasts; even if they invent still fancier machines, there'll still be savage beasts on board" (p. 53; "Ah! c'est une belle invention, il n'y a pas à dire. On va vite, on est plus savant. . . . Mais les bêtes sauvages restent des bêtes sauvages, et on aura beau inventer des mécaniques meilleures encore, il y aura quand même des bêtes sauvages dessus"). Likewise, the little circular plot is tangential to all the novel's linear chains. Jacques Lantier comes there because Phasie is his aunt, who raised him. The circumstances of the test of wills are essential conditions, as I shall show, in Flore's chain. Séverine inherits from Grandmorin a house virtually next door, in which she will be murdered. Indeed all the major events of the novel take place within sight of la Croix-de-Maufras.

Finally, the Misard chain stands in a structurally symbolic relationship to the rest of the novel. *La Bête humaine* is a story about steam locomotives. In these engines, the back-and-forth movement of the pistons is translated through the drive rods tangentially into the circular movement of the wheels, which again translate it into the rectilinear movement of the train. The reciprocal nature of the causal model represented by the Phasie-Misard relationship is not without resemblance to the reciprocating steam engine. Their alternating and mutually stimulating cruelties toward one another, having become a continuous power-seeking circularity, drives the marriage in a straight line to its murderous conclusion. The self-contained subplot thus functions by analogy to overdetermine the symbolism of the locomotive. And the tangentially linear chains involving Flore and Jacques work, so to speak, like drive rods. As the little circular chain acquires contrastive, symbolic, and overdetermining formal functions in the *histoire*, the "seriousness" of events is diluted: they appear less reality-referential and more self-referential, causation serving a logical purpose which the *récit* attempts to mask as mimetic. Textualized causation is diverging from "real" causal relationships.

Phasie's discovery of Misard's secret (the poison in the salt) cannot halt the destructive process; he finds a new means (the poison in Phasie's enema solution), and she dies, without revealing the whereabouts of the "treasure." He will die without having found it, and it will remain lost for all time. Reciprocating engines wear out, their energy at last dissipated: Serres's "law" of entropy in Zola's fiction is herein validated.[12]

2. *Flore's chain.* Significantly, it is a cracked drive rod that brings Jacques Lantier to la Croix-de-Maufras. This mechanical failure in his "Lison" exemplifies the "chance occurrence": it is physically caused, but the chain of events that produce the tiny crack is too minute and too complex to follow. The timing and location of the breakdown were unpredictable, and it appears as a "random event," although one may suppose in fact that it was not. Such "chance" occurrences, frequent in the novel, are not a denial of physical causation, but rather an indication of human inability to observe, and hence to textualize. And, although la Croix-de-Maufras is easily accessible from Le Havre, where the breakdown occurs, Jacques's decision to spend the two-day enforced layoff at Phasie's also appears the result of a whim: there may be deep-seated reasons, but they are unknown.

What is known and clearly explained is the "fêlure héréditaire," the hereditary flaw or crack he brings with him (p. 61): an inherited predisposition to kill women when they arouse him sexually. The inferred author does not entrust this explanation to the narrator, but presents it himself in indirect discourse as an element of Jacques's thoughts. The engineer sees himself as paying, in his mental illness, for all the alcohol consumed by the "générations d'ivrognes dont il était le sang gâté" (the "generations of drunks whose tainted blood flowed in his veins"), as the product of a "slow poisoning" of the family blood—shades of what is happening to his aunt Phasie! Cumulative causation, whether the gradual accretion of metal fatigue in a drive rod or of poison in the blood, lacks the apparent temporal boundaries of an "event"; it is therefore unobservable as cause, although the effect may be well delimited, sudden, and disastrous, when the *fêlure* appears.

Like a drive rod himself, Jacques is both impellor and impelled, both victim (of heredity) and perpetrator (of crime), transmitting the past into the present like a superior link in a causal chain. It is as such that he reenters Flore's life. The events of the "Flore" sequence are clearly interconnected, from their first reunion near la Croix-de-Maufras, in the countryside at night. Jacques attempts to kiss her; she resists, then yields herself entirely. Jacques seizes her scissors, raises them to stab her, then flees, overcoming the homicidal impulse. But she, eyes closed in blissful submission, fails to see the murderous gesture: she is henceforth in love with Jacques. When she later learns of his involvement with Séverine, she determines to kill the lovers. She drags a quarryman's loaded wagon onto the tracks in front of the oncoming train which Jacques is driving, and in which Séverine is a passenger, off for a weekend tryst with the engineer in Paris. In the ensuing bloody derailment, Séverine escapes unharmed; mighty Flore herself pulls Jacques alive from beneath the wreckage. Then she goes off and kills herself. The major motivational links are self-evident: love, jealousy, murder, remorse, suicide.

But seen in detail, the chain includes two other sorts of unpredictable causation: the intermittent series and the coincidence. Jacques is able to conquer his desire to kill, and his hereditary mania is not therefore a necessary cause. Indeed the temptation to kill does not always even surface in sexual encounters: he will be able to carry on an affair of some duration with Séverine. (He apparently is not a man who always kills on the first date.) His temptation and the strength of his resistance to it are variables, and while events may cause their variation, it is impossible to predict when, in conjunction, they will produce an attack. On at least one occasion, an exterior force intervenes to prevent his violence, and exterior interventions are also variable. So the series of his sexual aggressions is an intermittent one, and all an observer can say is that sometimes he is dangerous to his partners, and sometimes not. Sleeping with Jacques might be compared to Russian roulette, except that with him the variables are more complex and the data on which to calculate chances of survival less readily available. Causation is functioning, but it is not observable in such a series until after the fact.

In a coincidence, two or more causal chains intersect; events in each are observable, perhaps predictable, but the unforeseeable temporal conjunction of particular occurrences on the chains opens the door to astonishing, unusual happenings. The single most influential event in the novel is just such a coincidence: Jacques, wandering by the tracks in a daze after his aborted attack on Flore, catches a glimpse of Séverine and Roubaud murdering Grandmorin on an express train speeding past. Flore's chain involves several coincidences; two examples will suffice to illustrate their function.

First, to become crazed with jealousy, Flore must confirm her suspicions that Jacques and Séverine are conducting an adulterous affair, and indeed she catches them in an embrace. To bring about this crucial discovery, the inferred author creates the following chain of events: (a) Séverine almost always takes Jacques's train to Paris on Friday and spends the week-end with him there; (b) one Friday, during a blizzard, the train is brought to a halt by huge snow drifts; (c) the train gets stuck some three hundred meters from the Misard home at la Croix-de-Maufras; (d) some of the passengers, including Séverine, take refuge there; (e) Séverine knows Phasie personally because of the Grandmorin property next door, and she is there-fore ushered into Phasie's sickroom to sit down, instead of waiting in the kitchen with the other passengers; (f) Jacques too comes in to greet his bedridden aunt while Séverine is there; (g) Phasie falls asleep before her visitors leave; (h) Jacques and Séverine seize this moment "alone" to ex-change a kiss; (i) Flore happens to open the bedroom door at the right moment to observe the embrace.

Most of the events are plausible, including the stolen kiss—this love affair is characterized by audacity. But, even allowing for nineteenth-century railroad equipment, and presuming some difference in meteoro-logical conditions over the past century, one could surely have travelled the Le Havre-Paris line every Friday for many years without becoming snow-bound, and for several lifetimes without being trapped in the snow near a specific house. Since no topographical features are mentioned, like a steep incline or a ravine, to make *enlisement* more likely at this spot, the statistical probabilities of an impassable snowstorm on Friday morning must be mul-tiplied by the probability of blockage at a particular, unexceptional point on the line. Thus causation of each event is explicit and clear; each individ-ual event is believable and possible; yet the conjunction of events is highly unlikely. Whence the reader's problem: to suspend disbelief because causes are clear and possible, or to sense manipulation of events by the inferred author to achieve a future result, because of the statistical improbability. Ambiguities of this kind may well leave our belief intact ("this is a realistic story") while making us aware of the inferred author ("this is not a true story"). Coincidence thus tells us that textualized causation is partly "real," partly structural, emphasizing the distinction between linguistic construc-tion and life.

Flore's entry into the bedroom at just the right moment is similarly ambiguous—plausible because she is bustling about the house serving food and drink to the stranded passengers, implausible because of the narrowness of the critical time frame: the duration of a kiss. Just as she had her eyes closed at the right moment to avoid seeing Jacques poised to strike her, she has them open just in time to learn the truth. Coincidence, even when the intersecting chains are themselves plausible, points to manipulation, to a level of *narration*, and thus to "textuality."

Another coincidence in the Flore sequence brings together three important chains, Flore's, Cabuche's, and the Misard "circle," all to create the dramatic train wreck. Cabuche's arrival with a wagonload of stone blocks is plausible: hauling stone is one of the quarryman's tasks. His arrival at Flore's crossing just before the passage of Jacques's train is the coincidence: nothing suggests that his trips are regular or that Flore expects him at that moment. Flore has the motive; Cabuche brings the means. But how can Flore detain the wagon for several minutes until the train arrives? How can she separate Cabuche from his horses, so that she can pull horses and wagon onto the tracks? Phasie has just expired! He can scarcely refuse Flore's invitation to stop in to pay his last respects to the deceased, leaving his rig unattended at the crossing. And where is the only outside force that could prevent the wreck, the signalman who could stop the train or halt Flore's action? Misard, freed by Phasie's death, is not at his post, but is wildly digging for treasure in the back yard! Thus the Misard "reciprocating-engine" chain vents its last energy, throwing Flore like a broken drive rod straight into the spokes of the onrushing express. The fact that the inferred author had attributed to Flore a workable plan to wreck the train by removing a rail—a plan she abandons only when Cabuche comes into view—just demonstrates that this coincidence was "unnecessary." The indexic author is at once suspect: does Cabuche arrive in order to facilitate connection of the Misard chain to Flore's, as she runs amok?

Finally, like intermittent series, coincidences put in doubt the value of causal knowledge for predicting. We may be aware of all the causal forces at work in the two approaching chains; without precise knowledge of when they will intersect, we cannot predict the outcome. As soon as Flore falls in love with Lantier, we may foresee that she will come to no good, but how and when we cannot imagine. Only after her suicide can we look back, following Nietzsche's dictum, and construct the chain that led, "inevitably," to her demise.

3. *Parallel chains.* From the time that Roubaud learns of his wife's adolescent sexual involvement with her guardian, Grandmorin, and brutally forces Séverine to be his accomplice in the wealthy old man's murder, the couple's lives run in close parallel. From the moment Jacques observes

the murder, although too fleetingly to be certain of the criminals' identities, his chain is tied to theirs, most tightly after Séverine seduces him as a way of preventing his casting suspicion on her at the hearings. Table 4.1 lists the principal causes and effects, vertically, in these three narrative lines, showing also the horizontal points of interconnection.

Table 4.1

Lantier	Séverine	Roubaud
Hereditary illness.	Reveals to Roubaud her liaison with	↔ Learns of Séverine's past liaison.
Broken drive rod.	Grandmorin.	
Visit to Misards.	Beaten, forced by Roubaud to be accomplice in murder.	↔ Wants Grandmorin dead, forces Séverine to be accomplice.
Observes murder.	↔ Takes part in murder.	↔ Kills Grandmorin.
Called to testify.	↔ Called to testify.	↔ Called to testify.
Seduced by Séverine.	↔ Seduces Lantier to obtain his silence.	Takes to gambling with money stolen
Séverine's lover.	↔ Lantier's lover.	from Grandmorin.
Plots Roubaud's murder.	↔ Plots Roubaud's murder.	↔ Argues over money with Séverine.
Kills Séverine.	↔ Murdered by Lantier.	↔ Discovers wife's body in Cabuche's arms.
Philomène's lover. Discovered with Philomène by Pecqueux. Killed in fight with Pecqueux.		Arrested for complicity with Cabuche in Séverine's and Grandmorin's murders. Convicted.

These narrative lines represent true causal chains, in which nearly every effect is the cause in turn of a subsequent effect. If we are seeking a Zola who is "anti-Gide," *anti-absurde*, it would seem that here we have found him. The unpredictable occurs, but it is always explainable, in Kantian fashion, after the fact. There is coincidence in Jacques's witnessing of Grandmorin's murder, and a quasi-coincidence in the fact that Jacques's hereditary "time bomb" chooses to explode precisely when the plot to kill

Roubaud has given him means and opportunity—and a skillfully pre-arranged alibi. One may argue that the very circumstances of the planned crime—waiting alone in complicity with Séverine, knife in hand, for the victim to walk into their bloody trap—were the trigger of Jacques's latent violence. But this is not the first time they had plotted to waylay Roubaud. And if present circumstances have major causal force, then the causal role of the genetic impulse is somewhat diminished. Still, causes, if not timing, are generally assessable in retrospect. One could scarcely predict, for example, that Jacques would begin sleeping with Philomène, his fireman's mistress, shortly after slaying Séverine; in hindsight, however, it is easy to accept the explicit notion that he needed to test himself, to see whether his crime had purged him of the hereditary curse: curiosity about his own intermittence becomes itself a cumulative causal force. That Cabuche should find Séverine's body is well prepared by the narrator: adoring Séverine with almost canine fidelity, he is always "hanging about." Roubaud's arrival to find Cabuche with the corpse (their joint presence on the scene is one cause of their arrest) is an impeccable link in the causal chain: he is the intended victim, arriving, as prearranged, for his own murder. A primary effect of such carefully structured causation is the comparison it permits with Denizet's version of these events as the magistrate reconstructs them.

Reduced to their simplest terms for later comparison with the Denizet explanation, the major causal chains link the states or conditions of the characters as shown in diagram 4.1. The notion of "love" (" + ") in the diagram receives its broadest meaning, ranging from the most ethereal and idealistic adoration, represented by Cabuche's worship of Séverine (not causally related to anything in the novel except his own subsequent conviction for murder), to simple sexual relations (Lantier and Philomène), to brutal possessiveness (Roubaud and Séverine). The multiple meanings subsumed under the idea of "love" evoke another sort of parallelism indicative of the "laboratory" study of causality being carried out in the novel.

As the diagram shows, jealousy is the prime mover, the underlying dynamic of action in the text. The inferred author sets up no fewer than five love triangles, resolving the potential instability they represent each time in a different way. Nothing suggests more clearly that the novel is experimenting with the notion of causal laws. (1) Roubaud and Grandmorin love (have loved) Séverine. (2) Flore and Séverine love Lantier. (3) Lantier and Roubaud love (have loved) Séverine. (4) Pecqueux and Lantier love Philomène. (5) Lantier and Cabuche love Séverine. Instability is triggered by

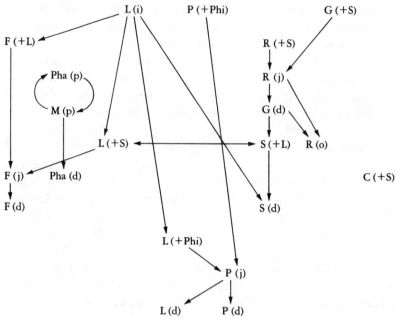

Diagram 4.1   Capital letters are characters' initials ("Pha" = Phasie; "Phi" = Philomène), and other symbols designate the conditions: "+" = "loves," "d" = dead, "i" = mentally ill, "j" = jealous, "o" = obsessive gambler, "p" = power-seeking.

perception: one of the lovers becomes aware that he or she has a rival for the affections of the beloved. Triangle 1 illustrates what might be called the standard or traditional mechanism for resolving instability: the husband punishes both the lover and the beloved, as Roubaud beats Séverine and kills Grandmorin. If this is the "law" of the jealousy reaction, the other triangles demonstrate that it can often fail to work. In triangle 2, the "aggrieved" party strikes out at rival and beloved according to the "law," but the event fails through a series of doubtless caused, but apparently random, occurrences. Flore's clumsy choice of means, a train wreck, kills and maims unpredictably a number of unrelated persons, while leaving Jacques and Séverine fortuitously alive. Thereupon, in remorse, the "aggrieved" party kills herself. The mechanism of the "law" may thus be readily derailed by chance.

Triangle 3 illustrates a potential instability that is never triggered. One rival (Lantier) knows from the start that his love is married; he has obviously won her affections, and jealousy does not occur. The other rival

(Roubaud) undergoes perception, learns that Séverine and Lantier are lovers. But, having apparently lost all desire for his wife through participation in triangle 1 and having thereafter substituted gambling for sex as his principal obsession, Roubaud feels no jealousy. Once his bomb has gone off, so to speak, it cannot explode again. This triangle has every possibility for stability, and it is Séverine of course who destabilizes it by seeking her freedom to marry Jacques. When Roubaud refuses a divorce, needing her inheritance from Grandmorin to gamble, she draws Lantier into the murder plot. Thus we would have the "aggrieved" party (Roubaud) slain by the two others. But this solution to the triangle also goes awry, when Jacques's genetic *fêlure* breaks at last. This interference of series changes the character of the situation, and this time it is the beloved who dies. Triangle 3, had the standard mechanism been set in motion, would have furnished a neat and balanced ending to the novel (*clôture*): Roubaud, discovering Séverine and Lantier together, kills them both and goes to the scaffold for his crimes. But the inferred author has other things in mind; Lantier's genetic flaw must play a role in Séverine's causal chain, and it must go unobserved, to prepare the Denizet explanation.

Triangle 4 brings us back to the basic mechanism: Pecqueux strikes out at his rival and kills him. But circumstances again influence the outcome: having chosen to fight Jacques on the platform of a moving locomotive, Pecqueux puts himself in jeopardy, and both fall to their deaths, leaving a driverless train speeding off, symbolically, with its passengers into the night. As for triangle 5, it engenders no violence, for Cabuche's love is both pure and unrequited. All three survive in this stable situation, although Séverine will die through participation in triangle 3, which seems to ignite Lantier's hereditary predisposition.

Of the eight possible mortal outcomes of triangles, the inferred author has used five, which can be summarized like this (A = aggrieved party, B = rival, C = beloved; capital letters indicate survivors): (1) AbC; (2) aBC; (3) ABC; (4) abC; (5) ABC. Of the three remaining possibilities—aBc, Abc, and abc—the first is difficult to arrange in context. The second and third would be quite plausible, but were not selected as outcomes for triangle 3, when the genetic flaw intervenes: Roubaud never has the chance or the desire to eliminate Jacques and Séverine. Besides, to arrange all twelve deaths necessitated by the eight possible solutions, writer and readers alike would have to expend a great deal of emotional energy on an exceptionally large cast of characters. The five examples suffice to show that, from parallel initial causes, very different effects may ensue, either as a result of poor

planning (Roubaud is better at arranging murder than is Flore) or of unpredictable influences, elements either unknowable (Pecqueux cannot foresee
his death) or unknown (Séverine is unaware of Jacques's *fêlure*). What this
experiment "proves," then, is that, while we may be able to spot a motive
force, such as raging jealousy, in an individual, or recognize an unstable
situation, such observations cannot serve as predictors of the outcome:
causality involves an interplay of forces too hidden and too complex to be
observed except (perhaps) after the fact. It also attests that genetically
acquired homicidal mania, if there is such a thing, is only one type of
hidden cause; without such hereditary baggage, Roubaud, Flore, and Pecqueux launch similar sex-related violence, of equal or greater brutality, on
the simple basis of jealousy. By wrecking trains, Flore, and probably Pecqueux, intervene unpredictably in the causal chains of the lives of many
otherwise unrelated passengers. A crack in a drive rod, if it goes un-
detected, can destroy the orderly succession of numerous lives. And such
cracks are often impossible to detect until it is too late.

 4. *Denizet's explanation.* But what about after the fact? Even if it is too
late to avoid damage, can we not at least look back and construct causal
chains in our minds and thus "make sense," if not of the future, at least of
the past? The inclusion of Denizet's explanation in the novel provides an
answer to these questions, no longer about causality as a real, if often
unobservable, phenomenon, but about cause and effect as mental constructs.

 Denizet's hypotheses form a kind of embedded narrative in the novel, a
structure Todorov compares to the imbrication of subordinate clauses in
longer sentences.[13] As such, it forms a part of the *histoire*; it has a cause
(society's desire to find and punish the guilty) and an effect (the convictions
of Cabuche and Roubaud). It occupies a precise position on the timeline of
the story and is thus contingent upon the causal forces then operative. It is
an "event" created by the inferred author. But it is also *histoire*-referential, a
recasting of many of the same events we find in the rest of the novel, but
recombined and reconnected in new and different causal chains. The inferred author thus creates a narrative that is itself contingent upon events
and places it in competition with the narrator's apparently gratuitous tale,
so that each functions as a critique of the other.

 Denizet's analysis (pp. 277–83) develops the following points. At the
inconclusive investigation of Grandmorin's murder, Cabuche, the poor,
unlettered quarryman, had come under suspicion for three reasons: he was
an ex-convict; he had expressed hatred for Grandmorin (the aging lecher
had mistreated a young girl thereafter befriended and cared for by

Cabuche); and Roubaud, to avoid suspicion, had claimed to have seen a man of Cabuche's description boarding the murder train. When the investigation is renewed following the murder of Séverine, Denizet's convictions about Cabuche are confirmed, for he is found blood-spattered and holding the corpse in his arms. The murder wound was similar in both crimes (Séverine had preserved the knife and planned for Jacques to use it in slaying Roubaud). Cabuche is therefore a prime suspect in both cases. A search of his cabin after the first killing had turned up nothing, but a second search, after Séverine's death, produces Grandmorin's gold watch (Séverine and Roubaud had stolen it, along with some money, to mask the motive as theft; Cabuche had later pilfered a handkerchief of his adored Séverine, only to find the watch, by coincidence, wrapped up in it), the essential link of evidence tying Cabuche to both crimes.

The motive for the second crime gives Denizet pause, for Cabuche seems to have worshipped Séverine. This difficulty leads the magistrate to have Roubaud arrested. Denizet's theory holds that Roubaud coveted the legacy his wife was to receive from Grandmorin. A coward incapable of murder, Roubaud had paid Cabuche to do in the rich old man, thus speeding up the inheritance. Afterwards, since it was apparent to all that the Roubauds were on the outs, it was supposed that Séverine had refused to sell the house at la Croix-de-Maufras, as Roubaud wished, to stake his gambling. Whence the need for a second murder. Cabuche was hired again (a rape before the killing would surely satisfy the "adoration" of such a brute!) to do the deed.

Tortured by hours of questioning in Denizet's effort to prove the accuracy of this construction, Roubaud at last confesses to the truth: he had killed Grandmorin himself in a jealous rage. This confession, part of the causal chain of the investigation and not of the murder itself, could well destroy Denizet's theory of a prearranged plot. But the magistrate resists it as a ruse to weaken his case for premeditated murder. Aware that Roubaud had tolerated Jacques's affair with his wife, he prepares to describe to the court a Roubaud incapable of jealousy, a man who married for money, and who conspired with Cabuche to kill to get it. (The proof of the veracity of Roubaud's confession exists. Séverine's letter to Grandmorin, written at Roubaud's violent insistence to ensure that the old man would be on the train with them, was found among Grandmorin's papers after his death. But the person who found it, judging that it could compromise Grandmorin's reputation and thereby weaken the Emperor's government—all prominent supporters of the government must appear irreproachable, after all—de-

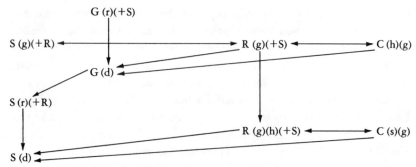

Diagram 4.2 Characters are designated by their initials; "+" = cohabiting with, "d" = dead, "g" = motivated by greed, "h" = motivated by hatred, "r" = rich, "s" = motivated by sexual desire.

stroyed it: a post-crime interference of series.) As for Séverine's true murderer, the alibi Jacques established, by slipping out of, and then back into, his hotel room through a window, arranged to cover Roubaud's killing, works just as well for Séverine's. Besides, from Denizet's position, it is unreasonable to suppose a man would kill his mistress, with whom he was on the best of terms.

Denizet's reconstruction, with which he wins his case, is represented in diagram 4.2. Comparison with diagram 4.1, the narrator's construction of events, will bring essential discrepancies to the surface.

Differences between Denizet's mental construct and "reality," as best we know it from the *récit*, have three primary sources: (1) Denizet's subjective predispositions, which are a major subset of (2) the causal dependency of the explanation itself, as an effect of the causes within its own time frame, and (3) the necessity to construct it logically, which is to say, counterchronologically.

As for his predispositions, Denizet is arrogant, materialistic, and bigoted. His arrogance is apparent in his own self-assessments, reported by the narrator: "As he used to say, he had a nose for truths" (p. 279; "Comme il le disait, il flairait des vérités"); "in one of those moments of inspiration when he believed in the genius of his perspicacity" (p. 280; "dans une de ces minutes d'inspiration où il croyait au génie de sa perspicacité"); "Never had he delved so deeply, he said, into human nature" (p. 283; "Jamais, disait-il, il n'était descendu si à fond dans la nature humaine"). His own materialism emerges from his imputation of greed to others. Indeed, as the diagram shows, greed has replaced jealousy in his causal system as the primary dynamic of the action. From his standpoint, acquiring wealth is a most understandable motivation. His prejudice against the poor, who have failed to acquire material possessions, is evident in his judgment of Cabuche. Uneducated, untrained in self-expression, doubtless ill-clothed and unprepossessing, he is in difficulty with Denizet from the outset. It is reasonable, on these grounds, to read Denizet's explanation as a satire of the judicial system, run by the well-to-do for the well-to-do, at the expense of the poor. Certainly perception of cause and effect can be twisted by class values. But there is more.

Events occurring during the investigation influence its course. Roubaud's initial lies implicating Cabuche in the Grandmorin murder (cause: Roubaud's desire to save his own skin; effect: Cabuche's inculpation); Roubaud's later confession (cause: fatigue, discouragement; effect nullified by Denizet's predispositions); discovery of Grandmorin's watch in Cabuche's cabin (cause: Denizet's determination to convict Cabuche, whence the second search, and Cabuche's fetishistic thefts from Séverine; effect: Cabuche's conviction): all such events belong to causal chains exterior to the murders, yet they influence the explanation. Denizet's prejudices are a part of this subsequent influence, including one tendency we have not mentioned: the inclination to preserve a preestablished theory in the face of new evidence (such as Roubaud's confession), to read the evidence so that it fits the theory, rather than to change the hypothesis to accommodate the facts. Yet despite all the personal criticism we can address to the magistrate on the basis of the text, an epistemological problem remains: if the search for causes of previous events is contingent upon a causal chain inherent in its own time frame, it cannot uncover what it purports to seek, except by coincidence. This places the very principle of a posteriori causal explanations in doubt. Denizet cannot be blamed for that.

Finally, the antichronological logic required to construct explanations differs by nature from the chronology of causality and therefore fails to explain it. When Roubaud admits to having killed Grandmorin in a jealous rage, Denizet reasons backward: Roubaud was quite tolerant of Lantier's long affair with Séverine; therefore he is either not sexually possessive by nature or not sexually possessive of his wife. In either case, jealousy could not therefore be the motive for killing Grandmorin. If he married Séverine for her inheritance, however, it is possible to explain Grandmorin's murder (greed) *and* the absence of jealousy when Roubaud learns that Jacques is bedding his wife. Thus he establishes a causal system which explains two events, but which omits an intermediary cause present in reality: psychological change in Roubaud after the first murder. Unobservable causes—

causes which are not "events" but evolutions, slow accretions—can find no place in a logical structure built backward from event to event. Asked about the apparent discrepancy, Roubaud can only state the facts: "J'ai tué l'autre, je n'ai pas tué celui-ci" (p. 282); "I killed the other one, I didn't kill this one." In an explanation, however, it is not the facts that matter but their causal interrelation. For these facts, a posteriori, none can be found. As Roubaud will conclude at the trial, "what good was it to tell the truth, since it was the lie that was logical?" (p. 288; "à quoi bon dire la vérité, puisque c'était le mensonge qui était logique?").

Likewise, explanations lose their logical rigor if they reject an over-determined hypothesis in favor of an implausible coincidence. Cabuche is a rough and boorish ex-convict, present at the site of the second murder and probably at the site of the first. It would be logically easier (and not only for Denizet) to believe that he killed Grandmorin and stole his watch than to believe that he took a handkerchief as a keepsake from his beloved and found, by chance, the watch inside. As for Jacques's intermittent urge to kill, if that is unobservable to all those who knew him well in the present, it is totally undiscoverable in hindsight. "Backward" reasoning connects only visible events and prefers the simplicity of broad, general causes to the complexity of interfering series (coincidence) and of irrational, unpredictable behavior. In these ways, causal analysis is foreign to the reality it pretends to explain. Here again, the problem lies not with Denizet or a particular judicial system, but in the realm of epistemology: logic can neither see nor reconstruct causation after the fact. In this instance, the primary error is a belief in inertia: once a condition exists, it will persist until an "event" intervenes to change it. If Cabuche was once a criminal, he still is; if Roubaud once failed to be jealous of Séverine, he never was. Yet the basic principle of causal logic, that states of being are the result of events that cause them, rests upon this belief in inertia.

The diagram of Denizet's explanation thus appears far simpler than the one we have constructed on the basis of the narrator's *récit*. The cast of characters is smaller. Lantier is erroneously omitted, for he is invisible to logic. With him go a number of "extraneous" characters: the Misards, Flore. (But are they extraneous? Without Phasie, Jacques would never have become involved in the chain of events at la Croix-de-Maufras. And if Flore had kept her eyes open, Jacques's mania might have become public knowledge in time to save Séverine.) And for the characters retained, Denizet makes far fewer vertical connections, since his logic sees only events and not evolutions and coincidences. He prefers instead horizontal connections, indicative of conspiracy, thus pulling Cabuche into the action.

The narrator's tale, then, is critical of Denizet's, which the inferred author requires him to include in it. Denizet's explanation is "false." But if Denizet is in error partly for epistemological reasons, how can the narrator's tale be "true"? How can we believe anyone who explains in the past tense? In this work, the narrator is reduced to an objective observer, a simple "scribe." [14] Causal connections are expressed by the characters themselves, for the most part, even if that requires understanding doubtless beyond their capacities (i.e., Jacques's comprehension of the genetic origins of his mania). [15] Thus causation appears to the reader to come in the form of "visible" events—characters' thoughts, actions which we and the perpetrators alone perceive. The narrator lacks even the class identity his language patterns gave him in *L'Assommoir*, and the inferred author dominates throughout this novel. His dominance reveals an intent of *narration*, and it produces a text in which the "gaps" require no creativity or symbolic activity on the part of the reader.

Why read a work in which our own creative activity is thus reduced? The function of *La Bête humaine* appears essentially didactic. The inferred author instructs by example, and the lesson is the weakness of causal theory. In this inside-out detective story, where we "know" the causal chains from the point of view of the criminals and can thus make sport of the wildly erroneous explanation of the "detective," the implausibilities serve less to liberate us from the inferred author than to accomplish his ends: making life difficult for Denizet. Ripoll points out, on the basis of Zola's preparatory notes, that the author was intentionally breaking the structural code of the detective story; [16] Serres notes that the intervention of random occurrences produces a new state of systematics. [17] For the "system" persists: everything in *La Bête humaine* has a clearly inferable cause. The questions are: In an open and uncontrolled system, can causation be observed? Can it serve as a useful predictor? Can it be textualized, reconstructed linguistically after the fact? The answers are all essentially negative.

Were the deaths of specific passengers on the train wrecked by Flore in any useful sense "determined"? No one—not even Flore—could have predicted them. And Zola leaves the reader in a similar situation at the close of the novel: who, if anyone, will die on the driverless train? The causes are all in place, but the precise results remain unpredictable. Séverine could not foresee her own death as she made love with Jacques while waiting to kill

Roubaud, nor could Jacques himself predict her murder, as he slipped out of his hotel and made his way to the lonely house by the tracks. But there are surely few readers who fail to predict it. For readers ask questions not only about fictional events, but also about the *narration*. Why create a homicidal maniac, unless he is going to kill? Why create such a beautiful, trusting, and evil character as Séverine, if she is not to be a victim? Why establish means, opportunity, and alibi for Jacques, unless he is to kill *now*?

The ability to ask such metacausal questions puts readers in contact with the *narration*. It is not gaps or weaknesses in the causal chain that send us there this time, however, in search of explanations. In the excitement of this adventure, where the past seems self-explanatory, we are interested rather in foresight. If we can often be, as readers, more prescient than the characters of this narrative, it is precisely because we have recourse to a level of *narration*, with its novelistic conventions, which is unavailable to the characters, visibly unaware of their fictional status. Our privileged knowledge, our "reason for inference," is that nothing is included in traditional mimetic fiction which does not, sooner or later, have a bearing on events. A second impulsion for readers to look to the intent of *narration* is a gap—not a break in the causal chain, but a crack in the logic. The logical abyss that separates the two competing narratives of the crimes, the narrator's and Denizet's, points to a more general intent of *narration*, which we have just observed. Why present two competing *récits* of the same *histoire*? This time, our reason for inference resides in the differences between the two *récits*, the inferred causes of those differences, and the privileging of the narrator's tale. Even behind the intricate, densely woven *histoire* of *La Bête humaine*, a level of *narration* is manifest, defining the distinction between "text" and "reality."

Notes

1. Emile Zola, *La Bête humaine*, in his *Oeuvres complètes*, 6 (Paris: Cercle du Livre Précieux, 1967). Further references in the text are to this edition.

2. Etienne, who ended up in *Germinal*, was originally intended to play Jacques's role, according to Zola's notes as quoted in Roger Ripoll, *Réalité et mythe chez Zola* (Paris: Honoré Champion, 1981), pp. 823–25.

3. J. H. Matthews, *Les Deux Zola* (Geneva, Paris: Droz, Minard, 1967), p. 11.

4. Emile Zola, *Le Roman expérimental*, in his *Oeuvres complètes*, 10 (Paris: Cercle du Livre Précieux, 1968), 1178.

5. Zola, *Le Roman expérimental*, pp. 1180–81.

6. Fredric Jameson, *The Political Unconscious* (Ithaca: Cornell University Press, 1981), p. 85.

7. Paul Valéry, "Regards sur le monde actuel," *Oeuvres*, II (Paris: Gallimard, Pléiade, 1960), 916–17. Original edition, 1931.

8. Quoted in Ripoll, pp. 823–25.

9. Ripoll, p. 825. The awkward construction of *s'arranger* strikes me as an unconscious reiteration by Zola of the illogicalities of *Le Roman expérimental*: is it the events or the author that does the "jibing"? (Ripoll's transcription is accurate, as I verified on microfilm of the notes at the Bibliothèque Nationale, Nouvelles Acquisitions Françaises, ms. 10274, folio 353.)

10. Gérard Genette described the interplay of causal chronology and antichronology in his *Figures II* (Paris: Editions du Seuil, 1969), pp. 92–99; I shall return to his analysis in the next chapter.

11. Ross Chambers, *Story and Situation* (Minneapolis: University of Minnesota Press, 1984), p. 4, evokes another polysemic reading of "to relate."

12. Michel Serres, *Feux et signaux de brume: Zola* (Paris: Bernard Grasset, 1975).

13. Tzvetan Todorov, *Poétique de la prose* (Paris: Editions du Seuil, 1971), pp. 82–85.

14. Seymour Chatman might well call this a "narrator-absent" novel; see his *Story and Discourse* (Ithaca: Cornell University Press, 1978), p. 33. My position is that a narrator is always present, simply because her or his characteristics constitute an option of the text. "Neutrality" and "transparency" are narratorial characteristics; to select them, the text had to reject a "southern accent," "judgmental tendencies," etc.

15. This exemplifies J. H. Matthews's insight in his *Les Deux Zola*, p. 38.

16. Ripoll, pp. 803–4.

17. Serres, p. 23.

5
Inference, Causality,
and the Levels of Narrative

Histoire et narration n'existent donc pour nous que par le truchement du récit. Mais réciproquement le récit, le discours narratif ne peut être tel qu'en tant qu'il raconte une histoire, faute de quoi il ne serait pas narratif . . . , et en tant qu'il est proféré par quelqu'un, faute de quoi . . . il ne serait pas en lui-même un discours. Comme narratif, il vit de son rapport à l'histoire qu'il raconte; comme discours, il vit de son rapport à la narration qui le profère.

(Thus *histoire* and *narration* exist for us only through the intermediary of the *récit*. But reciprocally the *récit* assumes its identity as narrative discourse only insofar as it tells an *histoire* [otherwise it would not be narrative . . .], and only insofar as it is proffered by someone [otherwise . . . it would not of itself be a discourse]. It owes its existence as narrative to its relation to the *histoire* it tells; it owes its existence as discourse to the *narration* that proffers it.)

—GÉRARD GENETTE

Suppose—erasing for a moment what we have written under erasure—that we return to our initial position: there is no causality as such in fiction. There may be words, credible or not, referring to it, but causation remains invisible: nothing causes anything in novels unless a reader infers it.

What then are those "gaps" and "weaknesses" we have uncovered in "causal chains"? A gap does not depend upon the presence or absence of inference, but on the degree of assurance with which a reader hypothesizes. Consider two potential gaps in *L'Assommoir*: Coupeau falls four stories to the street below, and then he is found to have injuries; Gervaise is energetic and self-disciplined, and then she demonstrates traits of slovenliness and laxity. A relationship of implication, based on life experience (or on newspaper accounts thereof) makes us confident in supposing that Coupeau's fall caused (or explains) his injuries, while Gervaise's apparent transformation provides little ground for inference. Hubris theories, notions that success leads to failure, may fit the *récit*, but they are highly speculative, espoused with misgivings on the basis of meager evidence. The gap lies not in the inference as such, but in the relative doubt that surrounds it. Texts may or may not allow for ready inference.

"Weakness" in a "causal chain" is characterized by implausibility, but not all implausibilities weaken our inferred connections. Here, it is perhaps less life experience than the story itself which determines how weak an implausibility appears. Again, two contrastive examples illustrate the principle: Coupeau's survival and complete recovery from a four-story plunge; and the incredible sequence of events we have already described leading, in *La Bête humaine*, to Flore's discovery of Jacques's and Séverine's mutual passion. The implausibility in *L'Assommoir* appears unnecessary to the causality of the *histoire*, since Coupeau is cured and ends up working in Etampes as if nothing had happened. Thus the fall could, for all its surface consequences, have been eliminated from the *histoire*. It could also have been used to explain (had there been lasting physical or psychic damage) Coupeau's drunken decline, but the text eschews that function. The apparent gratuitousness of the implausibility makes of it a "weakness" and sends us looking for writerly reasons, for the intent of *narration*. On the other hand, Flore's wrecking of Jacques's train and her subsequent suicide seem integral parts of a causal *histoire*, implied by jealousy. Readers may be more willing to accept a most unlikely series of events when they are linked together by plentiful reasons for inference to achieve an obvious purpose. Refusing to believe in a specific train becoming snowbound near Phasie's house, or in Flore's opening the door just in time, means rejecting all the rest, all the dramatic consequences of these events. Flore's discovery and the excitement that follows make it easier to "swallow" the causally incredible preparation. Our foresight ("when Flore finds out, there'll be Hell to pay!"), based on inferred understanding of the intent of *narration* at this point, keeps us going, accepting the implausible as possible.

Thus implausibility is not of itself a "weakness." Again it is a matter of the ease of readerly inference: if we can readily infer the *narrative* necessity for an event, if we can easily see why, for the purposes of *narration*, it is required, we are more likely to suspend disbelief; the alternative is rejecting the story as a whole. When we have doubts about narrative purpose and the incredible event's place in it, the implausibility appears as a "weakness" in the "chain." Whether we perceive a gap or a weakness, the plane of *narration* has a crucial role: if we are confident we understand its purpose, we can fill the gap, accept the implausibility; if we are unsure of the intent of *narration*, we are impelled to look ever more closely to uncover it, in extratextual allusions, metaphors, and other elements of comparison.

Ease of readerly inference and intent of *narration* are thus prime determiners of the nature of fictional texts. Brief examination of each will help us begin to define the nature of the changes that have arisen in twentieth-century fiction.

Creation or obliteration of readerly uncertainty in inference is a classifying characteristic of novels. Devices that create uncertainty—absence of inferable causes in the *histoire* (Gervaise's unexpected *avachissement*) or in the *narration* (Coupeau's "gratuitous" and "inconsequential" fall)—represent a lack or "ungrammaticality" in the chain of textually inspired causal inferences. I borrow the term Michael Riffaterre has so masterfully applied with respect to poetry[1] with some hesitation: it implies a "grammar" of implied causation; it implies a "norm," although none exists. But if grammar is defined as presence of causal implication, then its absence, like an ungrammaticality, provides an entry into, or reason for recourse to, the *narration*.

It should be obvious that dozens if not hundreds of minor gaps (not all causal) appear on each page of traditional novels, all of which are open to reader inference. Most of these surmises are doubtless made without reflection, on the basis of personal experience. We infer that, if a character steps off a sidewalk, she or he is in a street, where there may be carriages (horsedrawn or automobile, according to place and time), other people about, buildings on either side, and a sky above; we assume that a character called "Marceline" has at least the same genetic makeup as a character by that name mentioned forty pages earlier. Although they are individually of minor importance, the sheer numbers of these small hypotheses required by texts produce a wider range of indeterminacy than is often recognized. Indeterminacy goes unnoticed precisely because, in mimetic fiction, it is mostly inconsequential. One of the times we become aware of the essentially hypothetical nature of fictional reality is when a minor inference proves unsound: we suddenly learn, perhaps, that the busy thoroughfare we had created in imagination is "at this hour deserted." But the "realistic" tradition usually contrives to spare us such shocks: the essential (i.e., causally consequential) details are provided in advance, a technique reminiscent of the now outmoded cinematic convention according to which a scenic space is filmed in its entirety before the cameras move in to show characters acting within that space, so that viewers may integrate them mentally into their surroundings. The avoidance of shock by elimination of the potential for erroneous hypotheses in fiction might be termed, in our "grammar," the "rule of prepared consequentiality." Not only must consequential details be provided in traditional novels, but they must be proffered sufficiently in advance to forestall incorrect inferences.

The operation of this rule points to an effort in mimetic fiction to conceal from readers the degree to which the fictional world they enter is open to inference. Our little hypotheses must be automatic, obvious, and apparently error-free, so that our imaginary scenes will seem firm, familiar, and safe for us as readers, no matter how dangerous they may be for the characters. When we imagine fictional people in settings, whether it be Gervaise in her laundry or Jérôme and Alissa in the symmetrical garden at Fongueusemare, there are two areas of potential inference: those elements of the scene which will have a function in events, and those which will not. For the second area, our imagination is relatively free: Jérôme may be imagined, for example, with or without a mustache, for that detail remains inconsequential. But, for a familiar-seeming fictional world, prior presentation of consequential details is a requisite, whether it be explicitly in the *récit*, implicitly in the *histoire* (characters out-of-doors may be presumed to be under a sky), or by convention (fictional "existents" such as characters and settings are assumed to remain the same unless we are made aware of the intervention of a force to change them, for example). If Virginie's fortuitous inheritance may appear to be a weakness in the structure of *L'Assommoir*, it is because it forces readers to revise the scenario; they have no reason to infer early on that she might be related to anyone who could accumulate a nest egg. Such shocks require us not simply to reevaluate past events, but to redefine the parameters of the possible and the probable in a preestablished situation. They are a standard part of the fictional esthetic nowadays, as we shall see, but destroying readerly inferences after the fact, on the level of the *histoire*, breaks the rule of prepared consequentiality, a fundamental metonymic dictate of "realism." This rule for guiding readerly inference in matters of consequence is a primary basis of what Roman Jakobson calls the "profound affinity" binding realism to metonymy.[2]

As for the "inconsequential" inferences, they constitute the reader's freest creative participation in traditional novels. Through them, we insert ourselves and our life experience into texts, possibly recreating our own identities and injecting our psychological defenses, as Norman Holland suggests,[3] into the background of the action, thus coloring the reading of the text as a whole.

The notions of "textually conditioned" and "free" inferences are, of course, not absolute, but a matter of degree. As I have noted, hypotheses are by definition conditioned: X is a necessary condition that I infer Y. Without the condition, we are in the realm of fancy or guesswork. Even "free" inferences are limited by our experience and conditioned to some extent by the text (in a novel of the 1870s, a "voiture" must be imagined as horse-drawn; there are no blue horses; etc.).[4] Likewise, textually conditioned inferences are partially free: our imaginary visual image of a character may acquire far more detail than a text gives us. Thus the condition of inference is the point at which readers' experience and propensities on one hand, and textual data on the other, conjoin.

If hypotheses are limited on one end by the requirement that there be a condition of inference, they are constrained on the other by the necessity for at least some doubt. By definition, no hypothesis is, as yet, proven "true." A proven hypothesis about a story would be truth itself. Where causal relationships are concerned, such truth is never totally obtainable.

When inferences concern causes and effects in fiction, they rest upon that other set of hypotheses we call the levels of narrative. The *histoire* itself, as a preexisting series of events, is inferred; the *récit* is a condition of that inference, although our experiences and penchants also participate in the condition. The idea of an "author" is also inferred from the existence of a narrative text; in addition to the voice speaking to us from the page, there is an inventor of events for the voice to relate. And the final inference is that of intent: if things happen as they do in a story, there is, so we infer, a purpose behind it. Like all hypotheses, this one is of unassured veracity. As a text-based assumption, it cannot claim to reveal the "true" intentions of any "real" author. It presumes merely that what indeed happens in a novel fulfills an inferable purpose, which we have called the "intent of *narration*." This inference is conditioned by the existence of *récit* and *histoire* taken together, as well as by readerly experience. In this instance, however, it is our acquaintance with literary and other texts which will doubtless provide our personal conditions for inference, rather than our general knowledge of "life." We infer the intent of *narration* more from what we know about texts than from what we know about living.

In discovering these levels, as if they lay one above the other, we are engaged in making what might be termed "vertical" hypotheses. The causes and effects we infer on any one of the levels lie in "horizontal" relationship to each other. Thus, the levels appear to mask one another, to impede our vertical inference. Believable causal statements in the *récit* obviate the search for possible hidden causes in the *histoire*, and strong, plausibly inferable chains of cause and effect in the *histoire* tend to reduce our questioning of the *narration*. Insofar as the mimetic tradition follows the rule of prepared consequentiality, providing creditable conditions for satisfactory inference in advance, the "author" seems to disappear from the text, in casual reading; the *histoire* itself seems to be the only "intention."

In his essay on verisimilitude and motivation in *Figures II*,[5] Gérard Genette calls attention to the contrarieties of causal logic inherent in fiction of mimetic tendency. While he is not really discussing cause and effect as such, but rather relationships of implication among functional narrative units, he brings causal vocabulary into the discussion by evoking the causal logic of a seventeenth-century critic (Valincour) to explore the chronological direction of such logic in *La Princesse de Clèves*:

> . . . M. de Clèves ne meurt pas *parce que* son gentilhomme se conduit comme un sot, mais le gentilhomme se conduit comme un sot *pour que* M. de Clèves meure, ou encore, comme le dit Valincour, *parce que* l'auteur *veut* faire mourir M. de Clèves et que cette finalité du récit de fiction est l'*ultima ratio* de chacun de ses éléments.[6]

> (. . . M. de Clèves does not die *because* his gentleman behaves like a fool, but the gentleman behaves like a fool *so that* M. de Clèves may die, or even, as Valincour says, *because* the author *wishes* to have M. de Clèves die, and because that intention of the fictional narrative is the *ultima ratio* of each of its elements.)

What the Genette-Valincour argument points to is the difference in causal direction, by narrative levels, which we have observed. If the rule of prepared consequentiality impels "realistic" fiction to provide the causes before revealing the effects in the *récit* and the *histoire*, the *narration* has the effect "in mind," and invents the cause afterward so that the effect may occur. As Sartre's Roquentin discovers (before Genette, but long after Valincour: see chapter nine, below), the beginning of a story implies a purpose, an "end":

it is the effects that have given rise to the causes. Why does the text of *La Bête humaine* inform us (p. 61) of Jacques's hereditary flaw? The answer is to be found in the murder of Séverine (p. 270). On the plane of *narration*, the plan for Séverine's death "causes" the insertion early on of a reference to Jacques's mania. It is of course possible for a real author to create a homicidal maniac and to decide later how to use him or her, but limits of potential use in mimetic fiction are already inherent in the character. We have encountered other examples of the *narration*'s reverse logic. The cause of Virginie's humiliation near the start of *L'Assommoir* may be inferred to be the symmetrical humiliation of Gervaise by Virginie near the end. Coupeau's fall from the rooftop subsequently appears symbolic of his moral decline. By inference, readers may conclude that the planned moral decline caused a "desire" for a prefigurative symbol. Coupeau's miraculous recovery separates the incident from all causal chains: with no explicit causes or effects, the incident appears relevant only if it serves a metaphoric function. Just as, for example, in the case of a homicidal maniac who never kills, readers would be faced, if it were not for potential symbolism, with an irrelevancy, and irrelevance is never an assumption in conventional fiction. A causal relationship, at least on the level of *narration*, is assumed for all details.

Genette calls the anterior details ("caused" by a plan for ulterior events) the "motivation." It is a "false" causality inserted in the *histoire* to mask the "true" causality, which I situate in the *narration*, and which is antichronological and based on intent. The function of such masking, for Genette, is verisimilitude.[7] If we know the reasons for an event before it happens, if it is "motivated," it appears more plausible, verisimilar: prepared consequentiality is in operation. But I would suggest, based upon what we have seen about reader assurance in inference, that the relationship has reciprocal elements. For if a world described in a fiction is familiar, verisimilar, readers will be all the more confident in their ability to draw causal assumptions. Thus verisimilitude helps us perceive tightly knit causal chains, gives us assurance in filling the myriad little gaps (and the larger ones, too) between events. Causation is always to be inferred, and familiar worlds reduce the uncertainty in inference. Thus verisimilitude facilitates *histoire*-level causal inference, just as, reciprocally, ready inference may give an impression of the verisimilar.

But while forward logic in the *histoire* gives an impression of "reality," it is the backward logic of the *narration* (which is also, lest we forget,

Denizet's logic) which sets texts apart from the verisimilar reality they pretend to describe. We infer (on solid grounds) that the future-of-text is known on the plane of *narration*; it is difficult to infer such exterior foreknowledge in our real lives. The inferred causality of the *narration* is by nature indexic,[8] as smoke is an index of fire, as a photograph is an index of a camera. Coupeau's fall is, on the level of *narration*, indexic of a project to symbolize; on the level of the *histoire*, it is, in literary transmutation, iconic of the moral fall to follow. Cabuche's fortuitous theft of Grandmorin's watch is indexic of a project in the *narration* to have him falsely accused of murder; in the *histoire*, it is exemplary (perhaps iconic) of coincidence: the "interference of series," the intersection of two otherwise unrelated causal chains. In each case, the apparent structuring of the past by the future in order to bring itself into existence, to justify its existence, marks a divergence from the "real." Textualization, as the result of an inferred intention, can create only a pseudoreality; the hidden inverse logic of the *narration* undermines the realism of the most realistic *histoire*.

Always inferred as in the *narration*, causality in the *histoire* may seem at times explicit, when words referring to it spring up in conversations, interior monologues, etc. But these are themselves *histoire*-level events: the credibility of such language, as we have seen with Gide's Jérôme, is a matter for reader inference in context. In realistic *histoires*, cause normally precedes effect. Although we have seen no examples of it, narrators can obviously, in the *récit*, give the effect before the cause, which appears in a flashback; thus, in Mauriac's *Thérèse Desqueyroux* for example, the judge gives his verdict of "non-lieu," the reasons for which we will learn half a novel later, at the end of a long analepsis. But analepsis, whether it occurs in the memory of an intradiegetic character as in the Mauriac novel or through another device, is really a strategy of the *récit*. Readers end up reconstituting a chronological *histoire*, presumably with cause before effect if it is realistic.

That is not to say the analeptic (or proleptic) option is of no effect once readers have mentally reestablished chronology; questions concerning why it was selected simply concern the *narration*, while the notion of "how" is to be found in the *récit*. But for purposes of normalization, I will describe analepsis as a divergent form: the "standard" traditional novel is recounted in chronological order of events. Causal elements in the *récit* are explicit and, as such, they call for no direct inference on the part of readers. Indeed, they express inferences of the text, whether they are opinions of the narrative voice or causal assumptions inherent in the linguistic code. The reader's task at this level is thus to attempt to provide explanations where they are lacking and to determine whether the explanations given are to be believed. Belief, for example, in Jérôme is not essential to the comprehension of his story; statements about it by Juliette, Abel, and Alissa tend to confirm his facts. But his interpretation of events may be put in question, and so his intermittent, clustered explanatory vocabulary is an instrument for judging him rather than for making sense of the *histoire*. In contrast, the narrator of *La Bête humaine* must be believed in all he says, or the *histoire* is senseless: Denizet's *récit* must appear erroneous (based as it is upon antichronological logic, which the narrator seems magically able to eschew) in light of it. The narrator's uncanny, apparent ability to "discover" the past as it happens constitutes a virtually invisible subversion of mimesis—invisible because it is based on absence.

Thus the inference that we are referring to here as causality not only exists on the traditional levels of narrative, but it characterizes and constitutes those levels. Whether our causal hypothesizing is in search of an *idea* as the *ultima ratio* of a text (*narration*), or proposing relationships of implication among *incidents* (*histoire*), or gauging the credibility of *words* (*récit*), it is the *readerly quest for causes* that brings narrative levels into existence. As inferences about the text, they do not precede it nor belong in essence to the writerly world. Table 5.1, particularly in columns three and four, summarizes the causal distinction among levels.

Table 5.1's typology is "normalized" essentially in that it does not allow for nonchronological *récits* (analepsis, etc.), to which I accord special status, and in that it does not admit of causation explicit in the *histoire* through conversations and verbalized thoughts. These latter are not abnormalities in traditional fiction, but as "events" in the *histoire* they are read rather than actions; their linguistic component shares the characteristics of the *récit*, like small *récits* embedded in the narrator's larger one. What normalization brings to light, particularly in the "cognition" and "direction" columns, are the fundamental distinctions among levels arising from causal analysis.

If the inferable existence of *narration*, with its counterchronological logic, separates the fictional text neatly from "reality," what may we infer as its source? The "indexic author" is not real. All we can say is that he, she, or it is the sum of linguistic, social, cultural, psychological, and anthropological codes funneled through the mind and the pen of "someone": as Genette affirms in *Figures III*, a text is "proffered by someone," who is also the

Table 5.1   Normalized Typology of Construed Causation

Level	Expression	Cognition	Direction
narration	ideal	inferred	antichronological
histoire	incidental	inferred	chronological
récit	linguistic	explicit	chronological

narration ("proféré par quelqu'un . . . la narration qui le profère").[9] Both the proffering (*qua* event) and the codes are place- and time-specific: fictional texts are a part of history.

But if history is to be significant, differences in causal strategy should be apparent across the years. In what sense, for example, are Zola's texts causally anterior to Gide's? Obviously, the narrator in Zola has not yet acquired the importance as causal interpreter which he or she will attain in later fiction. Zola's *récit* is most often transparent, a slightly tinted glass through which we look directly on the facts and the events of the tale. Causal relationships are usually readily inferred, almost self-evident, or characters explain their motivations in honest conversation or in interior monologues. If, on occasion, a narrator appears only partially reliable, readers are all the more encouraged to seek out causal relationships in the chain of events itself, in the *histoire*. In the canon of modern fiction, from Proust to the new novel, the *récit*, linked by narrators' perceptions of causality, will be powerfully interposed between reader and *histoire*. (Tastes change, and therefore so do "canons." But what has been viewed as "typically best" of early twentieth-century French fiction has a strong *récit*, usually by an intradiegetic narrator who provides her or his own causal explanation of events—or who, like Jérôme, fails to do so—events whose causes are often not self evident.) Zola might well be seen as the culmination of the *histoire*-dominant tradition. *Récits* with narrowly limited perspective have existed all along—notably in the eighteenth century, with the epistolary *Liaisons dangereuses* or *Candide* as prime examples, but also in nineteenth-century France (one thinks inevitably of Fabrice at Waterloo)—but ease of causal inference at the level of the *histoire* is characteristic of the mimetic tradition from Balzac to Zola. Denizet is a quasi exception. Arising out of the *histoire*, he serves as a substitute narrator, providing a competing explanation of events to the one we receive from the narrative voice. In *La Bête humaine*, his circumscribed reconstruction loses in context;

but historically he wins. From Michel and Jérôme to Marcel, Roquentin, and Rieux, the circumscribed, intradiegetic voice dominates, and without competition from a transparent *récit*. Thus the narrator's magic capacity, bestowed by the *narration* to achieve its *ultima ratio*, by which he "discovers the past as it happens," begins to disappear. In this sense, Zola's successors may be more "realistic" than he.

Then too, prepared consequentiality will diminish. Narrators limited to normal, human capacities often discover and relate causes, in Nietzschean fashion, after the effects. Jérôme (apparently) discovers the reasons for Juliette's engagement to Teissières after the fact (although some astute readers may suspect them in advance), and he presents Alissa's diary near the close of his *récit*, at the point in the timeline of the story when it entered his life, although it may provide some causal explanations (or aid in inferring them) for elements of his foregoing *récit*. With certain exceptions, of which I shall evoke an example or two, stories will tend to admit to the inverse logic of *narration*, instead of seeking to conceal it.

Furthermore, Zola appears willing to allow for confident inference of causation within narrative sequences. Typically, major gaps in the causal chain occur between sequences; the long, explicitly connected chains of *La Bête humaine* are doubtless the exception.[10] Readers are free to surmise relationships that would unite the fragments, but Zola's texts provide a mythic, metaphoric substratum, which guides our choices and tends to limit readerly interpretation. Indeed, the vocabulary of the "mythical anthropology" Jean Borie uncovers so convincingly in the *Rougon-Macquart* novels can be read as a lexicon of pre-Freudian psychology: mythic motivations are, in any case, "causes," although their expression is metaphoric rather than metonymic. Causes can, in this sense, be readily inferred for most of the events in the *Rougon-Macquart* series: "Satanic forces" is perhaps as reality-referential as a metaphor for human motivations as is "Oedipus complex." Even *La Bête humaine* appears to accept the principle of causation, while raising doubts about human ability to observe and textualize it in open systems, either before or after the effect. Obviously aware of the loss of truth value in tendentious explanations (Denizet), Zola's texts are not above using causation to mask (in the manner described by Genette) as mimetic certain plot deviations developed apparently for structural effect: the Gervaise-Virginie reversal, the Misard chain. The underlying presumption in this practice is clear: readily inferable causation works hand in hand with verisimilitude. The assumption that the verisimilar illusion is "realistic" has less currency in the twentieth century, as the circumscribed narrator replaces the omniscient one. Truth value will gain in importance at the expense of an illusory mimesis.

If we view novels as devised solely for our entertainment, concealment of the *narration*'s manipulations behind the chronological causality of the *histoire* is perhaps less than crucial. But if we see the text as providing a "lesson in life," truth value reasserts itself and the problematics of textualization acquire a new seriousness. When novels appear to convey epistemological, ontological, or ethical knowledge, as we saw with Gide, readers become wary: the "age of suspicion," as Nathalie Sarraute called it, has arrived.

Notes

1. Michael Riffaterre, *Semiotics of Poetry* (Bloomington: Indiana University Press, 1978), pp. 1–22 and *passim*.

2. Roman Jakobson, *Essais de linguistique générale*, tr. Nicolas Ruwet (Paris: Editions de Minuit, 1963), pp. 61–67.

3. Norman N. Holland, "Unity Identity Text Self," in *Reader Response Criticism*, Jane P. Tompkins, ed. (Baltimore: Johns Hopkins University Press, 1980), pp. 118–33.

4. For reciprocal constraints on the verisimilar text, see Gérard Genette, *Figures II* (Paris: Editions du Seuil, 1969), p. 93.

5. Genette, pp. 71–99.

6. Genette, p. 94.

7. Genette, p. 97. He concludes by defining the "value" or "profitability" (*rendement*) of a narrative unit as its function minus its motivation. Thus Cabuche's theft of the kerchief (*cum* watch) would seem relatively "profitable," since it has a simple motivation (easily acquired adoration for Séverine) and an important function (the irony of his conviction for murder). On the other hand, Flore's suicide serves no *histoire*-level function at all, causes

(implies) nothing; yet it is motivated by a long and extraordinarily complex chain of events. The suicide would appear to be a total loss as a unit, unless its "profit" derives from the very drama surrounding it.

    8.   According to the definition of C. S Peirce, in *Philosophical Writings of Peirce*, Justus Buchler, ed. (New York: Dover Publications, 1955), pp. 102–3.

    9.   Gérard Genette, *Figures III* (Paris: Editions du Seuil, 1972), p. 74.

    10.   Néide de Faria, in his *Structures et unité dans "les Rougon-Macquart"* (Paris: Nizet, 1977), p. 217, affirms the predominance of spatially distributed, described scenes over narrated events in Zola. This strategy is, of course, productive of causal gaps.

Part II
Nonrectilinear Causal Strategies

6

Track and Sidetrack

Thus the story of the Odyssey can be stated briefly. A certain man is absent from home for many years; he is jealously watched by Poseidon, and left desolate. Meanwhile his home is in a wretched plight—suitors wasting his substance and plotting against his son. At length, tempest-tost, he himself arrives; he makes certain persons acquainted with him; he attacks the suitors with his own hand, and is himself preserved while he destroys them. This is the essence of the plot; the rest is episode.

—ARISTOTLE
(trans. S. H. Butcher)

Paul Bourget's novel *Le Disciple* (1889) tells the story of Adrien Sixte, a mild-mannered psychology professor of deterministic convictions who leads a sheltered, well-ordered life, and of Robert Greslou, a young, self-appointed "disciple" of his, to whom he has provided counsel in his approach to graduate study. Greslou sends his former mentor a disturbing communication, a kind of clinical study of his own psychology. In it he reports that, obliged to work for a living, he had found employment as a tutor in a well-to-do noble family. Having taken a dislike to the proud and athletic eldest son and heir, André de Jussat, he determines to seduce his sister Charlotte, using the mechanistic causal principles he had so avidly gleaned from Professor Sixte's writings. Man's animal nature, conditioned response, total dominance of environmental and hereditary forces in determining the course of human lives: such notions form the theoretical basis of his plan to seduce the daughter of the aristocratic family with whom he now lives. Ever the scientist, Greslou describes his strategy in terms of a psychological experiment, something of a novelty at the time, when psychology was little more than a philosophical theory. At last, Charlotte yields herself

and her honor to the young tutor, but for one night only, with the understanding that she and her lover will both commit suicide thereafter.
Charlotte eventually carries out her part of the suicide pact, but Greslou
quickly discovers he has lost interest in suicide, and he fails to keep the
bargain. Profiting from circumstantial evidence, André de Jussat has
Greslou indicted for murder, even though he knows the truth of Charlotte's
suicide (she had written him a deathbed confession), for he hopes to conceal
her dishonor. Awaiting trial in jail, Greslou has drafted his report and sent
it off to Sixte. Having learned that Sixte also knows the facts, André at last
tells the truth, and Greslou is released—only to be shot dead by André.

The power of causal chains is evident here on two levels. First,
Greslou's successful seduction demonstrates the dominance of psychological
forces over will: Charlotte's fears, sympathies, and animal desires have
combined with the environmental influences of her upbringing and the
wiles of the young tutor to produce, not only her moral downfall, but her
"inevitable" suicide. Second, Robert Greslou is likewise the product of his
hereditary nature and environmental influences, notably that of his middle-
class origins (whence his inability to grasp Charlotte's aristocratic concept
of honor), and particularly that of the kindly professor with the deterministic doctrine. But the text is constantly working to undermine its own
causal structure. Obviously, it paints Charlotte as delightful and admirable, while Robert Greslou appears as a self-centered and calculating
scoundrel. If readers are morally outraged by Greslou's conduct (and it is the
"point" of the story that they should be), it is because they are insufficiently
convinced of the inevitability of Charlotte's fate to absolve him from responsibility for his calculated actions. It is difficult to believe that, despite his
influences, he could not have turned back, could not have done otherwise.
Then too, Robert, in his own embedded, first-person "report," is surprised
to discover that he feels remorse after Charlotte's death; if he is merely the
plaything of determining causal forces, why should he feel responsibility?
And Sixte, in his free-indirect-style reflections, wrestles with a parallel
problem: why should he feel guilty for the influence of his books on a young
man's life? Greslou failed to understand Charlotte (he understood her well
enough to seduce her, but not well enough to forestall her suicide) or
himself; Sixte had no notion of Greslou's dangerous potentialities, nor of his
own capacity for guilt. Thus the basic question to be asked of the *narration*
("Why is the 'author' telling us this?") brings to light the conflict between
the inferred author's view and that of Greslou's *récit* and Sixte's thoughts. For

the inferred author, psychological causation, while apparently similar to the laws of cause and effect in the material world, has other, spiritual dimensions that render it far more complex. Notions of morality and honor escape the determinist's grasp.

While the quasi-religious and perhaps anti-intellectual underpinnings of this tale may make its message suspect, it uses causal chains in an interesting way to undermine causation as applied to the human psyche. The problem is that, with its traditional linear form, it must use what it condemns and understand what it presents as beyond understanding. It reveals the causes of the characters' failure to grasp certain causes, and precisely what causes they were unable to comprehend.

If the human psyche is to be portrayed as a world apart, with respect to causal influences, from the material world in which a cue ball imparts specific impetus and direction to a billiard ball, in which effects are predictable and quantifiable, then other sorts of novels, with different causal structures, are required for the task. From the Bergsonian-Saussurian era on, forms have been discovered (and rediscovered) which allow for the separation of the psyche from "everything else." Many of them are peri-causal, in that they seek to elude or "go around" the problems imposed by linear causal structure, particularly in portraying the human mind and emotions. Some are structured to evoke kinds of causation specific to the psyche and different from physical causation. In this and the chapters to follow, I will illustrate six primary strategies that alter the rectilinear causal chains associated with psychological causation in traditional fiction, and with language itself.

Episodic structure has been around at least since the *Odyssey*, and it is still thriving. In the simplest terms, it provides a unifying central track, along which a number of sidetracks branch off. These may or may not lead back to the main line; when they do not, the reader is required to leap across a causal gap to find the central track, before setting off down the next branch. The branches are not causally connected to each other, except insofar as each has some causal bond to the main line. Many novels include the odd episode, but in truly episodic fictions they occupy far more space than do the elements of the unifying track.

In standard analysis, the main line is referred to as the *plot*. According to E. M. Forster's time-honored definition in *Aspects of the Novel*, a *plot* consists of those events that are interconnected by a causal chain. But, as we have seen, such interconnections can be made on all three levels of narrative, and the notion of *plot* has thus become a highly complex one. Furthermore, Forster's definition contains an implied expectation of stasis: things would remain the same, he seems to say, unless causation intervened to change them. Causation is that which makes the "beginning" change to become the "end." But one can just as well start from an underlying expectation of change and see causation intervening to produce constancy. Our main line may involve change or constancy, and causation may be inferred as much for one as for the other. Its primary structural function is to provide an explicit or inferred basis for the sidetracks, which make up most (or even all) of the *récit*.

Since our subject is the strategies used to weaken or subvert linear causality, the particular structure under consideration here is that in which the sidetracks lead to dead ends. Indeed, insofar as any episode can be defined as distinct from *plot*, it must have an ending of its own, from which we leap back into the main course of events, or ahead into another distinct episode. These dead ends are breaks in the causal chain, but breaks of a specific kind, far different from the fragmentation we will examine in later chapters.

J.-K. Huysmans's *A rebours*,[1] a standard *roman à tiroirs*, provides a clear example of a traditional linear plot dominated by multiple episodes. In it, Jean des Esseintes, ultimate scion of a degenerated aristocratic family, withdraws, fleeing the turbulence of Parisian life, to a *thébaïde raffinée* in Fontenay, where he leads a hermit's existence, until neurosis and disease force him to return, on doctor's orders, to a more social existence in Paris. The elements of the plot are few. The initial cause is the effete young man's extreme sensitivity, doubtless of hereditary origins, which produces in him a neurotic fear of disorder, and an equally neurotic desire to see himself as different from the common horde. The first event is the withdrawal to Fontenay. The second "event" is the establishment of a style of life which is at once ordered and different. He lives by night and sleeps by day, thus avoiding contact with his servants; with strict punctuality, he eats the simple meals set out for him according to menus established four times a year. His surroundings are both unusual and thematically organized: one room of his apartments is decorated like a ship's cabin; his bedroom imitates a (remarkably luxurious) monk's cell; his library, done in blue and orange, offers him the company of his exquisitely decadent collection of books; he steeps himself in rare wines and liqueurs, surrounds himself with exotic plants and perfume-making equipment. The third event is the actual physical illness and exasperated neurosis arising from solitary nights passed in such surroundings. The final event is his decision to return to Paris, taken with a prayer on his lips: "Seigneur, prenez pitié du chrétien qui doute . . ." (p. 269); "Lord, take pity on the Christian who doubts . . ."— suggesting a rebirth of faith. From the initial stative event onward, the story is that of a problem and an attempted solution which merely aggravates the situation, leading to admission of failure. The events just listed are the *noyaux* or "kernels" of the "plot," as Chatman calls them, and readers perceive them as "important," for the primary meaning of "important," with respect to traditional fiction, is "consequential," i.e., "belonging to a causal chain."[2]

The episodes are examples of ways in which des Esseintes spends his time while ensconced at Fontenay. That these occupations contribute in some measure to his worsening health, there can be little doubt. But their contribution could easily have been summarized in a single chapter, if demonstrating their importance were the only aim, instead of the thirteen chapters (III through XV) that they actually fill. As examples, some of them at random could have been omitted, or they could be rearranged in a different order without altering the central track of the story. But they are more than examples: that the episodes dominate the central track is apparent, not only from their sheer volume, but also from their power. At one point, to illustrate that travel is a matter of perception rather than of action (the distinction between psyche and reality mentioned above), the inferred author has des Esseintes undertake a voyage to London; he gets no farther than the Gare Saint-Lazare—by that time he has seen enough fog and Englishmen, and eaten enough English food, to satisfy his craving for foreign travel. In order to insert this illustrative episode (chapter XI), the inferred author is obliged to postulate a sudden and causeless amelioration in des Esseintes's health, so that he is mentally and physically able to travel. Thus the linear direction of the main line—from bad to worse—is temporarily altered for the sake of an interesting episode. The main line will be moved, if necessary, to switch us onto a sidetrack.

Despite the frequent transitions, sidetracks are not causally interrelated. One of them begins, for example, with des Esseintes selecting plants to ornament his seclusion. He chooses bizarre hybrids which simulate metals or human flesh in leaves and petals. These choices, made as a consequence of his neurosis, lead to fevered sexual imaginings and finally to what we would call today a highly Freudian nightmare. The following chapter (IX) begins: "These nightmares recurred: he grew fearful of going to sleep" (p. 136; "Ces cauchemars se renouvelèrent: il craignit de s'endormir"). To fill the sleepless hours, he decides to reorganize his collection of Goya prints. At this point, we have reached a dead end and started off down another sidetrack. The causal chain does not continue, for the fear of sleep furnishes the condition for reexamining the Goyas, but not the cause: any one of numerous other activities could have been selected. When he discards the offending plants before turning to the prints (p. 137), we have reached a causal block. As for the new Goya branch, organizing the prints turns out to be purposeless, since des Esseintes fears to hang them: some fool might see and admire them, thus ruining the egocentric pleasure they hold for our hero. Here we reach another causal block and return to evocations of the feverish restlessness characteristic of the neurosis. The next branch begins with a decision to read "emolient" literature, to "refrigerate" his overheated brain: Dickens! But the chaste and blushing maidens he finds there, instead of calming his nerves, end up by reminding him of his own, less virginal loves—an American acrobat named Miss Urania, a female ventriloquist, and a young man who had sought directions of him in the street.

Thus the episodes, separated by causal blocks, form a series rather than a sequence; superficially connected at times by transitions, they are also often attached at their beginning to the main line, to show that they are causally born of the malady itself. Indeed, of the sixteen chapters, seven (VII, IX, X, XI, XIV, XV, XVI) leap back from a dead end to reconnect in this way at the beginning to the central track. The movement within the episodes is typically caused, however, and the direction of causation is usually from "real" stimulus to psychic state. Hideous houseplants evoke nightmares; readings (Dickens, medieval Latin texts) provide memories; the neighborhood of the Gare Saint-Lazare creates a mental image of London; perfumes resurrect the past. It is these psychic states—dreams, memories, hallucinations—which constitute the essential dead ends of the sidetracks. This particular causal organization is worth examining in both its structural and its thematic effects.

Structurally, this track-and-sidetrack mechanism establishes potential parallelism among the branches. Part of what the text loses in linear unity, it recaptures in unity-by-resemblance. The movements from present physical reality to psychic states create a pattern that sets repetition up as a competitor with causation for the "honor" of satisfying the readers' quest for unity in the novel. Repetition encourages reading of the text not as line but as space, an activity calling forth all manner of similarities: between the pet tortoise, whose shell des Esseintes gilds and bejewels to enliven the rug on which it crawls (thus caparisoned, it promptly dies), and our hero himself (also dying, in splendid isolation); between des Esseintes's taste in house-plants and Baudelaire's *Les Fleurs du Mal*, which he admires; between the blending of liqueurs in the famous "mouth organ" and the blending of perfumes; among underlying similarities in all des Esseintes's preferences in art and literature. Indeed, the ubiquitous references to artistic expression—prose, poetry, painting, music, interior decoration—establish the *récit*, by repetition, as highly "specular."[3] The description of the Gustave Moreau paintings of Salome's dance (chapter V), as a vision of the undermining of rational authority by the animal appetites, can be read as a model or matrix for Huysmans's novel, where life (corporal needs) destroys order (the per-fectly regulated *thébaïde*): "Tel que le vieux roi, des Esseintes demeurait écrasé, anéanti, pris de vertige devant cette danseuse. . . ." (p. 89); "Like the old king, des Esseintes was left crushed, destroyed, overcome with vertigo as he beheld this dancer. . . ." John the Baptist's head, shining terrifyingly upon the platter in the watercolor, seems to prefigure the temptation of faith in the Lamb of the last page of the novel: will return to faith in Christ be still another dead-end hallucination or at last a truly liberating vision? The very creation by des Esseintes of the rarified atmo-sphere of his hermitage coincides with Huysmans's creation of the text, as it in turn becomes the reader's *thébaïde*. It is toward such fundamental connec-tions that readers are guided by the parallelism of the sidetracks, and con-nection by comparison undermines the linear concatenations of causality.

Since causation is both potential structure and potential theme, when causal structures are nonrectilinear as in this novel, texts are weakened in their capacity for expressing, on the thematic level, the deterministic power of causation. But weakened or not, the determining forces here are far from powerless. The strong central chain, along which neurosis becomes psycho-somatic illness, drives des Esseintes ineluctably to Fontenay, and just as ineluctably drives him out again. Causation does, however, tend to dissi-pate in the branches. His is then, in the Bergsonian sense, an interiorly undifferentiated psyche (one could not say what element of his conscious-ness led him, for example, to his Goya prints in particular), and at the same time an exteriorly differentiated one (a reader could scarcely predict that, by turning to Dickens, our hero would revive memories of his earlier exotic lusts and moments of impotence, for the reader is not des Esseintes). But absence of clear causation here on the level of the *histoire* raises questions, as in Zola, on the level of the *narration*: why is the author breaking the chain? Since many sidetracks end in psychic states, it is apparent that the branches treat mental deterioration, while the central track, with its linear causation, has as its destination the physical degeneration of des Esseintes's body. Arrival, along the sidetracks, at various psychic states is effected primarily by the mechanism of psychological association. While I will explore this special type of causation more fully in subsequent chapters, it is essential to note here that this sort of causal connection (associations between plants and women, between Dickens's heroines and certain memories) is functional only in the mind; it is explainable but unpredictable. Odd hours, diet, and inactivity, on the other hand, are predictably ruinous to the body. One answer to our question is thus that the "author" is breaking the chain in order to distinguish between psychic causation on the sidetracks and physical causation on the main line of his story.

A second plausible answer is that the "author" wishes his character to have moments of unpredictability, moments when his reactions cannot be foreseen. Thematically, des Esseintes makes common cause with Taine (and "Adrien Sixte") in deploring the unpredictable and the spontaneous in his surroundings. He finds the inanimate more desirable than the animate, preferring locomotives to women and requiring that his live houseplants appear artificial. The famous tortoise with the gilded carapace soon obligingly becomes the decorative object it was purchased to be, when it dies; and the ornamental artifice of Fontenay is killing its master's body just as surely. Des Esseintes is delighted to recall that, by a psychological ploy, he was able to destroy a young marriage, and he is troubled by the thought that a similar deterministic experiment of his was apparently unsuccessful in transforming an indigent and abused lad into a thief and a cutthroat (chapter VI). Our former dandy adores the predictability of rigid, mechanistic physical causality, but the application of such unwavering order to living things has its dangers. Either the unpredictable disorder of life will break through in hallucinations and dreams (psychological causation), or the unrelenting forces of physical causality will kill.

There is something of Rimbaud in des Esseintes's "visions," and both had tried nearly "all forms of love, of suffering, of madness." But Rimbaud was seeking freedom from determinism in poetry; des Esseintes is unproductive, and his visions are abortive dead ends. Indeed, in their very dead-endedness, they doubtless contribute to his physical deterioration and the collapse of the noble experiment in Fontenay. Unless the last, religious "vision" is productive, des Esseintes belongs to the inevitable.

Huysmans, in his own life, was already on the way to selecting the religious sidetrack and making it his main line when Zola upbraided him for publishing *A rebours:* "with somber glance," as Huysmans recalled, "he criticized me for the book, saying that I was dealing a terrible blow to naturalism, leading the school astray . . ." ("l'oeil devenu noir, il me reprocha le livre, disant que je portais un coup terrible au naturalisme, que je faisais dévier l'école . . .").[4] The track-and-sidetrack structure is indeed more than a different way to organize the *histoire* of a novel. It is another sort of causal strategy, distinguishing between causation of the mind and of matter, exemplifying the richness of numerous parallel structures, and thus attacking as insufficient the mechanistic, rectilinear causality on which many of the most admired nineteenth-century novels had been plotted.

But after *A rebours*, how far could such a counterstructure go? The surrealist novel is perhaps the extreme example of the sidetrack approach. These novels are characterized by the fact that the psychic causation exists on the main line, while physical causes, such as there are, reside in the branches; by the strongly reality-referential character of the branches (these texts treat primarily real people and real places); and by the fact that the main line itself is present but scarcely explicit. Psychic causation still runs on a track separate from the physical in both our examples, Aragon's *Le Paysan de Paris* (1926) and Breton's *Nadja* (1928),[5] but its new position on the central track gives it the upper hand.

Le Paysan de Paris, which Pfromm calls felicitously "fiktionale Autobiographie,"[6] consists of two itineraries; first the narrative voice takes us on a stroll through the Passage de l'Opéra (since destroyed to make way for the boulevard Haussmann), and then we follow a walk, taken by Aragon with Marcel Noll and André Breton in the Parc des Buttes-Chaumont. The commercial establishments in the covered pedestrian walkways that made up the Passage are described in the order in which one would come upon them if one followed a specific course through the mall. If some mysterious or long-forgotten causal chains determined which shops should be neighbors, no allusion is made to that here: the establishments simply pop into the text in the order foreordained by reality itself, and without causal connection to one another. What makes this one come "before" that one and "after" that other one is the movement of the narrator's itinerant psyche, as he passes along the walkways. The timeline, which here makes up the central track, is that of the moving, observing, narrating mind; each commercial establishment it passes, it expounds upon, thus producing a series of dead-end sidetracks. The narrator here has the same name, and presumably the same personality traits, as the author who signed the manuscript. If the narrator is "real" and the Passage is "real," where is the fiction? It lies precisely in that double distortion which comes from seeing first, and then from writing. The narrator's vision is conditioned by all of his past experience and by his mood and preoccupations of the moment; his choice of words is influenced by everything from his vast cultural baggage to the reader he is imagining for his text. Narrator and author conjoin in this work to make up the implied author, who is himself the fiction.

The transformation of things into language through the medium of a reacting psyche is the fictional mechanism. Aragon is well aware that, as narrator, his vision is at all times fictionalizing reality, projecting the workings of his psyche upon it: "la nature est mon inconscient" (p. 153); "nature is my unconscious." Under his mythologizing eye/pen, gasoline pumps acquire, for example, the identity of one-armed divinities or idols (p. 145). Aragon's narrative is at once *his* world and *his* text:

> Il y a dans le monde un désordre impensable, et l'extraordinaire est qu'à leur ordinaire les hommes aient recherché sous l'apparence du désordre, un ordre mystérieux, qui leur est si naturel, qui n'exprime qu'un désir qui est en eux, un ordre qu'ils n'ont pas plus tôt introduit dans les choses qu'on les voit s'émerveiller de cet ordre, et impliquer cet ordre à une idée, et expliquer cet ordre par une idée. (P. 234)

> (There is an unreasonable disorder in the world, and the extraordinary part is that ordinarily men have sought, beneath the appearance of disorder, a mysterious order, which is so natural to them, which expresses nothing but a desire which lies within them; and no sooner have they projected that order into things than you see them marvel at that order, and implicate that order into an idea, and explicate that order by an idea.)

One of the primary pleasures of reading this text is the discovery of the identity of the narrative voice through its linguistic reflection in things, seen and described. If the Parc des Buttes-Chaumont is henceforth for me vaguely vulviform, it is because the Aragonian psyche/text reflects it that way. Aragon and his two companions "attendent de ces bosquets perdus sous les feux du risque une femme qui n'y soit pas tombée" (p. 166); "dans les jardins publics, le plus compact de l'ombre se confond avec une sorte de baiser désespéré de l'amour et de la révolte" (p. 174); "Dans les plis du terrain où tout les sollicite, ils sont les jouets de la nuit" (p. 175); "il y a *cette* femme dans chaque idée qu'enfin je cerne" (p. 208); "Ainsi l'univers peu à peu pour moi s'efface, fond, tandis que de ses profondeurs s'élève un fantôme adorable, monte une grande femme enfin profilée, qui apparaît partout" (p. 209); "Ainsi retrouvant l'inflexion heureuse de ta hanche ou, le détour ensorceleur de tes bras dans le plus divers des lieux, . . . je ne puis plus parler de rien que de toi-même" (p. 211); "tu t'es levée sur ce parc" (p. 212).[7] In this evolving feminization of the park, if causation enters the process, it is on the level of the *narration*: why is the author/narrator seeing/writing the world this way? The origin of the constant "desire which lies within" him, of the order that he has "projected . . . into things," is nowhere explicit. But some velitation between id and superego is being mediated on the page.

Thus a vast domain is opened to reader inference. Two places in Paris of which readers supposedly have some memory form the matter of the *récit*. Comparison of our vision of the places to the Aragonian description suggests the nature of the difference between each of us and the inferred author. That difference will lie in the kinds of mental connections he and we tend to invent among the multifarious realities—that "unreasonable disorder"— in order to reason the inherently meaningless chaos. And since there are two quite separate walks (the Passage and the Parc), we have two fictional Aragons, two inferred authors, to compare to each other and to ourselves. What such inference—doubtless different for each reader—yields is a set of psychic causes conditioned by a linguistic code; for, as the nature of the psyche itself is the cause of its reflection in the world of things, so the limits of textualization determine how that reflection becomes text.

In *Nadja* as well, André Breton's "je" is virtually the only referent to a continuous central track from which the branches spring. The sidetracks are a series of anecdotes from which the narrator (who is "André Breton"—what that name means is a central question) not only omits much causal vocabulary, but in which he also adopts the strategy of denying explicitly the role of human intentions in events. Consider the way he prepares, in this supposedly autobiographical text, the account of his first encounter with Nadja in the street:

Le 4 octobre dernier, à la fin d'un de ces après-midis tout à fait dés oeuvrés et très mornes, comme j'ai le secret d'en passer, je me trouvais rue Lafayette: après m'être arrêté quelques minutes devant la vitrine de la librairie de *L'Humanité* et avoir fait l'acquisition du dernier ouvrage de Trotsky, sans but je poursuivais ma route dans la direction de l'Opéra. Les bureaux, les ateliers commençaient à se vider, du haut en bas des maisons des portes se fermaient, des gens sur le trottoir se serraient la main, il commençait tout de même à y avoir plus de monde. J'observais sans le vouloir des visages, des accoutrements, des allures. Allons, ce n'étaient pas encore ceux-là qu'on trouverait prêts à faire la Révolution. (Pp. 57–58)

(Last October 4th, at the end of one of those completely idle and very dull afternoons I have the secret of spending, I found myself in the rue Lafayette: after stopping for a few minutes in front of the display window in the bookstore of *L'Humanité* and acquiring Trotsky's latest work, I was continuing aimlessly toward the Opera. Offices and facto-ries were beginning to empty; from top to bottom in the buildings doors were closing; on the sidewalk people were shaking hands; any-way there were beginning to be more people about. Unintentionally I was observing faces, clothing, ways of walking. Come now, those still weren't the folks we'd find ready to launch the Revolution.)

The initial date (Breton later specified the year: 1926), like the place names, is a phenomenological marker, denoting the nonfictional character of the events to follow. In reality, where events occur wordlessly, causation is never explicit; we observe what happens, but the "why" remains a matter for interpretation. As narrator, Breton appears to strive to keep his text "phe-nomenological," devoid of causal interpretation. But he goes farther: had he said nothing, readers might well infer, on the level of the *histoire*, that he had gone to the rue Lafayette to pick up a copy of the latest Trotsky. But Breton specifically blocks the inference: he was spending idle time and simply "found himself" there. Afterward, he walked "aimlessly," observ-ing passersby "unintentionally." The people about him seem scarcely more capable of willed actions: it is the inanimate offices and workshops that are closing, as if without human intervention. It is difficult to avoid the transitive verbs that imply causality, but Breton manages: simply and impersonally, "*there* were beginning to be more people about." Even the causation inherent in "faire la Révolution" is negated.

One may perhaps infer the causes of the negative conclusion: these workers are too satisfied with their milieu ("se serraient la main"), or too prosperous ("accoutrements"), or too mechanized by the routine that governs their lives (daily "rush-hour" events) to be ready to rebel. But the conclusion, like the purchase of the Trotsky text, is itself an event and therefore a potential cause. It is clear that serious political preoccupations are dominating the narrator's mind, so strongly that he carries out a political analysis of the crowd in spite of himself. But here again, a causal block falls in place. These events are not preparatory to the composition of a political tract: the narrator is about to "pick up" a young woman in the street. These then are noncauses, a narrative dead end; why give these details at all if they are not relevant to what follows? Their relevancy lies, of course, precisely in their stressed irrelevance: "There I was, thinking about the liberation of the working class, when this woman walked by. . . ." The inferable intent of the *narration* is to demonstrate the discontinuous, non-linear, noncausal character, both of real phenomena and of the consciousness that observes them. If there is to be any linear constant in this anecdotal text, it will have to reside in the omnipresent "I," but below the level of the consciousness. Gaps here, just as in Zola, send the reader to the level of the *narration*, in search of unifying links; that the inferred author knows of and seeks this reaction is apparent in his careful presentation of "extraneous" details in the context of a preparation, and in the strategy of causal blocks it conditions. If readers eventually conclude that subconscious forces were at work in Breton's life, it will be largely because explanations were available neither on the level of the *récit*, where the paucity of causal vocabulary eliminates them, nor on the level of the *histoire*, where blocking strategies deny them.

We will later learn that Nadja too was walking quite at random ("sans but aucun," p. 59), so that this first meeting seems to be a chance occurrence, an effect of *le hasard objectif*. Nadja is, of course, "l'âme errante" (p. 69)—"the wandering soul"—the very essence of movement without conscious cause. She invites Breton to make up a story of random elements, carefully underscoring the relationship of life to text:

Ferme les yeux et dis quelque chose. N'importe, un chiffre, un prénom. Comme ceci (elle ferme les yeux): Deux, deux quoi? Deux femmes. Comment sont ces femmes? En noir. Où se trouvent-elles? Dans un parc. . . . Et puis, que font-elles? Allons, c'est si facile, pourquoi ne veux-tu pas jouer? Eh bien moi, c'est ainsi que je me parle quand je suis seule, que je me raconte toutes sortes d'histoires. Et pas seulement de vaines histoires: c'est même entièrement de cette façon que je vis. (Pp. 73–74)

(Close your eyes and say something. It doesn't matter, a number, a first name. Like this [she closes her eyes]: Two, two what? Two women. What do they look like? They're in black. Where are they? In a park. . . . Then what are they doing? Come on, it's so easy; why won't you play? Well me, that's the way I talk to myself when I'm alone and tell myself all sorts of stories. And not just useless stories: that's even completely the way I live.)

With a new and spontaneous "choice" to be made for each word or phrase, the story comes to life more vertically (movement at each "choice" from subconscious to consciousness) than horizontally (movement from preceding words to following words). As a sample matrix or model for this fictional autobiography as a whole, Nadja's text simulates, in its interruptive questions, the causal blockers of Breton's prose; his apparently random selection of anecdotes mirrors her spontaneous choice of words. But the very surface fragmentation sets one searching for a deeper cause: in a novel, we seek it in the *narration*; in life ("that's even completely the way I live"), we look toward the subconscious. These surrealist texts conjoin *narration*, narrator's subconscious, and main line in a single entity.

Another model for *Nadja* is to be found in the story of *Les Détraquées*, a play which had so greatly impressed Breton that he saw it three or four times. In it, two deranged women, both teachers in girls' schools, do away with a student in the boarding school that one of them administers. The victim is drawn into the murderesses' clutches by a chance occurrence: a ball the little girls are playing with in the courtyard happens to bounce through a window into the office where the two women are, and their intended victim enters to retrieve it. As Breton tells the story, there is a suggestion that the teachers had killed another pupil the year before, but the evidence is purely inferential, as is indeed the explanation of this year's murder: spectators do not see the crime, only the girl's entrance and the subsequent discovery of the body. We may be certain, on the level of the *histoire*, that the women did her in, but Breton's interest is drawn precisely to the absence of explicit causal links:

Le manque d'indices suffisants sur ce qui se passe après la chute du ballon, sur ce dont Solange et sa partenaire peuvent exactement être la proie pour devenir ces superbes bêtes de proie, demeure par excellence ce qui me confond. (P. 45)

(The lack of sufficient clues about what goes on after the ball bounces, about just what Solange and her partner may be prey to in order to have become such superb beasts of prey, is what supremely leaves me perplexed.)

What is missing is not causation (Breton indeed infers that the women are prey to some diseased desire), but "indices" of its existence. That the author's analysis of the play points out the importance of causal gaps reveals the use he makes of causality in his own text: profiting from readers' need for it in the absence of all "indices," he employs a lack to make them discover or generate a profound psychic causation for what happens. Blocking inferences on the level of the *histoire*, he sends readers directly to the *narration*.

The relationship of this causal strategy to psychoanalytic dream analysis is obvious and explicit in the novel. In a rare causal link, the narrator recounts a dream he had, partly inspired by certain episodes of *Les Détraquées*, partly by his recent observation of a mother bird stuffing insects into the craws of its young. Conscious, waking impressions provide the vocabulary of our dream language, which the subconscious of course restructures, juxtaposing remembered impressions to fit a psychic syntax. Breton remarks on the "eminently revealing" role, "in the highest degree 'overdetermining' in the Freudian sense," which conscious images play in dream formation (p. 47). It is the search for the "revelation" in the psychic syntax, for the cause of the particular selection and structuring of dream images, that constitutes the groundwork of Freudian dream analysis. The logic applicable to psychoanalytic interpretation of dreams applies as well to the reading of this novel.

A markedly heterogeneous series of events, noted and remarked upon by a "same" psyche: for reading such a text, the logic required is simple abstraction—comparison of anecdotes, retention of those factors common to most episodes as representative of the informing psyche, and elimination of heterogeneous factors as related to dream vocabulary rather than syntax. Comparison of the sidetracks in *Nadja* hints at the presence of certain constants, a common preoccupation, a possible reason why these things should, in particular, stimulate the narrator's interest. A likely psychic state behind the selection of these episodes might be the tension between physical attraction toward women and fear of them, leading to fear of intercourse and possible impotence. (The dream just mentioned includes the "particularly reprehensible" fraud of inserting one *sou* in the slot of an automatic machine, where two were called for.) Although Nadja's vertically constructed, highly spontaneous style of life is strongly valorized in the text, the inferred author also perceives it as dangerous:

> . . . un soir que je conduisais une automobile sur la route de Versailles à Paris, une femme à mon côté qui était Nadja, mais qui eût pu, n'est-ce pas, être toute autre, et même *telle autre*, son pied maintenant le mien pressé sur l'accélérateur, ses mains cherchant à se poser sur mes yeux, dans l'oubli que procure un baiser sans fin, voulait que nous n'existassions plus, sans doute à tout jamais, que l'un pour l'autre, qu'ainsi à toute allure nous nous portassions à la rencontre des beaux arbres. Quelle épreuve pour l'amour, en effet. (P. 143)

> (. . . one evening as I was driving an automobile on the road from Versailles to Paris, a woman beside me who was Nadja, but who could have been any other—right?—and even *that* other, with her foot holding mine pressed down on the accelerator, and her hands seeking to cover my eyes in the forgetfulness an endless kiss procures, desired that we cease existing, doubtless forever, except for each other, and that we be borne thus at top speed to a meeting with the lovely trees. What a test for love, indeed.)

Whether this sexual tension truly subtends the text, whether it is discovered there or generated by my own propensities, are less important questions in this context than the logic used to reveal it. For that logic implies a parallel tension, between the unique (and therefore heterogeneous) and the comparable (and therefore repeated). Nadja herself signifies radical difference and the impossibility of repetition ("Les Pas perdus? Mais il n'y en a pas," [p. 70]; "Wasted Steps? Why there aren't any").[8] Yet the inferred author is constantly comparing, noting for example a perceived similarity between Nadja's eyes and those of the actress playing Solange in *Les Détraquées* (p. 58). Even in the automobile anecdote he keeps comparing—"any other," "*that* other"—in the narrative midst of what could have been for him a genuinely unique experience! Love and fear, he seems to say, the unique, the differentiated, the heterogeneous, but seek security in the repeatable, the constant.

What is disconcerting about reading surrealist novels as avatars of the plot-and-episode structure is that, in the plot, nothing happens. But that "nothing" is, precisely, an event. The real world, as we consciously perceive it, is multifarious, disconnected, inexplicable—a heterogeneous collection of unrelated existents. One should expect, in these conditions, that the perceiving mechanism, bombarded on all sides by multiple, radically differentiated phenomena, would itself be transformed from moment to moment. The astonishing thing is that, instead, it organizes, unifies, connects the flood of differentiated impressions that assail it, selecting for memory the most useful and making a mental language of them. This unexpected changelessness of the observer has a cause, in theory: the ineluctable functioning of the subconscious according to the Freudian system. The power of causation, of explicability and predictability, lies therefore on the main line just as much in Aragon and Breton as in Huysmans.

For the earlier novelist, the psyche is unpredictable, while the physical world is subject to relatively foreseeable causal factors. The surrealists have turned that around, while retaining similar structures. The central track (explicit in *A rebours*, inferable in the surrealist texts) is essential to an understanding of all three texts; it also plays a unifying role and generates the required contrasts: psyche/reality and unity/diversity.

And yet, what is this "understanding," this constant, unifying psyche, if not one more inference, by definition unproven? Is a changeless psyche behind it all, or have I, like Aragon's human observers, been introducing my own "natural" order into these texts, only to discover it there and marvel at it? The prime difference between Aragon's observers and readers is that the latter confront texts rather than universal chaos. Insofar as textuality is a *condition* of writing, texts are bounded by linguistic limits, which insinuate conceptuality (exemplified by the merger of "seeing" and "writing" we observed in Aragon) and intentionality into them, as surely as they consist of "discourse." For while it is theoretically possible to write without conceptualizing or intending, discourse, narrative discourse, would hardly be the result. The resources of language, of textualization, thus play a causal role, as a condition of our inferences. One can point to a "unifying textuality" (e.g., recurring words, metaphors, the gradual feminization of the landscape in Aragon's picture of the Parc des Buttes-

Chaumont) just as accurately as to a unifying unconscious: the intent of *narration* is intent of text, as well as intent of "author."

The purely inferential character of the main line in Aragon and Breton makes their structures easy to confuse with the absurdist fragmentation strategies and with the structures of mental representation, both of which we will consider later. This is perhaps the place to underscore the basic distinctions. Like episodic tales, absurdist fragmented stories include radical causal breaks and blockers, assemblages in the *histoire* of apparently unrelated events, and generally homodiegetic narrators. But the fragmented stories call into serious question causal explanations in general, including notions of a structuring or structured psyche; and despite the breakdown in causality (or perhaps because of it) chronological order reacquires significance. Even though events are unrelated in the *récit* and unrelatable in the *histoire*, it is inferably important to the *narration* that they occur in a given order: there can be little question of interchanging episodes, as in our three track-and-branches novels.

Novels of mental representations, common in France since the 1950s, string together a series of "mental images" as perceived by a psyche (whether in perception or memory, by hypothesis or imagination) and textualized. Des Esseintes's dream qualifies as an "imagination" of this sort, while subjective perceptions and recollections characterize the surrealist texts. But des Esseintes's nightmare, embedded as it is in a clearly referential third-person *récit* of specific detail, is obviously connected to a fictionally "real" world. The surrealists also rely heavily on objective reality—real people, places the reader knows. Breton provides numerous photographs with his text, perhaps as a means of marking the causally unrelated or (in the modern sense) "contingent" nature of reality, as it stands in contrast to the unifying subconscious of the *narration*. Recontextualized, the photographic images are also textualized, but they retain their differences from words. The more recent "novels of mental representation" tend to abandon their reality-referential components (even when they allude to historical places or events): the contrast psyche/reality is gone, and only the psyche (or the text . . .) remains. Reality, if we seek it in such texts, will be neither causally related nor "contingent," but what it is perceived to be; in the most extreme cases, referentiality will elude us, and with it the causal model, leaving only a text. Surrealism still pretends to an inferable intent, lurking beneath the seemingly disparate episodes.

Notes

1. Joris-Karl Huysmans, *A rebours* (Paris: Falsquelle, 1955). Further references in the text are to this edition. Original edition, 1884.
2. On these questions, see Seymour Chatman, *Story and Discourse* (Ithaca: Cornell University Press, 1978), pp. 53–56.
3. I allude, of course, to Lucien Dällenbach, *Le Récit spéculaire* (Paris: Editions du Seuil, 1977).
4. "Préface écrite vingt ans après le roman," *A rebours*, p. 21.
5. Louis Aragon, *Le Paysan de Paris* (Paris: Gallimard, 1926); André Breton, *Nadja* (Paris: Gallimard, 1963). Further references in the text are to these editions.
6. Rüdiger Pfromm, *Revolution im Zeichen des Mythos: Eine wirkungsgeschichtliche Untersuchung von Louis Aragons "Le Paysan de Paris"* (Frankfort-am-Main: Peter Lang, 1985), p. 39 *et seq.*
7. Aragon and his two companions "are expecting from these groves, lost beneath the fires of risk, a woman who is not there by chance"; "in the public parks, the densest of shade blends into a kind of desperate kiss of love and rebellion"; "In the folds of the terrain, where everything calls out to them, they are the playthings of the night"; "in each idea that at last I grasp, there is *this* woman"; "Thus the universe fades away for me and melts, while from its depths an adorable phantom ascends, an immense woman arises at last clearly outlined, appearing on all sides"; "Thus rediscovering the pleasant curve of your thigh or the bewitching bend of your arms in the most diverse of places . . . , I can speak of nothing but you"; "you have risen upon this park."
8. Nadja refers to the title of Breton's 1924 work, *Les Pas perdus*, which contains (among other things) an allusion to the term "salle des pas perdus"—"waiting room" ("room of wasted steps").

7
Associating with Proust

Proust wrote at length in order to create within the frame of his novel an interval of *oubli*, the forgetting which would allow the reader a true experience of remembering and recognizing.

—ROGER SHATTUCK

Le plus troublant de la métalepse est bien dans cette hypothèse inacceptable et insistante, que l'extradiégétique est peut-être toujours déjà diégétique, et que le narrateur et ses narrataires, c'est-à-dire vous et moi, appartenons peut-être encore à quelque récit.

(The most disturbing thing about metalepsis really lies in that unacceptable but insistent hypothesis, that the extradiegetic is maybe always already diegetic, and that the narrator and his narratees, that is to say you and I, are perhaps a part of some still other *récit*.)

—GÉRARD GENETTE

Causal analysis of *A la recherche du temps perdu*[1] reveals little new meaning in Proust's monumental novel that has not already been uncovered by the thousands of extant analyses, but it yields insight into Proustian strategies involving causation to relate the reader to the text. We have already seen how gaps in causal chains can *condition* reader reactions, allowing readers' needs for explicability and predictability to cause us to pose questions on other levels of the narrative; with Proust, we can observe strategies at work tending to cause reader reaction directly. Nearly all stories employ to this end the well-catalogued techniques of otherness, which set the reader up in competition with the text: curiosity, suspense, surprise, seduction.[2] Proust chooses techniques of similarity, which reveal the dynamic, narrative, causal substratum of metaphor itself.

At first glance, Proust's magnum opus seems to offer a brachiate, plot-and-episode structure: a linear temporal existence with occasional escape into "epiphanic" involuntary memories. Like des Esseintes, the narrator (who might as well be called "Marcel") suffers from a "disease," the inexorable progression of which forms the causal main line of the text: the biological and psychological aging process. We follow the narrator from childhood in the 1870s well into middle age. Just as maturation is programmed in the child, so physical deterioration inheres in the adult. Furthermore, with every mental change we undergo—new experiences, changing health, transient states of mind—the being that we were before slips away from us, so that a series of psychological "deaths" marks our relentless pathway to the physical tomb. That the narrator perceives these elements of his story as forming a causal chain is apparent in his references to the genetic and psychological "laws" of death (III, 850). By remaining youthful in appearance and attitude, Odette de Crécy strikes the narrator as having defied miraculously the "laws of chronology" (III, 984). It is of course against the ineluctable series of changes that lead to death that the narrator's text, with its astounding branching structures, is arrayed in battle.

The frequent recurrence of the words "law" and "laws" in the novel emphasizes the causal constraints that channel the irreversible course of characters' lives. Proustian "laws" tend to be more organic than mechanistic, allowing for some individual variation (Odette's apparent defiance of the aging process), functioning more nearly like laws of probability than like mechanical constraints. Yet they constitute codifiable tendencies, operative for the majority, aphoristic principles of the type: "Chacun voit en plus beau ce qu'il voit à distance, ce qu'il voit chez les autres" (II, 235); "What we see at a distance, what we see in others, looks more beautiful." Sexual orientation is a primary and influential example of such constraints, according to Marcel, although he finds homosexual and heterosexual attractions to follow the same "general laws of love" (III, 820): the tendency to select successive sexual partners who resemble one another, for example, or the predisposition, on the part of nervous, intense lovers, to pass from the search for love as pleasure to the addiction to love for the avoidance of pain. Marcel is acutely aware that no lover can ever possess the beloved (though that is the lover's desire), but only a perception thereof, a creation of the mind. This causal limit, and the inevitable "intermittences of the heart" (II, 756 ff.) which arise from it, influence both Swann (I, 300, for example) and the narrator (II, 831). Stupid people, Marcel suggests, are less apt to evade the organic laws that tend to govern their lives because they are unaware of them, although they reveal them in their gestures and their actions, where intelligent authors observe them at work (III, 901). Thus, without being crudely deterministic, the narrator creates a causal chain to be the central track of the novel, moving inexorably from life to death, from joy to pain (to joy again), each new emotional period owing its life only to the death of the preceding one.

The branching structures of the involuntary memories are obviously parallel, each beginning from a precise, physical occurrence on the central track and expanding into a mental representation, complete with emotions, of an earlier period on the chronological main track. The parallelism suggests that there is a "law" at work here too, and the *récit* provides a causal paradigm:

> Je trouve très raisonnable la croyance celtique que les âmes de ceux que nous avons perdus sont captives dans quelque être inférieur, dans une bête, un végétal, une chose inanimée, perdues en effet pour nous jusqu'au jour, qui pour beaucoup ne vient jamais, où nous nous trouvons passer près de l'arbre, entrer en possession de l'object qui est leur prison. Alors elles tressaillent, nous appellent, et sitôt que nous les avons reconnues, l'enchantement est brisé. Délivrées par nous, elles ont vaincu la mort et reviennent vivre avec nous. (I, 44)

> (The Celtic belief seems very reasonable to me whereby the souls of those we have lost are captive in some inferior being—an animal, a plant, an inanimate object—lost indeed to us until that day, which for many people never comes, when we happen to pass near the tree, gain possession of the object, which is their prison. Then they tremble, call out to us; and as soon as we have recognized them, the enchantment is broken. Freed by us, they have conquered death and return to live with us.)

In relating this myth to involuntary memories, the narrator is not comparing objects or states of being, but rather movements. The passage is verb-like, transitive, and causal. The "effect" is that the souls of the departed return to live with us; the "cause" is a twofold condition: physical proximity to the enchanted object, and recognition therein of the imprisoned soul. This is not a specific incident, but a general rule of Celtic belief and of involuntary memory as well ("Il en est ainsi de notre passé," [I, 44]; "So it is with our past"): if AB, then always C. The double cause (make contact with an object; recognize its relationship to the past) is inevitably followed by its effect: the past is resurrected.

The magical quality of causation in the legend (this is an example of causation making an event predictable though unexplainable) reflects the mystery of psychological association in the novel. The movement from recognized object to memory touches the chronological, unidirectional timeline of the main track in two places (the moment of recognition and the period remembered), but at each of these junctures it is disjoined from the irreversible linearity of causation. On the one hand, the contact-recognition event is consistently presented as fortuitous ("qui pour beaucoup ne vient jamais," "nous nous *trouvons* passer," etc., here), the recognition phase being sometimes arduous, as with the madeleine, even when one has the good fortune of random contact with the object. On the other hand, Marcel provides no explanation why, in the first place, the psyche selected a particular mental representation—image, odor, savor, position—as symbolic of the particular context, with all its emotional and sensory richness, in which it was first experienced. Why the taste of a petite madeleine dipped in linden tea should have become the effective synecdoche for all the summers at Combray is unexplained. Perhaps other sensations of the period were stored up in the memory as potential triggers for the same involuntary memories, but random contact was never made with those. The triggering sensation must be a rare one, for oft-repeated experiences quickly lose their association with the context. But the mystery of association remains. The triggering of Marcel's involuntary memories represents a particular kind of mental causation, not unrelated to certain of des Esseintes's experiences, but it remains apart, through chance and unexplained selection, from the central track's causal chain.

What lives in memory, of course, is not the object, nor even a mental representation thereof, but the experience of earlier contact with it: the self that the narrator was when he experienced it. The branches therefore all coexist in potential, running together in parallel to the central track, waiting for Marcel to find the talisman and become again one of his former selves, to leap out onto a parallel track. Readers' awareness of this temporal parallelism is awakened in *Du côté de chez Swann* with the description of the childhood walks Marcel took almost daily with his family along two invariable paths: "Swann's way" and "Guermantes' way." Instead of recounting what happens on several individual walks, the *récit* takes the form of a single outing in each direction.[3] The landmarks are presented in order of their appearance to those who follow the prescribed routes; as with Aragon's presentation of a walk in the Parc des Buttes-Chaumont, the order of succession has no apparent basis in physical causality. But the single walk, in the linear *récit*, from landmark to landmark, is composed of multiple promenades coexisting in the narrator's memory. The reader follows the walk as if it were a staff on a page of music, where each note (landmark) has the power to echo simultaneously on other lines of the staff, to become a chord. The hawthorns, for example, can evoke early childhood, when Marcel, arrayed by his mother in his infantile finery for the return trip to Paris, weeps out beneath their blossoms his despair at the thought of leaving them (I, 145). Or they can call up his pubescent surprise at the discovery of the awe-inspiring female (Gilberte) staring at him through their branches (I, 141–42). These two events did not occur on the same walk, could not have occurred in the same year, yet they are connected in a single narrative segment by a common landmark, the hawthorns of Tanson-ville. This is the "vertical" causation of association: the madeleine calls up the self-taking-walks; the walks evoke their landmarks; these in turn, contacted, recognized, give birth to other selves: self-weeping, self-seeing-Gilberte-for-the-first-time. All the selves so rediscovered are "horizontal"; they exist through chronological time, continuous and unchanged. Thus through the parallel structures of what Genette calls the "récit itératif," and the notion of causative association, the inferred author transforms linear prose into an active branching structure.

During the Balbec "epiphany" (II, 756–57), the narrator makes explicit the notion of multiple selves existing in parallel. Bending down to remove his shoes in his hotel room, Marcel rediscovers in a surge of involuntary memory the tenderness and solicitude of his grandmother, now dead, who had comforted him there years before. It is not she herself his memory revives, but a perception of her, another Marcel receiving her love, a Marcel who has since disappeared, replaced for a time by an "ungrateful, selfish, and cruel" young man, who had not suffered too much at her death. Now, bending down, he changes "sans solution de continuité" into the vulnerable and tender receiver of his grandmother's affection he had been before: it was, he remarks, "as if there were different and parallel series in time" ("comme s'il y avait dans le temps des séries différentes et parallèles").

But if he is to conquer the unidirectional flow of time, it will be necessary to reverse the one-way movement from cause to effect. In Balbec the vital pivot, which begins turning everything around, becomes most apparent. Just as an event on the central track can project the narrator into

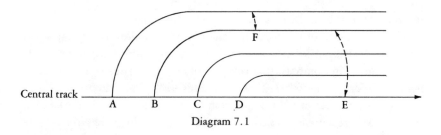

Diagram 7.1

another, extratemporal self, so the rediscovery of the other self can cause events to happen on the central track, for the narrator can feel, as a result, present joy or pain, can weep, as he does in the Balbec hotel room, very material and obviously caused tears. The causal bond between the main "plot" and the remembered "episode" is thus a two-way street: event triggers memory, which in turn triggers event. The tears themselves are of short duration and apparently cause nothing further, as des Esseintes's nightmares caused a merely temporary fear of sleeping. But the sum of these pivotal experiences—the madeleine, bending down in a Balbec hotel room, uneven paving stones in Paris, etc.—will become the cause, the creative origin of the text itself, intended to vanquish time and death. Thus the episodes will impinge upon and inflect by causation the main line of the plot.

The notion of parallel selves coexisting in time provides a spatialized vision of life, although one moves about in the space in a caused linear progression. This is also the vision of itself the text encourages the reader to adopt. The simplified graph in diagram 7.1 does not reveal the inflection of the central track, for which one would need, as we shall see, an additional dimension, but it summarizes the rest. A, B, C, D represent lived events in irreversible time. The branches they generate are extratemporal memories, constant and unchanging. E is a random event in time stimulating the reliving of event B, as the parallel self that originally lived it, and the return influence of track B upon the central track. F is an element of the events relived on B that triggers a memory of A (like Swann's hawthorns), which in turn enriches B. That movement in this space is linear, sequential, and causal there can be little doubt: the narrator must become an anterior self on A, B, C, or D before he can shed tears about it on the central track. But this linear movement in space is not only a theme of the novel; it is also a constituent of its lexical and thematic structure, which seeks to involve the reader in the game.

Comparable to the physical entities Marcel encounters that trigger his extratemporal excursions, lexical markers arise in the text capable of evoking readers' memories. In *Combray*, for example, the narrator notes that, with the exception of the recurring traumas surrounding the ritual of his mother's good-night kiss, he had forgotten nearly everything of his childhood summers in Combray, that this part of his life was dead for him. Then he asks: "Mort à jamais?" (I, 44; "Dead forever?"). The sentence is memorable for several reasons: it is a question in an overwhelmingly declarative text; it is a short sentence in a context of exceptionally long ones; the vehicle of the metaphor (forgotten = dead) may seem at this point to carry an exaggerated emotional charge in relation to the tenor; it is a verbless, elliptical fragment in a text remarkable for rigorous grammatical completeness. Finally, it is so situated that the striking madeleine "epiphany" provides the answer to its question. The brevity, interrogativity, and incompleteness of the phrase impress upon our minds not only the question's meaning but the words used to express it; the glorious answer it receives binds it in our memory to its context. So it is that, when "Mort à jamais?" returns several volumes later in *La Prisonnière* (III, 187), as a question asked this time about the novelist Bergotte, recently deceased, it can trigger in readers a leap into the other selves that they were when, some 2200 Pléiade pages earlier, they had first encountered the tiny query.

Thus repetition in Proust's text serves a causal function, helping us to move about in our (reading) lives as the narrator does in his life as *actant*. For repetition belongs at once to the temporal linguistic track that is the physical text (in this sense it is not quite repetition; among other reasons, in the first instance of our example, "mort" was the vehicle of a metaphor, while in the second, it denotes a "real" human demise, Bergotte himself having become metaphoric), and to the extratemporal branches of memory. Memories can, of course, be called "extratemporal" precisely because causation cannot intervene to change the course of events contained in them, nor the mood and predisposition of the self that lived them. But in the Deleuzian sense, repetition is always difference, for the same reason that one never uses the word "same" without having in mind at least two distinct entities.[4] Living consciousness, however, admits no difference: we can only be conscious as one self at a time. So the discovery of repetitions and similarities among parts of this text, or between part and whole, begins by a reader's leap from present self into another, a leap occasioned by linguistico-thematic phenomena. The words of the text function semiotically as an icon of the intent of *narration*, while they operate semantically in the *récit*. The interpenetration of levels thus achieved institutes a veritable metalepsis, as

Genette defines the term,[5] a crossing of boundaries between the act of telling and the thing one tells. So readers may begin to discover that they are characters, after all!

Bergotte's death is related not only to the potential death of childhood memories. It recalls for the reader the grandmother's demise as well, for she, like him, had been diagnosed as uremic (II, 318) and, like him, had gone out imprudently (on the advice of a doctor recommended by Bergotte) when she should have stayed in bed. The story of his death and the narrator's perception of it can thus trigger in the reader a number of branching, anterior selves.

Even the model of involuntary memory by association, the "Celtic belief" of souls imprisoned in objects, returns in *A l'ombre des jeunes filles en fleurs*. Out of friendship for the madam, Marcel had donated some inherited furniture, notably a sofa from Aunt Léonie's bedroom in Combray, to a house of ill repute. Thereafter, he could no longer frequent the establishment, where he would see the use to which these sacred objects of his childhood were put,

> . . . car ils me semblaient vivre et me supplier, comme ces objets en apparence inanimés d'un conte persan, dans lesquels sont enfermées des âmes qui subissent un martyre et implorent leur délivrance. (I. 578)
>
> (. . . for they seemed to me to be alive and pleading with me, like the apparently inanimate objects in a Persian tale, which have souls locked up in them suffering martyrdom and begging for their deliverance.)

Here the "Celtic belief" has become a Persian tale, and the retelling has a painful, rather than a joyous, conclusion, reflecting the degeneration characteristic of the main line. But the parallelism of the situation and the return of a complex of lexical items from the earlier passage (*âme, inanimé, délivré-délivrance*), trigger for the reader in the second instance the pleasure of recognition, the rediscovery of the self reading the earlier passage. Critics may compare the two passages, dispassionately and reflectively, but reading them means experiencing them in turn, and, upon reaching the second passage, undergoing a flash of recognition—not of words per se, but of oneself understanding words. The text, by providing lexical and thematic triggers, performs half of the causal task: creating contact with the enchanted object. The other element of the magic formula (recognition) is up to the reader—to his or her memory, predisposition, and desire.

The notion of the difference between the "critic's" kind of comparison, which is spatial, and the "reader's" kind, which is chronological, serves to explain as well the role of causality in the Proustian conception of metaphor. Proust's narrator, as critic, unites the two, in a well-known passage of *Le Temps retrouvé* (previously analyzed by Genette)[6] in which he seeks to define the nature of truth in art:

> On peut faire se succéder indéfiniment dans une description les objets qui figuraient dans le lieu décrit, la vérité ne commencera qu'au moment où l'écrivain prendra deux objets différents, posera leur rapport, analogue dans le monde de l'art à celui qu'est le rapport unique de la loi causale dans le monde de la science, et les enfermera dans les anneaux nécessaires d'un beau style; même, ainsi que la vie, quand, en rapprochant une qualité commune à deux sensations, il dégagera leur essence commune en les réunissant l'une et l'autre pour les soustraire aux contingences du temps, dans une métaphore. (III, 889)

> (In a description one can go on indefinitely enumerating the objects that were to be found in the place described, truth won't begin until the writer takes two different objects, affirms their relationship—analogous in the world of art to the unique relationship of causal law in the world of science—and binds them with the necessary links of a beautiful style; or even, as in life, when, by comparing a quality common to two sensations, he distills their common essence, by joining them to one another in order to free them from the contingencies of time, in a metaphor.)

In the last analysis, of course, it is not the writer who "dégagera leur essence," but the reader, who, discovering the substratum common to two images, will experience that which is neither, but a new mental reality made up of the overlapping semes of both.[7] When Proust writes, for example, "La haie formait comme une suite de chapelles" (I, 138; "The hedge formed, as it were, a succession of chapels"), the initial comparison bears upon a form: the arch formed by branches of aligned shrubs; the curve of gothic arches forming entrances to side-aisle chapels in a cathedral. The common substratum is an ideal curve, a mental image, to be found in no real ogival arch nor in any contiguous shrubs, but which we can imagine belonging to both. It is this ideal image that is here called "truth" (which will only "begin" when the writer "posera leur rapport"—it is up to the reader to complete the creation). The readers' experience of "truth" is triggered by the arrival, in the linear chain of words, of the second term of the comparison: "beau style" in the passage initiated our discovery of those semes of "anneaux" which signify here, and of the ideal relationship between "anneaux" and "style." In an earlier draft, Proust had ended this sentence, not with "dans une métaphore," but with "dans une alliance de mots" ("in a wedding ring [or "alliance"] of words"), a kind of meta-metaphor in which the wedding band of words (spiritual union) joins the necessary ring-links of a beautiful style to suggest a double band, of signifiers and signifieds: "anneaux" and "alliance" both denote "ring" and connote "union" (marriage/chain). This third entity, this newly created "truth," is, according to the text, freed from the contingencies of time.

The Proustian sense of "contingencies" is the etymological one, denoting connection—what Chatman calls "the stricter philosophical sense, 'depending for its existence, occurrence, character, etc. on something not yet certain' (*The American College Dictionary*)."[8] "Time" is precisely the domain of causation, and everything that exists in time appears subject to it, although the precise causes that will come to bear are still uncertain. Yet the general effects of time are wearing away, breaking up, destruction. What is admirable about "the unique relationship of causal law in the world of science" is precisely its character as a "law": the fact that it is eternally true and thus temporally (eternally) repeatable. The *law* of "contingency" is itself not "contingent."

Both metaphor and involuntary memory, according to the novel, share this characteristic of being both "contingent" in the Proustian sense and non-"contingent." Thus is established a threefold parallel, a metonymic order common to metaphor, to Marcel as character, and to the reader. That order may be described like this: $e_1 \rightarrow e_2 \rightarrow E$. Movement passes from a first "real" event to a second "real" event related to it by association, which triggers the discovery of an extratemporal entity—a "truth" or an extratemporal self in memory. This movement is precisely that of diagram 7.1: from B to E, and out to the extratemporal parallel arising in B. Just as the narrator moves from madeleine-tea in Aunt Léonie's bedroom to madeleine-tea in Paris to the resurrection of his childhood summers in Combray, just as the reader moves from "Mort à jamais?" in *Combray* to "Mort à jamais?" in *La Prisonnière* to resurrection of an earlier self, so readers also move in microcosm from first term of metaphor to second term of metaphor to an ideal, extratemporal "truth." Causality and metonymy play the same role in metaphor that they play, as we have observed them, in involuntary memory. Metaphor is a causal strategy, embedded in the linearity of language.

In this sense, Marcel is one term of a metaphor for which the reader is the other. Yet he is certainly different from most of us. Individualized in his experiences (affluent European childhood, hypersensitivity and neurotic propensities, aristocratic conversations in turn of the century drawing rooms, etc.), he is also limited in his point of view: he can only speculate on others' motivations (whence the famous "soit que . . ." constructions in his prose, offering multiple possible causes for others' actions, and sometimes even for his own). His differentiation makes him a difficult character with whom to identify. Yet the very difference of Marcel's life from ours, the very limited nature of his perspective, are the guarantee (metaphor is founded on the difference of e_1 from e_2) of the universality of his reported experience. Insofar as we understand him, learning to read his text (and eventually our lives) as he reads his life, we demonstrate that the specific differences that separate us from him are without importance. As Camus's Jean-Baptiste Clamence will do years later in *La Chute*, Proust's narrator reinforces the bonds by gliding imperceptibly from "je" to "nous":

> . . . cette réalité loin de laquelle *nous* vivons, de laquelle *nous nous* écartons de plus en plus au fur et à mesure que prend plus d'épaisseur et d'imperméabilité la connaissance conventionnelle que *nous* lui substituons. . . . (III, 895, emphasis mine)

> (. . . that reality far from which *we* live, and from which *we* are increasingly separated as the conventional knowledge *we* substitute for it grows ever thicker and more impermeable. . . .)

Manifestly, this metaphoric/metonymic structure complicates and indeed regenerates for its purposes the simple notions of *récit* and *histoire* with which we have been working. While one might compare the "plot" of *A la recherche du temps perdu* to a voyage of discovery, it would be excessive to suggest there is a traditional quest involved, since random occurrences make the discoveries serendipitous, and intent to discover cannot be given as the initial cause or primary desire which sets the *récit* in motion: the discovery is already made before word one. Yet the discovery of the narrator's multiple selves, each of which forms a branch of the central track, is not sterile: the branches are not dead ends, like des Esseintes's dreams, hallucinations, and involuntary memories; instead they succeed in inflecting the central track, bending it into a kind of circle. For the final discovery of the "plot"—that a properly constructed narrative endows its readers with atemporal selves, atemporal lives (III, 895–96)—becomes the cause of this novel's composition: its final sentence, in this sense, causes its first one. Hence its standard classification as a "roman du roman" and, *a fortiori*, as a "roman du (futur) romancier."[9]

Dällenbach has alluded to three illogicalities supposedly inherent in such circular novels, whose subject is their own composition: (1) *causal*, in that they present themselves as the product of their own product; (2) *temporal*, in that they refer to themselves as coming into existence in the future, whereas they are already completed; (3) *spatial*, in that they refer to themselves as a part of themselves, thus enclosed in what they contain.[10] But the novel seems closed in this infinitely reversible structure, echoing back and forth between "inside" and "outside," only until it is read.

Even a narrowly logocentric conception of reading, in which progression is seen as movement from sign to sense, from signifier to signified, leads toward openness when applied to this text. For the *sense* of "mon oeuvre" in the final sentence, its *signified*, generates for readers the signifiers "Longtemps je me suis couché de bonne heure," together with all the other lexical building blocks of the text they can individually recall. The inflection of end toward beginning, and the twist in the relationship of signifier to signified in the reader's mind, create a kind of narrative Möbius strip, along which the signifier is now relatively "on top" of the dividing bar, now "underneath" it (S/s). (Readers are invited to reproduce diagram 7.1 above, to extend the parallel lines along both sides of the paper until they join themselves near their beginnings, and to twist it into a Möbius strip, if they wish to see a diagram of the internal causal structure of the text.) The reversibility of the pair S/s does nothing of itself to open the apparently illogical circle, but it "promotes" signs to sense and makes sense a sign *for the reader*, as in the metaleptic *double emploi* of "Mort à jamais?" or of the complex "âme . . . enfermée . . . délivrance." The readerly act, which conditions all the reverses of which this text is susceptible (time and the extratemporal, metonymy and metaphor, sign and sense, etc.), transforms the reader into creator: the dichotomy writer/reader is thus reversible too. So that, while the text remains circular, it expands beyond itself in the transformed readers. It functions, as Genette notes, as an optical instrument to help readers read within themselves.[11]

The *récit* here, divested of "initial cause" and "final result," works a fundamental modification on the concept of *récit* as causal progression, for the *récit* becomes a closed circle. Whether the *histoire* is closed or not is another question. In the standard novel, including the Gidean stories analyzed herein, the *histoire* is a series of events, reconstructed (and reordered, if necessary) by the reader on the basis of data in the *récit*. Under the narrative pact, the *histoire* is presumed to have come first, to have been encoded in language by the narrator, and to be in turn reconstituted as *histoire* in the reader's mind. *A la recherche du temps perdu* can be read in this way, and the term *histoire* can thus have its usual meaning as a mediated and interpreted series of events. But if the reader begins to move about in the space of the text, to set off on antichronological explorations through recognition of such repeated signifiers as "Mort à jamais?" just as the narrator moves about in his memories, then the term *histoire* takes on other meanings. For subjective ordering on the basis of association is valorized at least as strongly in the text as objective chronological sequence: if all of the past coexists in memory, what does "sequence" mean? Yet chronology is essential if we are to create, and then rediscover farther down the line, the associative symbol which, upon re-cognition, liberates us from chronology. Thus there could be, for Proust's text, an *histoire (1)*, consisting of an objectively determinable sequence of events, and a series of *histoires (2 . . . n)*, each of which is a subjective ordering of events in the mind of a reader.

Once the reader is taken into account, causation is seen to trigger expansion: from single *récit* to plural *histoires*, from single symbol (madeleine) to multiple memories (part II of *Combray*), from individual signifier (second term of metaphor) to expanding signified (first term plus "truth"). In the purely metonymic associations (triggered memories of the narrator or of the reader), there are two caused functions: (1) association of symbol with contiguous context in e_1, and (2) production of expansion E, of which recognition of the symbol in e_2 is the cause. In metonymic/metaphoric association, the inferred author provides the contextual association; readers have only to recognize the ideal substratum of the metaphor, which recognition will yield in E the "expansion des choses infinies": Truth. By associating the narrator and inferred author to the reader, Proust's novel imposes on itself an external causation, impelling expansion outward from the circle.

Notes

1. Marcel Proust, *A la recherche du temps perdu* (Paris: Gallimard, Pléiade, 1954), 3 vols. Further references in the text are to this edition.

2. On these strategies, see Peter Brooks, *Reading for the Plot* (New York: Alfred A. Knopf, 1984); Ross Chambers, *Story and Situation* (Minneapolis: University of Minnesota Press, 1984); Seymour Chatman, *Story and Discourse* (Ithaca: Cornell University Press, 1978); Meir Sternberg, *Expositional Modes and Temporal Ordering in Fiction* (Baltimore: Johns Hopkins University Press, 1978).

3. On this "iterative" structure, see Gérard Genette, *Figures III* (Paris: Editions du Seuil, 1972), pp. 145–49. Marcel's post-puberty walks, taken alone in the summer of Aunt Léonie's final illness, are grouped separately (I, 153–65). But, as they deal essentially with the final landmarks on Swann's way, this section simply completes a single *parcours* for the reader, from Combray to Roussainville dungeon. The terms "Swann's way" and "Guermantes' way" are, I believe, inventions of C. K. Scott Moncrieff, from his impressive translation entitled *Remembrance of Things Past* (New York: Random House, [1941]), which includes Blossom's translation of *The Past Recaptured*. I have not consulted any published translation for the few sentences I translate in this chapter, but Scott Moncrieff is worth consulting!

4. Gilles Deleuze, *Différence et répétition* (Paris: Presses Universitaires de France, 1968).

5. Genette, pp. 243–46.

6. Gérard Genette, "Proust Palimpseste," in his *Figures* (Paris: Editions du Seuil, 1966), pp. 39–67.

7. On the semantics of metaphor and the underlying metonymy of metaphoric substitution, see Umberto Eco, *The Role of the Reader* (London: Hutchinson, 1979), pp. 67–89, and Jean Ricardou, "Miracles de l'analogie (aspects proustiens de la métaphore productrice)," in *Etudes proustiennes II* (Paris: Gallimard, 1975), pp. 11–42. Lucien Dällenbach notes the mutual exchange of properties Proust attributes to certain metaphors: *Le Récit spéculaire* (Paris: Editions du Seuil, 1977), p. 128.

8. Chatman, p. 47.

9. On whether this is a "novel of a novel" or even a "novel of a (future) novelist," see Dällenbach, p. 48, but cf. also Genette, *Figures III*, p. 237.

10. Dällenbach, p. 147. The "illogicalities" seem to me attenuated in Proust by a strict distinction between the fictional time of composition of the *récit* (as opposed to the author's real time of writing), and the fictional time of the *histoire*. Marcel's text exists not as itself in the *histoire*, but as project.

11. Genette, *Figures III*, p. 267.

8
Myth and Mythos

Le mythe a ainsi une portée ontologique: il vise la relation—c'est-à-dire à
la fois le saut et le passage, la coupure et la suture—de l'être essentiel de
l'homme à son existence historique.

(Thus myth has an ontological dimension: its aim is the relationship—i.e.,
both the sudden leap and the gradual passage, both the cut and the
suture—between man's essential being and his historical existence.)

—PAUL RICOEUR

I t is difficult to justify the inclusion of a chapter on myth, one of the
oldest forms of human expression, in a section devoted to modernist
and postmodernist texts; it is still more difficult to argue for its inclusion among "nonrectilinear causal strategies," when straight-line causation
is almost characteristic of myth. Suffice it to say that mythic expression was
not an unpopular vehicle in the modernist period, and that its rectilinear-
ity provides an interesting special case of that phenomenon, perhaps more
revelatory of causal logic than of myth itself.

Plot is the standard translation of *mythos* in Aristotle's *Poetics*; I use the
term here rather as a synonym for *histoire*. The foregoing Proust chapter
evoked the erosion of an objective concept of the *histoire*, as a term referring
ever more insistently to each reader's individual creation. In general, however, mythic *récits* can be read as exemplary, and thus as "authoritarian" in
Susan Suleiman's sense of the term:[1] redundancies overdetermine the possible inferences from the *récit*, so that readers tend to constitute the same
histoire—a series of causally connected events, that is, a traditional "plot."

But if Proust's causal strategies indicate the need for redefinition of
"*histoire*," the notion of "myth" raises questions, as the foregoing may

suggest, about the nature of "*narration*." The usefulness of the expressions we have adopted in this area—"intent of text," "intent of *narration*"—lies in the fact that they designate an underlying purpose in texts without suggesting that that aim is anterior to or causative of the text itself. For that is precisely what inference discovers: texts have an inferable purpose, but they are not necessarily themselves products of that purpose nor created as agents for its accomplishment. So long as it is understood that texts come first and reader inference about them afterward, ambiguity is avoided. In this system, texts generate, with readerly cooperation, certain meanings, which are in turn inferred to be their *ultima ratio*. The manifest circularity: text → meaning → intention → text (or *récit* + *histoire* → *narration* → *récit* + *histoire*, or story → inferred author → story), is useful and cleverly descriptive of relationships. But if texts are to be seen as productive of generalized essences, of meaning that lies beyond their own specificity and that of their readers, then it becomes interesting to know where the circle "begins," or where the generalized meaning arises.

Ricoeur would seem to start with the text, when he defines *myth* as "a symbol developed in the form of a *récit*." [2] (He might also have defined it—although he did not—as "a *récit* developed in the form of a symbol," or as "a *récit* read as a symbol.") Thus the symbol, with the cosmic, oneiric, and linguistico-poetic origins he posits for it, appears to precede its development as a *récit*. But symbolization is a form of human mediation of the real, a verbal mediation, a "matrix of symbolic meanings as words" (p. 18), so that the verbal stratum would appear to mark the "beginning" of a symbol, although textualization in the form of a temporal *récit* (production of myth) would appear to come later. Yet, when it comes to reading mythic texts, Ricoeur suggests that mythic meaning is part of a temporal reading sequence, for he describes a "signifié primaire," a primary and literal signified, reminiscent of what we have been calling *histoire*, and a "signifié second," a second signified based upon the first, and ineffable: an emotional, experiential signified. This second signified may "make us think," but it is not in itself a "thought." Is it the mediation of "reality" (cosmic, oneiric, poetic) in a text that produces myth, or is it the readerly experience, mediating the text to attain the "signifié second"?

The answer is important, and it seems to arise in Ricoeur's distinction between myth and allegory. How one reads, he seems to say, makes all the difference: what distinguishes them is a way of reading rather than a textual structure. With allegory, he points out, the first signified, the literal sense, is contingent, and the second signified is sufficiently exterior to it to be directly accessible. The relationship between the two of them is thus perceived as one of "translation": once we have deciphered the code, translated the literal *histoire* into its more general meaning, we can discard the *histoire* as useless. But historically, he shows, allegory was less a literary procedure for the artifical creation of pseudosymbols than a way of reading myths, less a literary than a hermeneutic concept. *Allegory* consists, in this sense, of treating myths as disguised philosophy, so that, once we have pierced the disguise, we can recover an intellectual "sense"—a thought or idea (p. 23). It would seem, conversely, that for myths to be what they are, to avoid being "allegorized," they must be read properly, that they must receive a mythic reading to achieve full status as myths.

Ricoeur points to a venerable tradition of allegorical interpretation, and it is with that tradition that our causal model obliges us to make common cause. Primed to recover inferable relationships, it is not suited to discovery by spontaneous intuition of essentially ineffable, experiential knowledge. All we can do is to infer, from the *récit*, the succession of specific events termed *histoire*; insofar as the *histoire* encourages interpretation in more general terms, search for the essential within the existential, we move toward a linear "signifié second," a series of relationships from which we can infer an intent behind the *histoire*. The second signified will have to be of a sort that can serve as *ultima ratio* for causal relationships in the *histoire*; our belief in comprehension by inference and in an authoritative narrative "act" thus leads us away from the spontaneity of mythic reading toward a more nearly stabilized, authoritarian reading. *Récit* conditions inference of *histoire*, which in turn conditions inference of *narration*: the level of *narration* now "becomes" the allegorical abstraction of myth. A method which infers "authors" and "intentions" will not readily admit of the direct, noninferential understanding necessary for the discovery of myth in mythos; it can, however, "allegorize" quite interestingly, as we shall see.

Myth and symbol are the ultimate generalities, expressing essence by means of existence. But myth differs from symbol in its development "in the form of a *récit*": chronology enters the picture. With a discrete symbol, a relationship is established between a primary and a secondary, more abstract signified. But a myth, operating in time, presents a relationship on the literal level of two or more events or signifieds, a relationship which must signify an analogous relation on the symbolic level. In order for a relationship to be generalized, to be of the essence, it must be unfailingly repeatable, replicable at each insertion into human experience. (Creation stories, such as those in Genesis, the union of Uranus and Gaea, and the Big Bang, are the obvious exception: first causes can be first only once.) It is the causal bond that insures the universal applicability of allegorical truth in myth, and it is literal-level causation that leads to the discovery of symbolic causation. From Eden to Achilles's heel, the functioning of causality is the subject and structure of mythic exemplary tales.

If myth is replicable in human experience, it must be also repeatable in texts: the same symbolic "message" may be rendered in different literal forms. Thus Jesus can tell us about the rejoicing in heaven caused by the repentance of sinners in three parables: the Lost Coin, the Lost Sheep, and the Prodigal Son. The myth of the Dying King (sons overthrowing fathers or father figures)[3] has been repeated from Sophocles to Shakespeare to Sartre. But in noting repetition, rather than replicability, in viewing myths spatially, like a series of surfaces that can be stacked in the manner of playing cards (so that vertical lines strategically passed through the "deck" would find at each card an identical mark),[4] we risk losing sight of the linear dynamics inherent in the causal links.

Mythic novels tell specific stories that are temporally and geographically related to the real world, but each refers, on the symbolic level, to an extratemporal causal matrix. Works since 1870 exhibiting such relationships of relationships include Camus's *La Peste*, Cocteau's *Les Enfants terribles*, Gide's *Thésée*, Giono's *Regain*, Malraux's *La Condition humaine*, and Zola's *La Faute de l'abbé Mouret*,[5] to all of which we may turn for examples of allegorical causation in mythic texts.

While these texts present no direct invitation to interpret, of the kind included in many of Jesus's parables,[6] they employ a number of allusive strategies (usually more than one per novel) urging readers to seek a "signifié second." Frequently one finds a direct reference to the existence of a more general superstructure, of a symbolic level on which the text can be experienced: *Thésée* and *La Condition humaine*, for example, evoke it in their titles, *La Peste* in its epigraph, and *Les Enfants terribles* in the text (pp. 83, 92). Proper names can also serve as an onomastic clue to the existence of a symbolic parallel: *Faute de l'abbé Mouret* (the Edenic "Paradou," in which the abbé Mouret "mourait"); *Peste* (Joseph "Grand," "insignificant and retiring hero," p. 1331); *Thésée* (proper names repeat directly those of the traditional myth). Clear parallels to a preexisting intertext, to another incarnation of the same mythic structure, encourage readers to experience the text on both literal and symbolic levels: *Faute de l'abbé Mouret* (the biblical Eden story); *Thésée*; *Peste* (relationship of characters' situation—notably that of Rambert and Rieux—to that of Sisyphus, and thus ultimately to Camus's *Le Mythe de Sisyphe*; noteworthy structural parallels to *Condition humaine*, suggesting a common myth as matrix for both); *Regain* (parallels to ancient fertility rites, to rites of passage, to cultural transformations relative to the passage of human societies from the condition of hunter-gatherers to agriculture); *Enfants terribles* (relationship to primitive and Freudian concepts of "taboo"). Novels also point to their mythic nature by metaphoric repetition or even by internal interpretation of their own symbols: *Faute de l'abbé Mouret*; *Regain* (e.g., burial of the dead described as planting of seed—Panturle's mother, Mamèche and her husband); *Enfants terribles* (e.g., repeated theater metaphors, spheres—white snowball at the beginning, black ball of poison at the end); *Condition humaine* (Gisors's general interpretations of specific realities, e.g., Kyo's failure to recognize his own recorded voice); *Thésée* (Daedalus's explanations, pp. 1430–38). And at times, causal implausibilities at the literal level suggest that the true reason for occurrences can be sought only on the level of the "second signified": *Faute de l'abbé Mouret* (incredible size of and unlikely flora in the walled garden of Paradou, an essential condition of the abbé's "fall"); *Regain* (uncanny ability of Mamèche to lead Arsule to Panturle, to be his bride, by flitting through the trees and grasses; remarkable powers of Gaubert's plow to produce a rich harvest in a bad year); *Enfants terribles* (unlikely death of Michaël before consummation of his marriage to Elizabeth; improbable return of the malefic spheroid). By such means, novels alert readers to the existence of a second level of meaning, to a symbolic matrix implicit in the *narration* informing their literal *histoire*.

This symbolic structure constitutes a second causal chain (often a simple, straight-line construction, although with "collective" novels such as *Condition humaine* and *Peste*, the organization can be quite complex), parallel to the caused events on the literal level. Mythic stories in which the literal causation appears implausible seem the most truly magical, for, to complete the causal chain of the literal *histoire*, readers must have recourse to the causation operative on the symbolic level, bringing myth "down," as it were, into mythos, where it appears to function magically, and thus promoting mythos itself to the level of myth. Peter Brooks describes such direct interaction between *narration* and *récit*, in my sense of these terms, as "a perverse logic of narrative," what classic rhetoric calls "metalepsis of the author," in which an action is attributed to the "author," when it should have an agent in the *récit*.[7] The relationship of metalepsis to magical happenings has already been hinted at with respect to *L'Assommoir* (if one admits metalepsis, a "mythic" reading emerges) and alluded to in reference to Proust (where readers acquire "magic" powers). And in *Regain*, for example, Mamèche's death remains unexplained on the literal level (is it from old age, starvation, overexertion?), but, since in dying she brings about the sexual union of Panturle and Arsule and thus the rebirth of Aubignane, her death appears a magically successful sacrifice, revelatory of the notion in *narration* that sacrificial death is a cause of renewed life in nature ("si le grain ne meurt . . ."). It seems all the more magical in that she foresaw it as inherent in her chosen action (laying out before departure her own burial sheets), and in her ultimate "burial" in the sheets in which Arsule and Panturle consummate their union—a random and hasty choice on Panturle's part, when fortuitous rats were discovered to have ruined her preselected shroud. What are mere odd coincidences on the literal level become injected with magic when causation from the matrix is imported to fill the void, to explain the implausible; and the *histoire* thus partakes of the atemporal, essential quality of the "second signified," inferred in the *narration*.

Such a "promotion" of the *histoire* is evident in *Les Enfants terribles* as well, where an element of the matrix structure presents taboo as a source of masochistic pleasure. Paul's beloved Dargelos (antihomosexual taboo) fortuitously provides Paul with a source of pleasurable suffering in the lung-disease-producing snowball, and at last in the ball of poison. Still more obviously fortuitous on the literal level is the uncanny resemblance of Agathe to Dargelos; she can only be understood as a socially acceptable (because female) reincarnation of the adorable androgyne. Her presence in the little coterie sets up the conflict between the anti-incest taboo (represented by Paul's dominating sister, Elizabeth) and homosexual desire, until Paul and Elizabeth's simultaneous death becomes, in the last pages, a mutual orgasm. Because the double return of Dargelos, in the person of Agathe and in the gift of the second baneful spheroid, remains unexplained, mysterious, the tale is elevated from a story of adolescents growing up unsupervised to a representation of the universal power of taboo.

By the same token, once the power of mythic causation is felt to be at work in a given *histoire*, such specific explanations as may appear in the *récit* are ironically downgraded. Arsule arrives in the region of Aubignane as a kind of cart-pulling slave to Gédémus, a knife-and-scissors grinder. Elizabeth meets Agathe when she goes to work in a fashion house where the latter models. Such particular information serves to render plausible the antecedents of the implausible. For the real purpose of specific causes on the literal level is to be implausible, or to bespeak by their presence their absence elsewhere. As we have seen, particular causal vocabulary establishes the expectation of explanation that will impel readers, when believable explanation is lacking, to interrogate the *narration*. Such questioning, when the reader finds the mythic answer that explains the implausibilities and fills all the gaps, produces a metacommunication; the *récit* transforms the *histoire* from a sequence of events into a language, into that code which, once deciphered, suggests the "second signified." And so the mythic *histoire* is elevated toward universality insofar as it assumes elements of metacausation from the matrix structure, while the causation of the *récit*, when it is credible and specific, is depreciated. At least, in the competition between the two parallel causal chains, that is what usually happens.

It is just possible, however, for the causes functioning in the *histoire* and present in the *récit* to win a kind of victory, ironically downgrading mythic causation in the *narration*. That is what happens in Gide's *Thésée*. When a given myth has already received a consecrated expression, retelling normally retains the causal matrix while changing characters and situation as well as temporal and geographical setting. Thus, in *La Faute de l'abbé Mouret*, Zola preserves the mythic causal chain of temptation-fall-expulsion, while imposing it upon the specifics of characters different from the biblical Adam and Eve, in a different place and time. *Thésée*, on the other hand, retains the characters, places, and events of the classical expression of the myth; what changes in the *récit* and *histoire* is the traditional causation.

Traditionally, for example, the labyrinth is a complex maze of passageways and the Minotaur a flesh-eating monster; in the Gidean text, the labyrinth turns out to be a palace of youthful pleasures that no one wants to leave (complete with a narcotic smoke, wafted on the air, to weaken the will), and the Minotaur a physically beautiful but stupid bovine. Thus, in the ancient versions, Theseus's escape is the result of strength and courage well used against royal power and vengeful cruelty, of cunning deployed against Daedalus's wise strategies; it is a conquest of youth over the power and wisdom of age, the stuff traditional rites of passage are made of. In the Gidean *récit*, the hero must overcome, not obstacles imposed by others, but his own youthful pleasure-seeking drives; Ariadne's thread is primarily symbolic ("tangible figuration of duty," as Daedalus puts it—*Thésée*, p. 1433). It represents the social responsibility of Theseus's royal origins—which, *noblesse oblige*, he fulfills remarkably well later on as king of Athens. Like its ancient counterparts, *Thésée* presents a rite of passage, but it involves a victory not over adult power but over the free concupiscence of youth. The cause of Theseus's triumph now is the sacrifice of individual pleasure for the eventual benefit of society. By changing the immediate and literal causes of struggle (complex maze becomes charming garden) and therefore the qualities required to win, the *récit* downgrades ironically the traditional mythic causal chain: socialization replaces strength and shrewdness as the modern means to adulthood. But depreciation of the traditional structure obviously does not divest the story of mythic qualities. Instead, the new causation creates a new and highly valorized myth in place of the old one. Change in causality at the literal level produces a displacement of the traditional myth at the symbolic level; retention of the original characters and setting makes the displacement evident.

So it is that the lesson of the myth, its allegorical "signifié second," is contingent upon the causal structures of the *récit*, rather than upon characters, times and settings. Where causation expressed in the *récit* is plausible and explicit, it appears superficial, weakened by irony. Where it is implausible or absent, it is replaced, by readers, with the mythic causes from the same chronological position in the matrix chain, causes that often seem magically powerful in context. If a given allegorical matrix has been previously expressed in a text, the choice for subsequent authors would seem to be to retain the causal matrix and change the contingent trappings (as in *La Faute de l'abbé Mouret*), or to use the same *personnages* and *décors* in which to animate a new causal matrix (*Thésée*), in competition with that of its "ancestor."

When a mythic novel seeks to unveil a matrix that has not been expressed before, it relies on allusive strategies like those listed above to awaken readers to the existence of its "signifié second." I have pointed out elsewhere[8] the mythic matrix common to Malraux's *La Condition humaine* and Camus's *La Peste*. I would argue that *La Condition humaine* (1933) is the first novel to present the Absurd as a mythic matrix. It indicates by the universality of its title a commitment to portray all humanity through the activity of individuals. The metaphysical notion of absurdity is subdivided in this "collective" novel into its constituent practical problems: notably inevitable suffering (despite our hunger for happiness), unavoidable death (though we wish to live), and ineluctable isolation (in spite of our longing to communicate with others). The *récit* presents a collectivity of individuals imprisoned in a closed city and facing a common enemy. Each character has his or her own story, with its literal causal chain; each one combats elements of the absurd dilemma. Thus the group, functioning as an individual and as the true "hero" of the novel, confronts the Absurd on all its levels. *La Peste* (1947) repeats the basic literal structure (closed city, collectivity, common "enemy") and evokes a similar matrix.

Both novels have characters who strive to escape the absurdity of the human condition: Clappique (*Condition humaine*), and Rambert early on (*Peste*). Each has characters who would like to conquer death (*Condition humaine*: Tchen, and perhaps Kyo, by martyrdom for "the Cause" and an afterlife in human memory; *Peste*: Tarrou, and perhaps Rieux, through medicine) and suffering (*Condition humaine*: Kyo, May; *Peste*: Rieux, Tarrou, and others). Both have characters seeking to overcome their isolation and commune with others: Katow succeeds temporarily through a gift of cyanide and a handclasp *in extremis* (*Condition humaine*); Joseph Grand "gets through" to Rieux in a sincere and symbolic prose sentence: "Ma bien chère Jeanne, c'est aujourd'hui Noël" (*Peste*, p. 1434). But the literally expressed causation of these individual stories is depreciated with respect to that of the matrix. For example, a primary reason why Kyo, Katow, and other communists are captured by the forces of Chang Kai-Shek is Clappique's failure to warn them; caught up in the fever of gambling, he remains at the gaming tables until it is too late. But on the level of *narration*, the mythic cause is obvious: Kyo and Katow must be shown imprisoned and awaiting the ultimate unpleasantness (burning alive in a locomotive's fire box) for the purpose of illustrating two possible reactions to a universal problem— the approach of death. Clappique's failure is a ploy on the literal level (*histoire*) to justify a symbolic segment. Such ploys are essential to mythic novels of the Absurd, where nothing can appear superficially implausible or coincidental. If indeed implausibilities or major causal gaps appeared, readers could infer mythic causation, as we have seen, thus importing potentially "magical" or "supernatural" overtones into a text that must deny all mystical power as antithetical to the Absurd. (But the "tragic" readings of Malraux—in the sense of classical poetics—that have crept in suggest that some gaps do exist.)[9] Thus the individual stories of the characters in these novels are set forth in generally clear and plausible causal chains (with historical justification in *La Condition humaine*), even though readers alert to the mythic dimension will see matrix causation as determinant and literal causation as a ploy.

Traditional myths are by nature judgmental: if you do A, B will result, and B is good (or bad). The rebirth of Aubignane is good (*Regain*); the inability of Elizabeth and Paul to overcome or escape the constraints of taboo is tragic (*Enfants terribles*). But with absurdity, nothing is ultimately good or evil in a universal sense: judgments of that ilk are a matter for individual determination. Both *La Condition humaine* and *La Peste* are remarkably free of judgment. Given the universal dilemma, each character acts in situation and faces the consequences of her or his choices. But the *récit* judges neither choices nor results. A fascist, for example, is given the chance to explain and defend his torturing of communists in *La Condition humaine*; neither Rambert (for seeking to flee) nor Cottard (for profiting from the epidemic) is condemned, in *La Peste*, for his decisions. The absurd myth impels the reader, likewise embroiled in the human condition, to judge which strategies against the common peril appear more nearly successful or more admirable.

The matrix of the absurdist myth is thus obviously not a simple, rectilinear causal strand. The conjoined paradigms which make it up resemble one another in that they have their original cause in the absurd paradox: on the one hand a human limitation and on the other a profound desire to overcome it. This tension has as its effect an action, which results, in the absolute sense, in failure. Some actions may be seen by readers as achieving partial, temporary success, or as representing, even in failure, more admirable attitudes. On the literal level, these "collective" texts share some characteristics with the "track-and-sidetrack" structure, with general parallelism among the branches, but pretension to universal truth establishes a "signifié second," a second level causally parallel to the literal récit and interacting with it.

The causally oriented, inferential spectacles I am wearing have thus served to uncover the allegorical traits in mythic tales. These are hardly without value: allegory announces the power of the general over the specific, of permanent causal laws over the seemingly random circumstances of daily life. Insofar as myths have ethical and religious overtones, allegory repeats and reaffirms moral and spiritual values in each new *histoire* that incarnates it. Retelling the power of mythic causation in ever different specific situations, as new mythic stories "repeat" old myths, constitutes a ritual act of renewal. La Mamèche of *Regain* is not Demeter, but death and rebirth find worthy celebration, in both human and agricultural terms, in Giono as in the early "Homeric" hymns. Even when mythic novels will not valorize religion (e.g., *La Condition humaine, La Peste*), they magnify the importance of the second signified by incarnating it in an emotion-filled context.

But the ineffable, purely mythic content to which Ricoeur points is an understanding born of comparison, of spatial relationships foreign to causality, which recall the helicopter-motorcycle comparison at the close of chapter three. From above, every element of the landscape stands in perpetual relation to every other; the dynamic, earth-bound motorcycle yields an inevitably reductive view. It is, like language itself, linear, directional, and temporal, while the completeness of the view from above, ineffable, escapes the linearity of language. For it is directionality that characterizes allegorical reading: there is a beginning (*récit*), a "primary" signified (literal *histoire*) and then a "second" one, which, once attained, supercedes its predecessor, thus left behind, discarded. The comparative view, the view from above, is nondirectional and extratemporal: all kinds of signifieds, regardless of the ordinal numbers that may be critically applied to them, coexist. Writing and reading are radically simultaneous; there is no beginning, no ending of a mythmaking "process." It is rather the directional optic of causality that imposes linear order. Where Ricoeur can see, for example, fear and purification as two views of a same reality (p. 40), causal analysts must observe cause and consequence. They can "compare" only perception and memory, not simultaneous perceptions. While language makes Ricoeur's analysis seem at times directional (primary → second, symbol → development), it remains spatial and ultimately comparative.

The causalist argument makes allegorical expression a part of the intent of *narration*, so that the general causal stance of *narration* (e.g., sacrificial death brings new life) is itself a cause of the *histoire* (Mamèche must die in *Regain* so that her death clearly brings about the rebirth of Aubignane), which allows us to infer the *narration*. Only readers' conditions of inference, springing from their own life experience, can guarantee, from the causal viewpoint, the "veracity," the universal applicability of the myth, for they are all that is outside the circular game of mirrors which is the text itself and its levels of narrative. Only readerly recognition of mythic qualities in texts can set essence and existence in relationship. Whence, from the etiological position, the basic (allegorical) structure: the parallel causal strands of primary and secondary signifieds, interacting and competing to supplant one another, often with delightful irony, across the *fêlure* or the cut or the suture that (un-)separates them.

The paradox of an absurdist "myth" lies of course with the fact that it must uncover the eternal and the universal despite nihilistic premises. Absurdist writers tend to present the Absurd as a primary cause of human unhappiness and revolt, while they express, on the other hand, profound doubts about the objective existence of causation; for them, derivation of causes and effects, of explanations, from observed phenomena constitutes subjective interpretation, in a world in which psyche and physical reality are irrevocably divorced. An absurdist strategy for portraying this problematical causal outlook forms the subject of the next chapter.

Notes

1. Susan Rubin Suleiman, *Authoritarian Fictions* (New York: Columbia University Press, 1983), pp. 149–97.

2. Paul Ricoeur, *Finitude et culpabilité, II. La Symbolique du mal* (Paris: Aubier, Editions Montaigne, 1960), p. 25. The arguments to follow are based essentially on pp. 11–30, and further references in the text are to this edition.

3. Sir James George Frazer, *The Golden Bough* (New York: Macmillan, 1935), 4, v–vi, 120–33.

4. See Claude Lévi-Strauss, *Anthropologie structurale* (Paris: Plon, 1958), pp. 233–41.

5. Albert Camus, *La Peste*, in his *Théâtre, récits, nouvelles* (Paris: Gallimard, Pléiade, 1962), pp. 1213–1474; Jean Cocteau, *Les Enfants terribles* (Paris: Arthème Fayard, 1951);

André Gide, *Thésée*, in his *Romans, récits et soties, oeuvres lyriques* (Paris: Gallimard, Pléiade, 1958), pp. 1413–53; Jean Giono, *Regain* (Paris: Grasset, 1930); André Malraux, *La Condition humaine* (Paris: Gallimard, 1933); Emile Zola, *La Faute de l'abbé Mouret*, in his *Oeuvres complètes*, 3 (Paris: Cercle du Livre Précieux, 1967), 19–270. Further references in the text are to these editions.

      6.   Suleiman, pp. 28–45, describes this phenomenon. Reading for cause and effect of course encourages the reading of mythic texts as *exempla*.

      7.   Peter Brooks, *Reading for the Plot* (New York: Alfred A. Knopf, 1984), pp. 83–84.

      8.   Roy Jay Nelson, "Malraux and Camus: The Myth of the Beleaguered City," *Kentucky Foreign Language Quarterly*, 13, 2 (1966), 89–94.

      9.   For example, W. M. Frohock, *André Malraux and the Tragic Imagination* (Palo Alto: Stanford University Press, 1952), and Bert M.-P. Leefmans, "Malraux and Tragedy: The Structure of *La Condition humaine*," *Romanic Review*, 44, 3 (October 1953), 208–14.

9
The Broken Line

Pour que soit possible une oeuvre absurde, il faut que la pensée sous sa
forme la plus lucide y soit mêlée. Mais il faut en même temps qu'elle
n'y paraisse point sinon comme l'intelligence qui ordonne. Ce paradoxe
s'explique selon l'absurde. L'oeuvre d'art naît du renoncement de l'intelligence à raisonner le concret. Elle marque le triomphe du charnel. C'est la
pensée lucide qui la provoque, mais dans cet acte même elle se renonce. Elle
ne cédera pas à la tentation de surajouter au décrit un sens plus profond
qu'elle sait illégitime.

(For an absurd work to be possible, the most lucid form of thought must be
involved in it. But at the same time it must not be visible in it, except as
the organizing intelligence. This paradox is explainable according to the
absurd. The work of art is born of the intelligence's refusal to try to reason
concrete reality: it marks the triumph of the physical. Lucid thought
instigates the work, but precisely in so doing it renounces itself. It will not
yield to the temptation to add on to what is described a deeper meaning it
knows to be illegitimate.)

—ALBERT CAMUS

Fiction that not only takes absurdity as its subject but also seeks to
mirror it in its form must elect to reveal a causally fragmented
histoire. The perceived divorce between psyche and exterior reality,
between "l'intelligence" and "le concret" in Camus's terms, presupposes
that physical causation is problematic; the relationship between cause and
effect in the world about us is part of the organizing grid imposed upon
perceived reality by the organizing eye. For the contrast between psyche
and reality to strike the reader's consciousness with convincing force, the

concrete reflected in the *histoire* must retain its causal disconnectedness before the narrator's eye and in the narrator's prose.

We have encountered fragmentation before, in the traditional fiction of Zola and in the causal blockers of the "track-and-sidetrack" texts. In traditional fiction, breaks in the causal chain of the *histoire* are relatively infrequent, while they are, in absurdist structure, ubiquitous, often more common than linkage. If neither the *récit* nor common sense nor personal experience helps readers of traditional fiction to fill a given gap between two events in the *histoire*, recourse to the level of *narration* will suggest what the inferred author is up to in breaking the chain at that point. Fragmented absurdist fiction discourages, in one way or another, any peek behind the scenery to discover an author at work. Indeed, it is on the level of *narration* that the absurdist paradox is, shamefacedly, hiding out, for despite Camus, "lucid thought" is never quite ready to renounce itself.

It may be useful to reiterate here as well the distinctions drawn in an earlier chapter between "track-and-sidetrack" fiction and "broken-line" texts. Episodic structure provides a break in the causal chain at the end of each episode (at least). Episodes are not causally related to one another; instead, they are usually connected by similarity—structural parallelism, common themes, a single dominant viewpoint. They exist as branches of a basic substructure or "plot," which they dominate by sheer volume. A digression or two does not constitute episodic structure; the sidetracks must take up more room in the text than the main line. Above all, episodes are generally interchangeable; the order in which they occur is not of the essence. Absurdist fragmentation, on the other hand, lacks the substructure of "plot"; the viewpoint of the narrator is not constant, but changes; and the segments of the *récit*, although not causally interconnected, must appear in the given order. A truly fragmented story is linear despite the extreme frequency of causal gaps; the linearity is determined by factors other than causation existing on the level of the *récit* or of the *histoire*.

As a prototype of the fragmented tale, Sartre's *La Nausée* (1938) will serve admirably. And Camus's partially fragmented *L'Etranger* (1942) can hardly escape analysis here, since, like a latter-day *Bête humaine*, it takes causality as its subject, and since the fascinating and voluminous scholarship that surrounds it disagrees with respect to the causal function.

While *L'Etranger* has elements of diarylike structure, Sartre's text adopts all the conventions of the fictional journal,[1] including a framing "Avertissement des Editeurs" and dated entries. The diary novel is eminently suited to absurdist fragmentation, most obviously because the fictional "time of composition" is itself fragmented. Written in a series of "present" moments, it reveals a narrator rooted in each one successively, with no knowledge of what the future then holds. The narrator cannot therefore construct a causal chain (an activity that requires reverse logic, reasoning from effect to cause) to connect beginning to end and to explain the *dénouement*. So fictional journals as a class must be causally disconnected at the level of the *récit*. It is often possible, however, for readers to infer causation at the level of the *histoire* just as well as in a Zola novel: one has only to think of Gide's *La Symphonie pastorale*, Malraux's *Les Conquérants*, or Mauriac's *Le Noeud de vipères*; sometimes one can discern even the allegorical paradigms of a "signifié second," as in Bernanos's *Journal d'un curé de campagne* or in the log entries of Tournier's *Vendredi, ou les limbes du Pacifique*. But *La Nausée* carefully segregates events—walks in the park, days in the library, conversations with the Autodidacte, meals in the café, a visit to the municipal museum, a trip to see Anny—grounding each in its own present. None of these can be said to "cause" any of the others, and such causal fragmentation reinforces the insight that the present alone exists: the "past" is present memories, present texts, and the future is at best a present project.

Fictional diaries share with all first-person narratives a limited point of view: we see the fictional world from behind a single pair of eyes. We can enter the psyche of the narrator alone, and all we can know is what is registered there now, with the distortions peculiar to the individual diarist. There is no omniscience and no objective viewpoint: if causation appears to be functioning at all in the world outside the narrator's mind, we can have no objective validation of it. When external causation appears in *La Nausée*, it often seems to have its origin in the observing psyche's distorted perspective: a pebble causing "a kind of nausea in my hands" (p. 16).

Finally, diarists, both fictional and real, are generally at the same time narrator and narratee in their texts. They write for themselves, often with an eye to greater self-understanding. Roquentin adopts this stance; his diary is not written for public consumption, but for his own edification. He is translating the daily events of his life to words, then reading (presumably) the words in order to comprehend the life. It is in the presumption that reading is enough like living for one to facilitate comprehension of the other that Roquentin's diary (along with the novel itself, in a sense) runs into trouble, as we shall see.

Like the texts of Huysmans and of Proust previously discussed, *La Nausée* traces the progress of a "disease." But the events of the story, apparently separate and random as they are, never function as digressions, never provide escape or even temporary remission from the progress of the symptoms. Events are ordered not by causal relationship to each other but to mirror the gradually increasing severity of Roquentin's suffering; as he becomes ever more lucid about the radical separation between his mind, in which his true self seems to reside, and concrete, exterior reality, horror and creeping psychological revulsion little by little take possession of him. The gradual progression, carefully arranged, of the symptoms, from initial anxiety to raving hallucination, to the deceptive tranquillity of the final pseudocure, defines the rectilinear character of the *récit*. The onset of this metaphysical disease, from which no other character in the text suffers, its relentlessly increasing severity, and the unrealistic "cure" all exist in the text without explanation: no cause is given for the rectilinear evolution of Roquentin's particular problem. We may well infer as readers that he is the victim of his own lucidity, of course, but neither the reason for his special insight nor the cause of his peculiar, carefully graded psychological reaction is inferable. Nothing in the characteristic of lucidity itself determines such an evolution. The text is informed by degree of severity of reaction, and by the fact that disease precedes cure, rather than by cause and effect.

As we are instructed at the outset, in the initial, abortive "feuillet sans date," the purpose of the diary is understanding ("y voir clair," [p. 5]; "to get a clear insight into it") and cure ("Je suis guéri, je renonce à écrire mes impressions," [p. 7]; "I'm cured; I'll quit writing down my impressions"). Thus Roquentin transforms himself, for therapeutic purposes, into a narratee, into a reader: he becomes one of us. From that transformation arises the persistent double meaning of the text, in its relationship to Roquentin for one part, and in its relationship to us (other) readers for the other.

Reading skill, I reiterate, involves ability to draw inferences, and in dynamic systems, such as novels and life, inferences have their basis, on one level or another, in causal assumptions. This is what Roquentin soon begins to discover. He becomes aware (pp. 46–50) that we cannot narrate our own adventures, that the term "true story" is an oxymoron, because of the causal logic inherent in stories. Begin to relate an experience, and the listeners or readers will know that you begin with a particular end in view: "C'est en réalité par la fin," concludes Roquentin, "qu'on a commencé" ("It's really with the end that you began"). What our hero is discovering is the reverse causal logic that functions on the level of the *narration*: if we are told A, it is in order to prepare for the subsequent occurrence of B, of which the inferred author, if not the narrator as well, is already cognizant. By assuming an author's intentions as prime cause in the narrative, we are associating text with mind, with psyche, as divorced from reality. Indeed, a primary distinction between life and story is that the latter has a "level of *narration*," while the former does not (unless, unlike Sartre, one envisages an inferred God). This discovery should already give Roquentin pause with respect to the therapeutic usefulness of his diary, but, situated *in medias res* and unaware of where his next entry is coming from, he can claim freedom from intentionality. Not so Sartre. Readers are correctly assuming a level of *narration* in *La Nausée* and can only read Roquentin's discovery as a warning that the novel itself, in its supposed referentiality, is a delusion. That Sartre was aware of the delusion is nowhere more apparent than in his *prière d'insérer*, where he notes the narrator's discovery that "there are no adventures," only to add, "Alors commence sa véritable aventure, une métamorphose insinuante et doucement horrible de toutes ses sensations; c'est la Nausée. . . ." (*Oeuvres romanesques*, p. 1695); "Then begins his real adventure, an insidious and sweetly horrible metamorphosis of all his sensations: Nausea. . . ." Finding no cause for the disease and its gradual progession, nor for the "cure" in the *récit*, and unable to infer any in the disjointed *histoire*, readers are impelled to seek them out in the *narration*: to attribute the "véritable aventure" to authorial intent. If Roquentin knows not what his future holds, Sartre does (see, for example, his outline of the projected novel, in *Oeuvres romanesques*, p. 1686).

Roquentin is perfectly aware of the uselessness of causal inference for explaining exterior reality, since it is on that shoal that his biography of the Marquis de Rollebon runs aground. The last sentence of his manuscript, the one upon which our hero gives up his biographic endeavor, is a causal explanation: "M. de Rollebon dut se laisser prendre à cette manoeuvre, puisqu'il écrivit à son neveu en date du 13 septembre, qu'il venait de rédiger son testament" (p. 116); "M. de Rollebon must have fallen for that maneuver, since he wrote his nephew as of September 13 that he had just drawn up his will." The logic of the sentence is precisely that of a reader constructing *histoire* from *récit*. The cause indicated by "puisque" ("since") is not that of an event in Rollebon's life, but the condition for Roquentin's own inference: $C \Rightarrow R (A \rightarrow B)$. The cause of Rollebon's reaction ("cette manoeuvre") is inferred ("dut"—"must have"), as is the reaction itself ("se laisser prendre"—"fallen for"): Roquentin creates an *histoire* on the basis of a *récit* (the letter to the nephew plus circumstantial knowledge of the "maneuver"), using inference as readers must. His rejection of such reasoning as unrelated to the objective reality of the events under consideration ought to raise questions for him about the value of narrating the events of his life in a diary in order to understand them, for understanding of texts presupposes causal inference. For readers of the novel, this incident points to the unreliability of readerly inference, as if it were warning them away from seeking to infer what is going on at the level of *narration*, where the paradox lies.

Despite his discovery that "you have to choose: live or narrate" (p. 48; "il faut choisir: vivre ou raconter") and his injunction to "Beware of literature" (p. 68; "Se méfier de la littérature"), Roquentin unfailingly "reads" his life. One foggy, rainy day, for example, when the proprietor of the café Mably did not come down to work, the idea strikes Roquentin, on a half-joking suggestion of an employee, that M. Fasquelle might be dead in his bedroom upstairs. This terrifying thought haunts him all through the varied events of the day (pp. 85–97). Like a reader, habituated to seeking meaning in the *narration*, for whom weather is a portent, and who knows that no self-respecting novelist would tell us that a character failed to appear for work unless that fact was the result of an important cause or the cause of a major effect, Roquentin fictionalizes, textualizes his life. It is in the diary's mixture of "living" and "narrating" that the paradox filters down into the text. It takes the form of a straight but broken line. In the example of the "dead" proprietor, the day is filled with causally unconnected events: breakfast in the café, overheard conversations, walks, morning and afternoon sessions at the library, a discussion with the Autodidacte, an encounter with a "flasher." But a constant mindset, the haunting thought of M. Fasquelle lying dead and undiscovered in bed, connects it all.

In another segment, preoccupation with his body, as a part of "concrete reality" and therefore distinct from his true inner self, unifies the multiple events in which Roquentin is engaged. First, he is aware of an uncontrolled twitch in his shoulder. Then he becomes conscious of his mouth: "Il y a de l'eau mousseuse dans ma bouche. Je l'avale, elle glisse dans ma gorge, elle me caresse . . ." (p. 117; "There's foamy water in my mouth. I swallow it, it slips into my throat, it caresses me . . ."). The quick shift from "Je" (agent) to "me" (patient) reinforces the separation of the observing mind and independent matter. Next, in the famous passage, his hand takes on a kind of animal life of its own. The notion of "body parts" unites the passage, makes it a "line," but no causal connective leads from one part to the next. Readers could not foresee the selection of organs nor the order of their presentation. But once the taxonomic principle is determined (independence of the material body from the mind), it is not hard to see where the line is going. It is hardly surprising therefore when, later on, his penis begins to operate autonomously. This leads to the horrifying discovery that he cannot always control his very thoughts, and that he can never stop them: the final line of separation fades. Progression in the passage is not causal but logical; the blockers of fragmentation fall between examples of a principle, not between a potential cause and its possible effect.

Given the continuity of prose and the discontinuity of events, it is hardly surprising that an inveterate "reader" like Roquentin should find a cure for his malady in language. "Le mot d'Absurdité naît à présent sous ma plume" (p. 152; "Now the word Absurdity springs to life beneath my penpoint"): this miraculous birth (there is no definable cause for it except Roquentin's terrible need for comfort) gives our narrator a linguistic tool, a name for the divorce that separates meaning from life, thought from reality, and *narration* from *récit*. But in this word the solipsism that has constituted the malady and the subject of the novel all along resurfaces, for Roquentin endows the word with meaning, with value, with the power to dominate through understanding: "je comprenais la Nausée, je la possédais" (p. 155; "I understood Nausea; I possessed it"). But now we other readers see what our hero does not: that the word "Absurdity" is no more meaningful, no truer in its pseudoconnection of psyche to exterior reality, than any other word. Like the notions of "causality" and "meaning" themselves, it is a mental construct: despite its capacity to name, the psyche never truly possesses anything, including itself. Roquentin will come to glimpse the problem: "Now," he notes later, "when I say 'I,' it sounds hollow to me" (p. 200; "A présent, quand je dis 'je', ça me semble creux").

But if, on the level of the *histoire*, the birth of the Word, with its magic power, appears miraculous, the event belongs to a clear causal chain on the level of *narration*. The novel is an "adventure," and, as Roquentin saw early on, the end causes the beginning. Our hero's initial anxiety, his lucid insights, and his psychological suffering, all existed in order for this Word, and its concommitant meaning expressed in other words, to come into being.

As I have noted, in his essay entitled "Vraisemblance et motivation,"[2] Gérard Genette evokes the conflict between the chronological causal logic of the *récit* and the antichronological causality inherent in the intentions of the *narration*. His use of the term "motivation" applies to all causal concatenations at the *récit* level:

> La motivation est donc l'apparence et l'alibi causaliste que se donne la détermination finaliste qui est la règle de la fiction: le *parce que* chargé de faire oublier le *pour quoi?*—et donc de naturaliser, ou de réaliser (au sens de: faire passer pour réelle) la fiction en dissimulant ce qu'elle a de *concerté*, comme dit Valincour, c'est-à-dire d'artificiel: bref de fictif. (P. 97)

> (So motivation is the outward appearance and the causalist alibi that intentionalist determination, which is the rule of fiction, establishes for itself: the *because* entrusted with driving the *what for?* from our minds, and thus with naturalizing fiction, or with realizing it [in the sense of "passing it off as real"], by dissimulating what is "concerted" about it, as Valincour says, i.e., what is artificial, in short, what is fictive about it.)

Roquentin's anguish and his resulting need for comfort are, in this sense, a causalist alibi constructed to bring the word "Absurdity" with its full baggage of meaning artificially into the text. But the paucity of causal connections between events in the novel, and Roquentin's position as observer before a succession of causally unconnected exterior happenings, sharply reduce the number of "alibis" in this fiction. We are constantly impelled to infer causation from the *narration* and to read at that level. But, as we already observed in chapter five, "motivation" in the *récit* is not a requirement for verisimilitude; *La Nausée*'s "alibi" resides rather in its verisimilar aspects: people, places, situations.

Genette seems to impugn "motivation," explicit causation in the *récit*, as a coverup for the "concerted," the "artificial," and the "fictive," which enter fiction through the *narration*. But intentionalist determination unconcealed would not be fiction (parables excepted), nor would a narrative without a level of *narration* to hide. But since the level of *narration* is simply a product of reader inference, one might suggest that Genette is using his own intentionalist assumptions to subvert what is fictional about fiction. It should be beginning to become apparent that the fictional enterprise requires cooperation of *narration* with *récit*, and thus of reader with text.

In *La Nausée*, the *narration* is concerted, artificial, divorced from reality, like the psyche, so that the tension between *récit* and *narration* constitutes a formal example of the paradox that is its subject. To reconcile the irreconcilable, the text decides to incorporate the project of another text: Roquentin decides at last, Proust-like, to write a novel, in the hope that it will reflect a moment of his present being upon the future, like the jazz artists "immortalized" on his favorite record. Like all fictions, it will dissimulate; it will have a *narration* level (implicit in the "hope" of the previous sentence) inexistent in the reality it pretends to describe. It is therefore a pseudosolution, for the absurd tension will remain between *récit* and *narration*, just as in *La Nausée* itself. This tension bears an obvious relation to the interlevel irony we observed in mythic stories (chapter eight), the importance of which I shall discuss in the conclusion.

While Roquentin's malady alerts readers from the start to the intentions of the *narration* (we may guess that Roquentin is headed for a "cure" or "death," rather than toward a linguistic pseudocure, but we know at least that the reverse logic of the *narration* warrants a guessing game), the *narration* is so eclipsed in the first part of *L'Etranger*[3] that we are nearly at the end of it before we realize that there is a game of causal logic afoot. In the *histoire*, the game is played for higher stakes: whether Meursault killed the Arab "en connaissance de cause" (p. 1196) is the question on which the homodiegetic narrator's life hangs.[4] The reader is in less jeopardy, but the competition between the *narration* we infer and the *récit* we read is so subtly waged that we grow aware of it only retrospectively.

Part I of *L'Etranger* is a fragmented, diarylike presentation (although it lacks the diary conventions of dated entries and introspection) of certain events in Meursault's life during the eighteen days, more or less,[5] that end with the murder. Part II is a straightforward narrative account of some of Meursault's experiences during the investigation, the trial, and his subsequent imprisonment while awaiting a pardon, which apparently does not come (the latest moments related in the novel, in the present-of-narration at the beginning of II, 5, suggest that Meursault has been moved to death row, and that execution, and the attendant final interview with the chaplain, appear inevitable to him). Part I thus provides no apparent causal chain leading directly to the murder, while part II, in the case developed by the investigating magistrate and the prosecutor, presents a *récit* connecting many of these events in a causal strand that attempts to demonstrate premeditation. We may call part I "*récit*-dominant," because it encourages readers to read at that level rather than constructing a causally linked *histoire*; the prosecutor's case is *histoire*-dominant, since it presents most of the same events in a causal relationship, virtually creating retrospectively the *histoire* for the reader. The confrontation of these two modes by the *narration* points to the notion that causation in human conduct is a matter of mental perception, not of pragmatic fact.

Since part I is fragmented, and since fragmentation is supposed to impel readers to seek causal explanations at higher levels of narrative, why do readers tend to accept the causal gaps in Meursault's *récit* unquestioningly? I propose three answers. First, the fragmentation is successful: the murder remains unpredictable until I, 6; therefore construction of a causal *histoire* remains impossible, and interrogation of the intent of *narration* fruitless. Second, the hero appears unthreatened until the end; our need to understand and predict is therefore somewhat diminished. Finally, the frequency of causal vocabulary in part I is extraordinarily high, giving a superficial impression that Meursault is indeed explaining, making the causal connections among the events in his life. The unusual density of obvious, optional causal connectives in part I has left critics at odds.

Sartre claims, in his penetrating "Explication" (1943), that, in a style like that of *L'Etranger*,

> . . . on n'organise pas les phrases entre elles: elles sont purement juxtaposées: en particulier on évite toutes les liaisons causales, qui introduiraient dans le récit comme un embryon d'explication et qui mettraient entre les instants un ordre différent de la succession pure.[6]

> (. . . you do not organize the sentences with respect to each other; they are purely juxtaposed; in particular, you avoid all causal linkings, which would introduce a kind of embryonic explanation into the story and set up between the moments an order which is different from pure succession.)

Subsequent critics—Ullmann, Thody, Fitch, Simon, et al.—have also indicated that the text tends to avoid causal connections. Sartre adds, in a more ambiguous sentence we shall examine later, that the world of this novel is one from which "causality has been carefully eradicated" ("dont on a soigneusement extirpé la causalité").[7] Yet Ignace Feuerlicht was able to list, in 1963, one hundred nine causal connectives in *L'Etranger*: *parce que* (60), causal *comme* (15), *à cause de* (13), *puisque* (7), *car* (6), *c'est pour cela que* (2), causal *ainsi* (3), *donc* (2), *par suite* (1).[8] There are also examples of causal *de*, of *pour* (accomplished intention), and of numerous transitive verbs indicative of causation (not to mention parataxis) not listed by Feuerlicht. A great deal of this vocabulary occurs in the "fragmented" part I: thirty-five of the sixty uses of *parce que* appear in that section. The frequency of the causal connectives cited by Feuerlicht in *L'Etranger* is indeed far higher than that in our Gidean sample (see appendix A)—quite high, I think, in absolute terms.[9] Our first-person narrator seems almost preoccupied with explaining "why," and yet the notion that he fails to make causal connections persists.

Close analysis of Feuerlicht's list (after the minor corrections indicated in note 8 above) suggests the reason for the contradiction. About sixty-six percent of the occurrences of causal terms are inconsequential or apparently evasive, or they involve mere inference or speculation on Meursault's part: such uses of the vocabulary cannot contribute to the generation of causal chains. Another nine percent are not part of Meursault's *récit* as such, but belong to the *histoire* as judgments of other characters quoted or alluded to by Meursault. The remaining twenty-five percent of occurrences of these "optional" causal terms reflect an awareness on the narrator's part of working chains of cause and effect, although seven percent of those appear to refer to the *narration,* of which Meursault is, theoretically, unaware. (For a statistical summary of my analysis of Feuerlicht's data, see appendix C.)

A few examples of this causal vocabulary will show how it often serves to give the impression of explaining without really doing so. Meursault writes, for example, that, during his vigil beside his mother's coffin, he fell asleep. Then: "Je me suis réveillé parce que j'avais de plus en plus mal aux reins" (p. 1133; "I woke up because my back was hurting worse and worse"). But no long-term consequences arise, either from awakening or from the sore back. No explanation at all is offered for dozing off (if one can ever explain such things), although it is falling asleep, rather than awakening, which will cause repercussions at the trial. The first morning after the return from the funeral, "J'ai eu de la peine à me lever," writes Meursault, "parce que j'étais fatigué de ma journée d'hier" (p. 1138; "I had a hard time getting up, because I was tired out from yesterday"). The cause-and-effect relationship is highly plausible, but the fatigue left him strong enough to go swimming that morning, to take Marie out that evening, and to prolong the date in his room into the night. Much of the causal vocabulary in this text explains in this way brief and inconsequential circumstances.

Less frequently, Meursault's causal vocabulary apparently evades a central issue, either by his intent or through his failure to grasp it. Two examples occur within three sentences when, after swimming, he and Marie put on their street clothes to leave the beach. She is startled, since he has just made a date with her, to note from his black tie and armband that he is in mourning, and he tells her his mother is dead.

> Comme elle voulait savoir depuis quand, j'ai répondu: "Depuis hier." Elle a eu un petit recul, mais n'a fait aucune remarque. J'ai eu envie de lui dire que ce n'était pas ma faute, mais je me suis arrêté parce que j'ai pensé que je l'avais déjà dit à mon patron. (P. 1139)

> (As she wanted to know since when, I answered, "Since yesterday." She backed off a little, but made no remark. I felt like telling her it wasn't my fault, but I held off, because it occurred to me I'd already said that to my boss.)

The initial *comme* introduces the reason for his responding, but not for his response; yet the problem lies there, for his mother had died, at the latest, the day before yesterday. Did he lie or err? As for the *parce que*, the fact of having said something once is not of itself a valid reason for not repeating it to another interlocutor. The construction of *parce que* with a mental "action" (*parce que j'ai pensé que, trouvé que, senti que*, etc.) is not, however, atypical of Meursault; he has no qualms about "explaining" actions on the basis of momentary judgments, illogical or not. He will give, parataxically, better reasons for his silence in the two sentences immediately following: "That didn't mean anything. Any way you look at it, you're always a little at fault" ("Cela ne voulait rien dire. De toute façon, on est toujours un peu fautif"). But precisely, the parataxis here, after the earlier *parce que*, leaves open the question of whether these reasons entered his mind while speaking to Marie or whether he thought of them later. Here again, he explains his (absence of) response, but not what he felt like responding. Why did he feel the need to disclaim responsibility for his mother's demise? Does he see her death as out of step with his usual style of life, rather than seeing his lifestyle as out of step with her recent passing? In such instances, Meursault explains the inconsequential—why he spoke (or did not)—while eluding the more crucial question of the cause behind his expressed (or unexpressed) ideas. So used, causal vocabulary creates no "chains of events."

Now and then Meursault uses the terminology of causation to draw inferences about the reality that surrounds him. While they let us see the world through his eyes, these inferences never explicitly influence his conduct. As he approaches the Arab he will soon kill on the beach, for example, he notes: "Maybe because of the shadows on his face, he looked like he was laughing" (p. 1165: "Peut-être à cause des ombres sur son visage, il avait l'air de rire"). If he took the inferred amusement on the part of the Arab as an affront, the text gives no indication of it; in the *récit*, the murder is caused by the sun, not anger. Indeed the causal term in this sentence serves to explain why the inference was of dubious validity. Occasionally too, our narrator chooses causal terms in developing hypotheses about future or other nonexistent "realities." Such speculations have no bearing on any action, and they occur essentially toward the end of the novel, as Meursault seeks to imagine what it will be like to be guillotined, or whether some other form of execution might be preferable (e.g., p. 1204, *Ainsi, Car, Par suite*).

But Meursault does make a number of substantial causal connections. The primary example in part I is the relatively clear causal chain, of which Meursault is conscious, leading from the relationship with Raymond Sintès to the initial confrontations at the beach, in Raymond's company, with the latter's Arab antagonists. Meursault knows that Raymond enjoys his company, "because I listen to him" (p. 1145; "parce que je l'écoute"). Such willingness to listen entangles the protagonist in Raymond's plot to brutalize further his former Arab mistress, who has been unfaithful, or, if he is her pimp, "unremitting." When asked if he will write a letter to draw her into Raymond's trap, Meursault says nothing; asked if he would mind writing it then and there, he replies, "No." There is no explicit causal explanation for that decision, but Meursault notes that he wrote the best letter he could, to please Raymond, "parce que je n'avais pas de raison de ne pas le contenter" (p. 1148; "because I had no reason not to please him"). Passivity— listening, not minding, having "no reason" to displease Raymond (although "avoiding violence" might have done in a pinch)— characterizes the explicit explanation at this juncture. From there, the causal chain continues, with others (Raymond, Masson) making the decisions and Meursault electing only to participate, until the first confrontation with the Arabs on the beach (pp. 1164–65). The causal link between that fight and the second encounter is not explicit, but Meursault infers a possible motive on Raymond's part (p. 1165). At the end of the second confrontation, our narrator takes a more active part, apparently to prevent Raymond from shooting his adversary. Here the causal chain ends. The third confrontation, in which Meursault returns alone to the beach and kills the Arab, is isolated from the preceding chain of events by the introduction of a new cause: "C'était le même soleil. . . . A cause de cette brûlure . . ." (p. 1168; "It was the same sun. . . . Because of that searing heat . . ."). Here the etiological term sets in motion a new causal chain, the most formidable of the novel: hearings, trial, conviction of premeditated murder.

In addition to the substantial causes Meursault sees, a number of causal terms in the text explain his emotional and mental states (e.g., "J'étais un peu étourdi parce qu'il a fallu que je monte chez Emmanuel pour lui emprunter une cravate noire et un brassard," [p. 1127]; "I was a little confused because I had to go up to Emmanuel's to borrow a black tie and armband from him"), but for the most part such states of mind are without consequence. A few may be seen, however, as actual causes of Meursault's final enlightenment. During the trial, our narrator once notes, "I had a crazy desire to cry, because I felt how much I was detested by all those folks" (p. 1189; "j'ai eu une envie stupide de pleurer parce que j'ai senti combien j'étais détesté par tous ces gens-là"). After conviction, he can still imagine himself alive and free. "J'avais tort," he explains, "de me laisser aller à ces suppositions parce que, l'instant d'après, j'avais si affreusement froid que je me recroquevillais sous ma couverture" (p. 1203; "I was wrong to let myself make these suppositions because, the next minute, I was so horribly cold I curled up in a ball under my blanket"). His final decision to cherish that which separates him from those who judge—and thus from life and free- dom—appears to be, at least in part, a result of such explicitly caused mental states.

A few causal explanations, inconsequential in the *récit*, seem in retro- spect to refer to the text itself, to what is going on at the level of *narration*; we will consider these later. The essential point is that, despite a causal vocabulary of exceptionally high density, the critics who see Meursault's account as causally fragmented are quite correct. Most of the obviously causal terms are "wasted" on the inconsequential or on apparently "evasive" explanations, particularly in part I. But the "waste" may have a dual purpose. First, it can give some readers at first reading the impression that Meursault is indeed explaining the events of his life, thus discouraging speculation, at the level of *narration*, about the indexic author's purposes. Secondly, it suggests a tension between words and reality, raising doubts about the veracity and utility of language, of linguistic "explanations."

Of course, if Meursault were writing, diarylike, the story of his life day by day as he lived it, it would be quite plausible that he might fail to note causal relationships that would become apparent only afterward: hindsight, after all, is the natural direction for causal reasoning. So it is that the question of when the text was composed by Meursault (present of narration) becomes central for analysts of causation. With it, the question of who is writing surfaces: is it the bereaved office clerk who writes I, 1, or the condemned murderer of II, 5, or both?

As several critics have noted,[10] evidence of proximate narration figures prominently in part I, suggesting a daily notebook or diary: in the first two paragraphs of I, 1 ("Aujourd'hui, maman est morte," [p. 1127]; "Today mama died"); in the temporal overlap of paragraphs two and three ("Je prendrai l'autobus. . . . J'ai pris l'autobus," [p. 1127]; "I'll take the bus. . . . I took the bus"); at the beginning of I, 2 ("c'est aujourd'hui samedi," [p. 1138]; "today is Saturday"); in I, 3, where the whole chapter could, without contradiction, be read as if composed at the close of the day recounted; in I, 4, which purports to have been written on Sunday ("Hier, c'était samedi," [p. 1150]; "Yesterday was Saturday"), but which ends with our narrator already in bed Sunday night (when did he write?). Beginning with I, 5, there is apparently nothing but postponed narration until the first sentences of II, 5 ("en ce moment," [p. 1202]; "right now"). It is easy to situate the segment of postponed narration as being composed during the period of incarceration, but the problem posed by the proximate narration is that Meursault gives such a full account of his activities that it is hard to imagine when he finds time to write.

Jean-Claude Pariente has proposed an ingenious solution: I, 1 through I, 4 constitutes a diary without indications of dates and times of entries; it was divided into parts and chapters by a transformed Meursault near the end of his life, when he also composed the long narration, I, 5 through II, 5.[11] Thanks to this latter-day textual division, breaks between moments of composition can occur in midchapter. Thus, for example, all of I, 1 after the first two paragraphs, plus the first two paragraphs of I, 2 (i.e., pp. 1127–39), was composed on Saturday, after the morning swim and before the evening date. That would allow perhaps some eight hours (minus time for meals) for the project: possible for a fast writer, but a grueling session. Meursault likes to explain his mental states, yet he never mentions distractions, or writer's cramp; indeed, he never alludes to work on the diary at all. If I raise the issue, it is to begin to suggest that no inferred solution, on the level of the *histoire*, can be completely satisfying.

Another difficulty with the early-chapters-as-diary theories is perhaps the ultimate causal question about the *histoire*: why, or for whom, was the "diary" written? Fictional diaries traditionally exist for cause, explicit or implicit;[12] Roquentin, one will recall, explains at the outset what impels him to write. *L'Etranger* provides no such indication. Fictional diarists almost always write for themselves alone, and the union of narrator and narratee furnishes for readers a guarantee of the narrator's sincerity.[13] Now, if Meursault begins a diary for himself, he need not explain those things he knows full well, such as the fact that the nursing home is in Marengo, eighty kilometers from Algiers (p. 1127), or that his bedroom overlooks the main street of the *faubourg* (p. 1140), or even that old Salamano occupies the other lodging in his floor (p. 1144). Such details imply another reader, one who needs orientation in an unfamiliar environment.

And, if diary there is, why does it begin precisely with the death of "maman"? Is it just an odd coincidence that the first event of the diarylike text is also the earliest element of the prosecutor's case? One critic, noting the problem, suggests that the text pretends to be retranscribed and edited after Meursault's decapitation, going so far as to imagine a possible editorial frame, which would indicate that entries prior to Mme Meursault's demise, being unimportant to the case, were deleted.[14] Of course, the notion of importance or relevancy is one of consequentiality, a causal notion whose adoption would presuppose an editor favorable to the prosecutor's case. And, if there were a *post mortem* "transcriber," could we attribute to her or him the insertion of the orienting details Meursault would not have written for himself? If so, what else did the *transcripteur* add or delete, given a bias for "relevancy" and public clarity? And if, as J.-C. Pariente has proposed, it is Meursault, at last capable of seeing his story objectively, as a "stranger" to himself, who performed the editing (division into chapters), did he delete entries prior to his mother's death and add the orienting explanations at that time, perhaps in view of presenting "his side of the story" to a wider audience? In that case, might he not have deleted a crucial causal term here or there, or inserted one of his "je ne sais pas pourquoi" ("I-don't-know-why" assertions) on occasion? A diary modified *ex post facto* by anyone is suspect, and one that takes account of external readers' ignorance is doubly so.[15]

On the other hand, if Meursault composed the whole tale in prison, when he presumably had ample time to write, the diarylike character of part I, with its indices of proximate narration, is a pure fabrication. With such hindsight, the absence of crucial causal connections and the misleading abundance of causal vocabulary could well be self-serving. In full knowledge of the prosecutor's reading of events, and aware that he was writing for others, he could propose another version of events, whether he believed it to have been "true" or not, as a condemnation of the judicial system and as his vindication before posterity.

So neither of these *histoire*-level readings is fully satisfactory; both leave doubts about the narrator and a suspect text. But it is precisely the impossibility of constructing a credible *histoire* that impels us to turn to the *narration* in search of an explanation. Novels that are complete and quite internally consistent in their *histoire* (like *La Bête humaine*, where Denizet's explanation fills the structural role occupied by the prosecutor's analysis of events here), while they may hint at their level of *narration*, do not oblige us to consult it. Inconsistencies in the *histoire* open a novel "at the top," raising our consciousness of the indexic author's intentions as we infer them, and increasing the importance of the *narration*. It is time to turn, therefore, to the metacausality in the *narration* of *L'Etranger*.

Meursault attends his mother's funeral, takes a mistress (in the parlance of the period), writes a letter for a friend, and kills an Arab. These four events occur in the fragmented part I, and again in the same order in the prosecutor's demonstration of premeditation. The difference lies in words: the absence of crucial causal connectives in part I and their presence in the prosecutor's reading of events. The *narration* presents first a *récit* with causal gaps, followed by an *histoire* of that récit, reconstituted by inference with the gaps neatly filled. The State's Attorney is merely reading part I as we have read Zola, making all the possible connections.

The metacausal function of part I is to make possible the prosecutor's *histoire*, while putting its validity in doubt.[16] The first-person narration throughout tends to keep readers' sympathy with Meursault. (The four final shots, for example, are not bullets penetrating a dying man's hide, but knocks on the gates of "malheur" for Meursault; the unfortunate victim remains nameless throughout: he is just "the Arab.") We read Meursault's version first, so that the subsequent, competing version must not only be plausible in itself (which is all we required of the first version), but must also overcome the established credibility of the prior account.[17] And Meursault will narrate the trial too, telling us he is disoriented, hurt, and astonished to see his actions debated as if without his participation. The *narration* appears thus to be seeking to ensure that we will see in the prosecutor's *histoire* a fabrication. For the point of the *narration* is that all causal explanations, coming, as they must, after the fact, are artificial constructs. Whether Meursault begins with a diary or not, whether he edited it or not, whether he used causal connectives innocently or to mislead, whether he wrote for posterity or for himself, the *narration* shows that two plausible versions can exist for the same events, that events can "exist" with or without crucial causal interconnections, and thus that causation is not inherent in them at all, but an exterior interpretation placed upon them by a human mind.

In addition to the causal terms treated earlier, there are eight examples of causal vocabulary in text-referential sentences. I hope to show that these examples, while inconsequential in the *récit*, point to the operation of the *narration* and thereby to the problematics of literary causation.

The three examples at the beginning of I, 6 (p. 1160) provide a significant lexical and thematic link between the mother's funeral and the murder, in the ironic company of "useless" causal vocabulary. The first example looks backward toward the funeral and contains a somewhat characteristic ambiguity: "Marie s'est moquée de moi parce qu'elle disait que j'avais 'une tête d'enterrement'" ("Marie made fun of me because she said I 'looked like I'd come from a funeral'"). The sentence can, of course, be understood in at least two ways: "Marie seemed to be making fun of me because she said . . ." (affirmation as cause of inference), or "Marie made fun of me because (as she said) I 'looked like I'd come from a funeral'" (facial expression as cause of teasing). Thus, while we may be at something of a loss about causation in the *récit*, the funereal mien that Meursault did not have when he first flirted with Marie the day after the funeral now appears, some two weeks later, sending symbol seekers to the *narration*. In the next paragraph, only five short sentences farther on, Meursault gives two reasons, with causal terms, for the sun's powerful effect on him as he left his building for the beach. There are no consequences, and he is soon enjoying the sun; but several hours later it will, he says, provoke his murderous act. Thus the text will organize a significant conjunction here between the funeral and the effects of the sun (a conjunction echoed just before the murder, "le même soleil"—the *same* sun as the day of the funeral, p. 1168). It will do so in the presence of three obvious causal terms; but the conjunction is by juxtaposition of naming words ("enterrement," "soleil"), while the words of causation ("parce que" twice, and "à cause de") are at best of superficial utility. Juxtaposition of events and causal interconnection of events are the two grids for observation of reality that the text provides. If this passage contains anything of significance, it lies in the juxtaposition: the *narration* appears to privilege that mode.

Words of causation are not, of course, the only "useless" vocabulary in circulation. Meursault notes that Masson's sentences are interlarded with "et je dirai plus" ("and I'll even go so far as to say"), although what follows usually adds nothing to what went before. He comments on it at the beach the day of the murder, adding, "je n'ai plus fait attention à ce tic parce que j'étais occupé à éprouver que le soleil me faisait du bien" (p. 1162; "I quit paying attention to this habit because I was busy feeling how much good the sun was doing me"). The earlier painful effects of the sun are now completely gone and their alleged causes of no effect. The meaningfulness of that causal vocabulary, through inconsequentiality, is annulled, as is the sense of Masson's habitual phrase, and for the same reason. Yet this sentence itself contains a "because": the indexic author appears to be pointing to causal vocabulary as a mere "tic" of our narrator's style.

Meursault's conception of his own identity is linked to four causal terms in the text, as his discovery of his separateness, his *étrangeté*, is brought to light, and as the meaning of "je" in the text is called into question. Early in the trial, Meursault describes a young reporter, with an asymmetric face expressing nothing in particular, who was observing him intently. He adds:

> Et j'ai eu l'impression bizarre d'être regardé par moi-même. C'est peut-être pour cela, et aussi parce que je ne connaissais pas les usages du lieu, que je n'ai pas très bien compris tout ce qui s'est passé ensuite. . . . (P. 1186)
>
> (And I had the strange impression of being looked at by myself. Maybe it was on account of that—and also because I was unfamiliar with the customs of the place—that I didn't understand too well everything that happened afterward. . . .)

What Meursault fails to understand specifically is the process of jury selection and the attorneys' opening statements, but he is here beginning to define his own separateness from judicial procedure in general. The "customs of the place," from which he distinguishes himself, include of course the causal linking of events; the fact that he gives his unfamiliarity with such things as a cause makes this choice of words ironic, when viewed from the level of the *narration*.

The presence of the journalist [18]—the other cause of the distraction—

evokes the startling prospect of becoming the subject ("he") of someone else's story; that the journalist should resemble Meursault calls up the notion of being the subject ("he") of one's own story ("I"). "Maybe it was on account of that" that Meursault feels estranged. If diary there is at this point, he has been (unknowingly?) dividing into a writing "I" and a written about "I-he" for some time. Whether he only now realizes the danger of this previous division, or whether he will realize it now and later assume the peril by writing, the estrangement from himself it implies produces here a failure to comprehend. "Being looked at by myself" implies distinctions between present self (observing) and present self (observed), between present self (observing) and past self (observed) and between present self (observed) and others (observing). Others, as strangers, cannot observe Meursault's past self, but only reconstruct it through inference. Yet inference about past events is inaccurate, because, when the events occurred, they were not past (and therefore subject to causal logic), but present. The diarylike text of part I reproduces in proximate narration, not a past self, but a series of present selves, none of which is inferable from any of the others since in the present there are no causal connectives. Meursault, for whom each of his selves was always already present, fails to comprehend the applicability of causal inferences to himself; the function in the *narration* of the juxtaposition of parts I and II is to bring readers to deconstruct the process of causal inference.

As Meursault takes the stand,

> On m'a encore fait décliner mon identité, et malgré mon agacement, j'ai pensé qu'au fond c'était assez naturel, parce qu'il serait trop grave de juger un homme pour un autre. (P. 1187)
>
> (They made me state my full name and occupation again, and, in spite of my irritation, I figured basically it made sense, because it would be just too serious to judge one man for another.)

But the naïve faith in a permanent *identité*, which causes our hero to overcome his "irritation," is precisely at the root of the problem. The injustice is indeed "just too serious," for the court is about to judge a Meursault-past, subject to causal reasoning, for a crime committed by a Meursault who was, at the time, quite present. Only if he returned to the beach with the gun, "looked at by himself" as a future self, inferring a potential killer-self, can premeditation be adjudged. The text cannot provide objective data on that matter, leaving readers with no tool but inference, and with nothing to discover but the inapplicability of the tool.

During the summation of the lawyer for the defense, Meursault is inattentive. "At one point, however, I listened, because he was saying, 'I have killed, it's true'" (p. 1198; "A un moment donné, cependant, j'ai écouté, parce qu'il disait: 'Il est vrai que j'ai tué'"). The substitution of "I" for "he" is the cause of Meursault's attention: he is discovering that the notion of consistent identity is a matter not of reality but of language ("Meursault," "je"). If an attorney can be said to have assumed temporarily the role of his client on the courtroom stage by a choice of pronoun, then Meursault (present in court) can see himself as having assumed there the role of Meursault (present on the beach). Only a naïve faith in the consistent truth value of language can cause these identities, so different in reality, to be perceived as one by the jury.

Causation, so readily expressible in language, is a means of giving persistent continuity to events; when it disappears, all the related assumptions—including the notion that "I" am consistently the "same person"—vanish with it. Causality returns for Meursault in prison, however, where the condemned man is forced to share his cell with a future self, ruled by a causality more inexorable than that of the prosecutor's argument: he is constrained to plan for his own dying. From that vantage point, he writes or completes his text. In his remarkable narratological analysis of *L'Etranger*, Nils Soelberg points out that what becomes of vital importance for Meursault at the end is precisely the unimportance of his life.[19] In a story, it is the inconsequential that is unimportant: causality defines importance. The episode of Salamano and his dog, while perhaps specularly revealing (and it involves a closed system of reciprocating causation, reminiscent of Phasie and Misard in *La Bête humaine*), is unimportant to his tale, and therefore highly important to its narrator. And a high density of causal vocabulary, used ineffectually, must be important to him too, for it demonstrates that causation is merely linguistic, and not inherent in his life.

Despite similarities, *L'Etranger* differs radically from *La Bête humaine* in that the modern work contains little true causation prior to the magistrate's reconstruction. Denizet gets the causes wrong; Meursault's prosecutor inserts causality where there (apparently) was none. At the level of the *histoire*, then, *L'Etranger* has the causal structure proposed at the outset, fragmented in part I and rectilinear in part II (see diagram 9.1). Part I is truly fragmented and not episodic, since the starting point and the order of

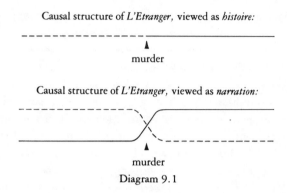

Causal structure of *L'Etranger*, viewed as *histoire:*

murder

Causal structure of *L'Etranger*, viewed as *narration:*

murder

Diagram 9.1

events are essentially predetermined by the need to allow the prosecutor to present a plausible causal explanation. But looking at the story retrospectively and from the level of *narration*, where the juxtaposition of the two versions of events sends us, the text seems to form a linear continuity: if Meursault did not premeditate the murder, the indexic author most surely did! On the other hand, the *narration* privileges the absence of causal chains, since it places the "causeless" version first. So it is that Meursault's *récit* undermines the prosecutor's *histoire*, making it a fraudulent imposition. Thus the apparent causal line we perceive from murder to guillotine seems fraudulent as well: at first reading, conviction is not a certainty, for if the jury learns what we know, if the diarylike account is inserted in the trial, premeditation may not be convincingly proven. If we accept the notion of a series of disconnected presents, everything that follows the murder is disconnected too, and our causal chain from murder to execution is a false retrospective imposition. Thus in hindsight, the linear and fragmentary tendencies have been continuously in conflict, the *narration* engaging them in chiasmic mutual destruction.[20]

Diagram 9.1 compares the causal structure of *L'Etranger* perceived as *histoire* and as *narration*. The upper half of the *narration* schema repeats, *grosso modo*, the causal diagram of the *histoire*; the lower half reflects the undermining forces present only in the *narration*: connective structure before the murder, and fragmentation thereafter.

The *histoire* pits two conflicting versions of events against each other. Criticism working on this level has sought to determine which version is privileged in the text by striving to unravel the enigmas of the *récit*: when Meursault wrote part I (question of sincerity), and how conscious the narrator was of causality (presence or absence of causal connectives). But the text can yield no conclusive reading of the *histoire*, for it is constructed to open upward upon the organizing intelligence of the *narration*. On that level, it sets in opposition "events" and the very idea of "versions" thereof. The coexistence of Meursault's diarylike *récit* and the prosecutor's *histoire* puts the value of both in doubt, along with the ability of language to recount events objectively.

This brings us back to the quotation from Sartre cited earlier; it should no longer seem ambiguous, for it will now be apparent that Sartre is analyzing neither the *récit* nor the *histoire*, but the *narration*:

> Mais peu à peu l'ouvrage s'organise de lui-même sous les yeux du lecteur, il révèle la solide substructure qui le soutient. Il n'est pas un détail inutile, pas un qui ne soit repris par la suite et versé au débat; et, le livre fermé, nous comprenons qu'il ne pouvait pas commencer autrement, qu'il ne pouvait pas avoir une autre fin: dans ce monde qu'on veut nous donner comme absurde et dont on a soigneusement extirpé la causalité, le plus petit incident a du poids; il n'en est pas un qui ne contribue à conduire le héros vers le crime et vers l'exécution capitale. *L'Etranger* est une oeuvre classique, une oeuvre d'ordre, composé à propos de l'absurde et contre l'absurde.[21]

> (But little by little the work organizes itself before the reader's eyes; it reveals the solid substructure which sustains it. There is not a single useless detail, not one which is not taken up again later on and added to the debate; and, when at last we close the book, we understand that it could not have begun otherwise, that it could have no other ending: in this world that is intended to appear absurd and from which causality has been carefully eradicated, the slightest incident has weight; there is not one which does not contribute to leading the hero toward the crime and toward the death penalty. *L'Etranger* is a classical work, a work of order, composed about the absurd, against the absurd.)

If the relationship between words and exterior reality is put in doubt, one might suppose that the literary enterprise that novels in general—and especially "classical" ones—represent is in jeopardy. Not so. Novels, with

172 • Nonrectilinear Causal Strategies

the artificiality apparent in their "level of *narration*," are admirably suited to speak to the human, subjective perception of reality, to our mental representations of the world about us, which are all we have. *La Nausée* and *L'Etranger* represent fragmented reality in paradoxically solid mental structures: the line is broken, but remains a line.

Notes

1. Jean-Paul Sartre, *La Nausée*, in his *Oeuvres romanesques* (Paris: Gallimard, Pléiade, 1981), pp. 1–210. Further references in the text are to this edition. On the conventions of the diary novel, see Valerie Raoul, *The French Fictional Journal* (Toronto: University of Toronto Press, 1980).

2. Gérard Genette, *Figures II* (Paris: Editions du Seuil, 1969), pp. 76–99. Further references in the text are to this edition.

3. Albert Camus, *L'Etranger*, in his *Théâtre, récits, nouvelles* (Paris: Gallimard, Pléiade, 1962), pp. 1123–1212. Further references in the text are to this edition.

4. The expression "en connaissance de cause," which functions in jurisprudence approximately like "with malice aforethought," literally means "with knowledge of the cause." Note that Gérard Genette classifies Meursault as a homodiegetic narrator with "external focalization," but he does so with reservations: *Nouveaux Discours du récit* (Paris: Editions du Seuil, 1983), pp. 77–89.

5. The length of time elapsed between the last event of I, 4 and the first event of I, 5 is not determinable with objective certainty; a week or two could conceivably have passed.

6. Jean-Paul Sartre, "Explication de *L'Etranger*," *Situations I* (Paris: Gallimard, 1947), p. 118.

7. Sartre, "Explication," p. 121.

8. Ignace Feuerlicht, "Camus's *L'Etranger* Revisited," *PMLA*, 78, 3 (December 1963), 606–21. Working from the Brée and Lynes edition of *L'Etranger* (New York: Appleton-Century-Crofts, 1955), Feuerlicht lists one example of *comme* which is not causal (p. 117, l. 8) and one of *ainsi* which is not causal (p. 99, l. 23). Of his two occurrences of

donc, one merely repeats the other for clarity and should not count as a separate occurrence. He fails to note *parce que* (p. 110, l. 16) and *c'est pour cela que* (p. 105, l. 2). He calls Camus's *c'est pour cela que* construction *"c'est pourquoi."* There are two errors in his line references: under *parce que*, "41/15" for 41/5; and under *c'est pourquoi*, "23/30" for 23/20. The analytical table in appendix C takes into account these minor corrections, but the accuracy of the Feuerlicht list remains impressive.

9. Feuerlicht, p. 612, note 3, agrees, on the basis of rapid comparison with Stendhal, Gide, Proust, Duhamel, Mauriac, Colette, Giono, Robbe-Grillet, and Sartre, among whom Proust alone showed a higher density of straightforward causal terms.

10. See especially Nils Soelberg, "Le Paradoxe du JE-narrateur: approche narratologique de *L'Etranger* de Camus," *Revue Romane*, 20, 1 (1985), 68–97.

11. Jean-Claude Pariente, "L'Etranger et son double," *Revue des Lettres Modernes*, 170–174 (1968), 53–80.

12. Raoul, pp. 29–30, 32.

13. Raoul, pp. 35–36.

14. Oscar Tacca, *"L'Etranger* comme récit d'auteur-transcripteur," in *Albert Camus 1980*, R. Gay-Crosier, ed. (Gainesville: University Presses of Florida, 1980), p. 97.

15. *La Nausée*, for example, seeks to elude this problem by presenting the diary intact, with an "editorial" note or two early on to supply orienting details for external readers.

16. Alfred Noyer-Weidner, "Structure et sens de *L'Etranger*," in *Albert Camus 1980*, pp. 79–80, notes that the events in part I are consciously ordered to permit creation of the pseudoexplanation in part II.

17. On the psychological basis for the importance of first impressions and the "primacy effect," see Meir Sternberg, *Expositional Modes and Temporal Ordering in Fiction* (Baltimore: Johns Hopkins University Press, 1978), pp. 93–99.

18. The Brée and Lynes edition of *L'Etranger* affirms, p. 104, that Camus considered the reporter to be an image of himself. If he did, it suggests that the author was indeed conscious of conjoining, at this point, *récit* and *narration*.

19. Soelberg, pp. 84–93.

20. Camus must have liked the structure, for a nearly identical chiasm occurs in *La Chute* (1956), with the "suicide" at its center point; there, however, it is not causal linking that is undermined, but the supposed coherence of the Western value system.

21. Sartre, "Explication," pp. 120–21.

10

Mental-Representation Fiction

. . . n'ayant eu des événements . . . que cette connaissance fragmentaire, incomplète, faite d'une addition de brèves images, elles-mêmes incomplètement appréhendées par la vision, de paroles, elles-mêmes mal saisies, de sensations, elles-mêmes mal définies, et tout cela vague, plein de trous, de vides, auxquels l'imagination et une approximation logique s'efforçaient de remédier par une suite de hasardeuses déductions—hasardeuses mais non pas forcément fausses. . . .

(. . . having had of events . . . only that fragmentary, incomplete knowledge, made up of a sum of brief images, themselves incompletely apprehended by vision, of words, themselves ill grasped, of sensations, themselves ill defined, and all of that vague, full of holes and voids, which imagination and a logical approximation strove to remedy by a series of hazardous deductions—hazardous but not necessarily false. . . .)

—CLAUDE SIMON

Having discovered themselves imprisoned behind the filters of their own problematic senses, postexistentialist inferred authors and their narrators could no longer evoke with the same authority and authenticity the truth about their fictional people and events. Fiction that recognized the difference between words and things could not talk without contradiction about what we used to call, with willing suspension of disbelief, "reality." Instead, the "new novel" (astutely tagged at first as "new realism") gradually replaced depiction of persons and events with descriptions of mental representations thereof, as they might appear in the mind of a character or narrator; in this fiction we would read less about things and more about mental images of things.

It may be argued that that is what we have been reading all along.

Narrowly viewed, that argument appears incontrovertible. When Flaubert offers us, in passages of *discours indirect libre*, glimpses of Emma Bovary's inner reaction to events, he is providing a look at her mental representation of them. Zola's third-person narrators give us in the *récit* their picture of the *histoire*. When Gide's intradiegetic narrators and Camus's Meursault express themselves in the first person and limit their tales to those things which they as characters perceived, they are presenting simply a mental image of a series of events. But the primary distinction between these elements of traditional mental representation and the innovative French fiction of the 1950s and 1960s is the ever-supposed presence of an observable offstage reality, of an arbiter of truth to which the mental representation could be compared. Emma Bovary's reactions will end up being in accord—or not—with the "reality" in which she lives. Third-person narrators, especially of the omniscient kind, consistently present themselves as factually reliable and base their authority on "truth." "Reality" will rise up to judge the skewed perceptions of the pastor in Gide's *La Symphonie pastorale*. *L'Etranger* is more innovative: Meursault (reminiscent of Gide's Jérôme) gives us two versions of events—his own and the prosecutor's—without providing the authority of an authentic "reality" to which we can compare them, in order to judge between them. Yet Meursault's personal belief in the existence of such a reality is a constant underpinning of his story: when he says, for example, that, in the shadow of the rock on the beach, the Arab appeared to be laughing, he is suggesting that the fact of the matter could have been verified by a well-placed, objective observer. And of course he wants us to believe that what he says happened to him in court and in prison corresponds to an objectively verifiable reality. The mental representations we meet in the "new" French fiction propose, in general, no such comparison.

Simon's *La Route des Flandres*, for example, presents a flood of memories and imaginations, with the only "present reality" being Georges's presence in bed with Corinne, to which only a few pages are devoted directly, and those serve to reveal Georges's perception of his surroundings. Alain Robbe-Grillet's *La Jalousie* provides a series of ruminations based upon the subjective observation of "real" things by an apparently jealous narrator, in whose mind readers dwell throughout. Nathalie Sarraute's "subconversations" are interior experiences arising during verbal interchanges between characters; the spoken words are assumed to be verifiably "real," but the subjectification of them is the privileged, important end product. Early "new" novels, like Robbe-Grillet's *Les Gommes*, still offer consequential and supposedly verifiable events: readers "know" that Dupont has survived the bungled attempt on his life, that he is in hiding to foil possible new efforts to kill him, and that his incontrovertible ruse to dissimulate the absence of a *corpus delecti* has successfully fostered among the detectives the belief that he is indeed dead. But even there, the mental representations of events in various characters' psyches are individually unverifiable subjective interpretations, with their source in personal perceptions of the "real," as in other "new" fiction.

The taxonomy of literary imitations of mental representations is highly complex.[1] Certainly the old terms "interior monologue" and "stream of consciousness" are less than adequate to this analysis, because they emphasize flow or continuity of mental images. A primary characteristic of the images we shall be examining (and they are not necessarily "images" either, since they need not be visual or visualizable) is their static quality, even when they represent action. A better metaphor for our purposes might be found in the field of stop-action photography, or in cinematic jump cuts, which immobilize a moment in time. As we shall see, such moments are indeed often interconnected in these novels, but by a single semantic thread, like discrete elements only partially conjoined. Claude Simon's well-catalogued discovery of the virtue of present participles for the expression of mental representations illustrates the unstreamlike character of fictional consciousness; in an imagined adultery scene, for example, the husband returns unexpectedly to find his wife, who has barely managed to bundle her lover into a closet, feigning passion for her spouse:

> . . . puis elle, là, puérile, innocente, désarmante, se frottant les yeux, souriant, lui tendant les bras, lui expliquant qu'elle s'enferme à clef par crainte des voleurs tandis qu'elle se presse contre lui, l'enlace, l'enveloppe, la chemise glissant par hasard sur son épaule, dénudant ses seins dont elle presse, froisse les tendres bouts meurtris sur la tunique poussiéreuse qu'elle commence déjà à dégrafer de ses mains fébriles, lui parlant maintenant bouche à bouche pour qu'il ne puisse voir ses lèvres gonflées sous les baisers d'un autre. . . .[2]

> (. . . then she, there, childlike, innocent, disarming, rubbing her eyes, smiling, holding out her arms to him, explaining to him that she locks herself in for fear of robbers while she presses herself against him, embraces him, envelops him, the nightgown slipping by chance from

her shoulder, baring her breasts whose tender, love-scathed tips she presses, rubs upon the dusty tunic she is already beginning to unhook with her feverish hands, speaking to him now with her mouth against his so that he cannot see her lips swollen from the kisses of another. . . .)

As the present participles stop the action in a series of "still" images which flash upon the consciousness of a character, the present tense in the subordinate clauses performs essentially a descriptive, not a narrative, function. Indeed, in the "new" French fiction, mental representations in general tend to be described states, as much fictional "existents" as recounted "events."[3]

My primary aim in this chapter is to describe the roles that causality can and cannot play in novels in which such mental representations predominate. First, however, we shall need to undertake a typology of the various mental representations one can experience. While I plan to draw examples from the mental representations attributed to fictional characters in postwar novels, allusions to the mental projections of readers will emerge, here and especially in the conclusion. Representing sights, sounds, and other sensations in the mind is an activity, even if it seems to stop the "action" of represented events; mental representations are therefore susceptible to classification in the manner of verb forms in the natural languages. Specifically, I suggest that they admit of analysis by voice, mode, and tense.

By *voice* I mean to designate the origin or stimulus of what we represent in the mind's eye. Voice may be direct or indirect, depending upon whether it is stimulated by perception or by a coded report from someone else. (Whether what I "perceive" is real or not, or whether "someone else" really exists, is unessential to the analysis. I am personally persuaded they are often quite real, but I seek no quarrel with idealists!) Indirect voice is always accompanied by direct voice, while the reverse is not so. One may directly perceive persons acting; one may also indirectly perceive persons acting (in the mind's eye), while perceiving directly a printed page on which words refer to persons acting. In this instance, indirect voice yields a message, while direct voice offers the encoded form of the message. (When the code is "music" or "film," the distinction is more complicated, for the code itself is both iconic and indexic. In these cases, only the indexic elements—in film, notably camera angle, distance, and movement with respect to the subject—are in indirect voice. But these subtleties are of importance in the novel, on the level of the characters, only when characters register mental impressions of music or movies.) In fiction, a character or represented mentality may perceive or experience an event (direct voice on the level of the *histoire*) or may know it vicariously through notification in a message (indirect voice on the same level); obviously, since a *récit* may be defined as a coded message to readers, at least two levels of indirectness may coexist. Examples of the distinction between voices in literature, as well as of the modal and temporal distinctions to follow, will appear later in the chapter.

Regardless of the directness or indirectness with which the representations arise in the mind, one may be aware of differences in their nature or "mode" of being. I use the terms *cognitive, hypothetical, counterfactual*, and *imaginary* to describe the modes of mental representation. In addition, we may attribute a relative time value or *tense* to the representations, associating them in general with past, present, or future.

In the cognitive mode, the tenses are *memory, perception*, and *prediction* or *project*. That is to say that, in this most common of modes, the mind may permit us to experience or envision again something we perceived in the past (past tense); it may also provide us an awareness of what we are experiencing now (present tense); furthermore, it may allow consciousness of what we intend (have already begun) to accomplish, or of what we firmly believe will inevitably occur (future tense). In the cognitive mode, as in all the others, each tense obviously admits of direct or indirect voice. We can be in direct contact with our own past, present, and future, and we can also take cognizance, through messages, or others' memories, perceptions, and projects. We have already examined the interrelationship between voices in the past cognitive with respect to Proust. When we read, for example, the childhood reminiscences in *Combray*, we are learning of Marcel's fictional memories (past cognitive, indirect voice). But when, in retrospect, we remember those memories, it is because they have become a part of us: we remember ourselves reading, living, particular passages, experiencing associated emotions. These memories of ours are quite direct. The reminiscences have reached us in indirect voice, but, as they and their narrator are assimilated into our own past, we transform them into past cognitive, direct voice. This capacity of memory to transmute indirect cognizance into direct experience places readers on a separate narrative level, symmetrical to the position of the author. For just as, for the writer, her or his *narration* includes and envelops the *récit* and its narrator along with the events and their *histoire*, so there exists for the reader a level of *lecture*, which assimilates his or her (re-)creation of the narrator's *récit* and the *histoire* it presents.

The hypothetical mode is a simple causal model based on memory, perception, and/or project. It is in this mode that we create the mental images which "make sense" of our world. To discover the past, for example, we reason from effect to cause (e.g., he must have studied ancient Greek, since he can translate this passage of Aristotle). We apply the same sort of logic to the present (it must be cold outside; people in the street are bundled up and shivering), and to the future (she will probably be in an unpleasant mood; she always gets angry when I am late like this). In each of these situations, through the use of a causal hypothesis, we are creating a mental representation of our environment—its past, present, or future. The future hypothetical is sometimes not readily distinguishable from the future cognitive. The difference lies in the degree of perceived inevitability: if you catch sight of a boulder a few feet above your head and falling, you are probably justified in forming a mental representation of disaster (future cognitive), but if you have time to envision a quick leap forward saving you, you are clearly in the future hypothetical. Firm intentions are future cognitive (e.g., I'll go to the phone and call my friend), while mental reservations (. . . unless the doorbell rings, . . . unless I can remember the information without bothering him) indicate rather the hypothetical mode.

Counterfactual mental images also follow a causal model, but they posit at the outset the absence of the cause (if he had been more charming, she would have invited him in; but he wasn't, and she didn't). Counterfactuals are most common in the past, where they are characterized by the mental image of a more successful, but alas unreal, self: I should have said . . . , *esprit d'escalier*, etc. In the present, they conjure visions of absent conditions (if I were rich, if I had time, if I were in London now . . .), pleasant or unpleasant (if I had missed this plane, I would be in serious trouble now). As for the future, it is, while not inherently counterfactual, usually not factual at all. Still, one may occasionally envisage impossible options to an apparently inevitable tomorrow: "If I had the wings of an angel, over these prison walls I would fly. . . ."

The final mode of mental representation is imagination or fantasy. In my experience of it, the time is nearly always a vague "present"—that is to say, any time at all. It may of course be specifically time-related, as in a fantasy about a particular period in the life of a person now deceased, but never necessarily so. The absence of tense as a required component of this mode indicates that causality is not necessary to it either. Indeed, the absence of perceived, essential causal relationships is what distinguishes the imaginary mode from the counterfactual. Counterfactuals have their basis in perceived reality, a "fact" to which they are contrary. While the imagination may possibly be grounded in "reality" (I may imagine myself in the amorous embrace of a woman whom I know, even when, in "reality," she has no interest in me), it remains pure (or impure) imagination, unless causation becomes involved. I may imagine the embrace occurring on the leather-covered divan in the sumptuous library of the seaside estate I wish I owned; the imagination does not enter the counterfactual mode until I begin to consider the luxurious surroundings as a necessary condition for the seduction (if I had the estate, the library, and the divan, then she would . . . , and so on). While imagination may have its origin in an identifiable time frame, in a memory, a perception, or a project, it is not internally dependent upon time, nor upon a causal model.

Robbe-Grillet's *Les Gommes* (1953),[4] although it contains elements of traditional third-person narration, provides clear examples of characters' mental representations and their causal functioning. The first paragraph of I, 2 (p. 51) illustrates how the modes of a character's mental representations interact to determine the future course of the text. Wallas, on his first morning in the city, has arisen and set out on foot, before sunrise and without breakfast, in a direction he supposes will lead him to the center of town, where he plans to make contact with Commissioner Laurent at the central municipal police station. Dawn has come, and Wallas still has not reached "downtown":

> Sans s'écarter de son chemin ni ralentir son allure, Wallas marche. Devant lui une femme traverse la rue. Un vieil homme traîne vers une porte cochère une poubelle vide restée sur le bord du trottoir. Derrière une vitre s'étagent trois rangs de plats rectangulaires contenant toutes sortes d'anchois marinés, sprats fumés, harengs roulés et déroulés, salés, assaisonnés, crus ou cuits, sauris, frits, confits, découpés et hachés. Un peu plus loin, un monsieur en pardessus noir et chapeau sort d'une maison et vient à sa rencontre; âge mûr, situation aisée, digestions souvent difficiles; il ne fait que quelques pas et pénètre immédiatement dans un café d'aspect très hygiénique, plus accueillant certainement que cet autre où lui-même a passé la nuit.

Wallas se rappelle qu'il a faim, mais il a décidé de prendre son petit déjeuner dans un grand établissement moderne, sur une de ces places ou avenues qui doivent, comme partout, constituer le coeur de la ville.

(Without deviating from his path or slowing his pace, Wallas keeps walking. In front of him, a woman crosses the street. An old man drags an empty garbage can, left at the curb, toward a porte-cochere. Behind a window, three rows of rectangular trays are stacked containing all sorts of marinated anchovies, smoked sprat, herring, rolled and unrolled, salted, seasoned, raw or cooked, kippered, fried, preserved, fileted and chopped. A bit farther on, a gentleman in a black overcoat and hat comes out of a house and heads toward him; middle-aged, comfortable income, frequent digestive trouble; he takes only a few steps and turns at once into a most hygienic-looking café, certainly a more inviting spot than that other one where he himself spent the night. Wallas remembers that he is hungry, but he has made up his mind to have breakfast in a big modern establishment, on one of those squares or avenues which must, like everywhere else, make up the heart of town.)

The conventional third-person narrator is obviously speaking here from within Wallas's mind, reporting to us whatever comes up on that interior viewscreen, including Wallas's judgments, and thus himself disappearing, replaced by the character's mental images. Wallas operates in the present cognitive for the first four sentences: awareness of the constancy of his own direction and speed, consciousness of others in the street, detailed perception of the contents of a delicatessen window. The fifth sentence, about the man in the black overcoat, slips into the realm of hypothesis: clothing, facial features, and expression (present cognitive) lead Wallas to infer the man's general age, his economic status, and the unfortunate condition of his digestive tract (present hypothetical). This is an example of intermodal causation, for perception is a contributing cause and condition for the inferences. The judgments passed on the café ("hygienic-looking," "inviting") also contain hypothetical elements: if it looks clean and friendly, I will probably be safe from disease and unpleasantness there. There is perhaps a further, unstated hypothesis: if the neighborhood dyspeptic, who could afford to eat anywhere, will have a meal in the place, it must be safe; this would exemplify intramodal causality, for it involves hypotheses arising from other hypotheses. With the comparison to the café over which Wallas had rented a sleeping room, memory also intervenes in the judgment. But when our hero "remembers" that he is hungry, memory is not really involved: the hunger pangs are present. The memory word merely evokes the notion that the hunger, although generally subliminal, has been present for some time; perhaps the memory of leaving "that other" café too early for breakfast calls to Wallas's attention the length of the fast. The paragraph has now reached its critical point, where the text could deviate from its consistent direction and speed. The detective could turn into the apparently hygienic café, taking his mental representations, and thus the text and us, with him. Detailed awareness of food has prepared Wallas (and us readers) for the choice, raising subliminal hunger to the level of present perception; hypotheses have led to the conclusion that this café is a satisfactory place to assuage it. The decision will be determined by intramodal and intermodal comparisons.

Beside the present temptation exists a project (future cognitive): Wallas's image of breakfasting in a large, modern restaurant, located on a wide avenue or city square. The existence of such squares or avenues in this city is present hypothetical ("doivent"): Wallas has never been here before. The hypothesis springs from the memory of other downtowns, from which a general law has been derived ("comme partout"): if downtown, then avenues and squares. Whence a further, implied hypothesis: if avenues, then large, modern restaurants. These hypotheses, while not linearly causal (downtowns do not cause avenues, nor avenues "big modern establishments"), arise from an underlying causal assumption: that the same socioeconomic forces that produce wide-avenued downtowns also lead to the establishment of a particular kind of restaurant in these areas. Wallas has enough confidence in this assumption to predict that he can safely take the text past the door of the clean, inviting café. But it is more than confidence; Wallas's future-cognitive image (his prior firm decision—what certain critics might call "desire") is stronger than present perception of hunger and of a potential, satisfactory means of relief. Thus, on the causal basis of a character's mental images, in which perception, memory, hypothesis, and project combine, the text will avoid diversion.

The imaginary mode appears in *Les Gommes* with respect to Garinati and to Wallas, notably in the latter's fantasies about his boss, the legendary Fabius, detective extraordinaire and master of disguise. Glimpsing (for example) a face in a window across the street from the scene of the crime, Wallas infers that it may belong to a habitual busybody, who might have caught sight, while keeping an eye on the neighborhood, of the "assassin" entering or leaving the area. Perhaps, he speculates, her attention was attracted by "a scream, an abnormal noise, or anything at all" (II, 3, p. 108). With this past-hypothetical sentence, the paragraph ends; the next paragraph begins:

> Fabius, ayant refermé la porte du jardin, inspecte les alentours; mais il n'en laisse rien paraître: il est un paisible agent d'assurances qui sort de chez un client et regarde le ciel à droite et à gauche, pour savoir d'où vient le vent. . . . Tout de suite il remarque un personnage louche qui l'épie derrière ses rideaux, à la croisée d'un second étage.

> (Fabius, having closed the garden gate again, inspects the surroundings; but he does so unnoticeably: he's just a peaceful insurance agent leaving a customer's house and looking at the sky, right and left, to see which way the wind's blowing. . . . Right away, he spots a suspicious character spying on him from behind the curtains, at a third-floor window.)

Now Fabius, according to the fictional reality of the novel, is elsewhere, and, even if he were to show up now at the scene of the crime, Wallas would surely approach him and speak to him; this is therefore not a fictionally "real" event but a mental representation in the imaginary mode: Wallas imagines what Fabius would do under the circumstances in which Wallas finds himself. In the rest of the passage, he pictures Fabius returning under the guise of an awning salesman, obtaining authorization on these grounds from the concierge of the apartment block across the street to call on all the south-side tenants (including of course the busybody), and thus gaining admittance to question a potential witness, without alerting the concierge to his identity as a detective. After the successful exchange of conversation between Fabius and the building superintendent, we read: "Wallas sourit à cette pensée" (p. 109); "Wallas smiles at this thought." Thus we return from the imaginary mode to present cognitive, wherein Wallas will adopt a different and even more promising ploy to dupe the concierge and to interrogate the busybody.

Until the word "pensée" just cited, the four-paragraph mental representation is never tagged as such; absence of the standard markers (such as "Wallas drifts into a daydream" or "Wallas can imagine Fabius . . .") not only makes the mental-representation status of the passage a matter of reader inference on first reading, but it also diminishes the role of the narrator, as explainer of the tale, almost to the vanishing point. The reader is here essentially in direct contact with the *histoire*, of which this mental representation is an element. And indeed the Fabius fantasy fits into the causal chain of the *histoire* just as if it were a physically perceivable "event": arising from Wallas's reverence for Fabius and his methods and from a project or "desire" to interview the busybody without disclosing his own identity, it leads Wallas to discover the parameters of a successful ruse in this circumstance. Mental representations, although relatively closed and static blocks or *Gestalten*, can have causes and effects, even when they are imaginations or dreams.[5] Although this reverie has the superficial earmarks of the counterfactual mode ("If Fabius were here, he would . . ."), Fabius does not qualify as an "absent cause": it is Wallas who invents Fabius's ruse, and who will profit from the experience to find a still better one. Only if we read it as in the imaginary mode can it here take its place in the causal chain of the *histoire*: imagination leads to project (future cognitive), which immediately becomes present cognitive as our hero acts.

Furthermore, the eclipse or ellipsis of the narrator (the words *éclipse* and *ellipse* play a significant role in the story: III, 4, p. 170) places the reader in immediate contact with the mental representations that are "events" in the novel. The words of the text seem less a coded communication from a narrator to us readers than the verbal transcript of characters' thought processes. The "voice" of the text for the reader, while by definition indirect, thus shifts toward the experiential and the direct, toward the supreme form of narrator-absent fiction, which is theater. Much has been written on the use of theater vocabulary in *Les Gommes*, often to suggest a relationship between its plot and Sophocles's tragedy, *Oedipus Rex*, a subject to which I shall return. But the theater connection also turns on the shift toward direct voice, a device common to much "new" fiction. At the theater, spectators observe most of the *histoire* without the intervention of a narrative voice and the causal connectives it can supply; narratorial tags ("she exclaimed," "he said," etc.) disappear, as we experience "directly" the source and interrelationship of acts and utterances: the *récit* is largely "mimed." *Les Gommes* has, in this sense, aspects of a play performed in the theater of characters' minds, as readers experience the mental representations of a number of characters—Wallas, Garinati, Laurent, the *patron* of the café. Mental representations pass from mode to mode, from tense to tense, for causes which the reader infers.

Whatever it is for readers, the Fabius fantasy is direct voice for Wallas.

But indirect voice, on the level of the characters, can lead to inference as well, as Wallas discovers when he asks directions of the woman with the broom (I, 2, pp. 54–56). The inferences she draws from his verbal communication nearly suffice to unmask his subterfuge, intended to conceal his police connections. Her inferences arise from causal questions: why is he looking for a post office, and why does he insist upon going all the way to the main post office, when there is a substation nearby? Her detective work mirrors the causal structure of a major portion of the text, which is in the hypothetical mode.

Indeed, the primary conflict of the novel is between the hypothetical and the cognitive modes. Wallas pounds the pavement in search of the realities of the crime. He is the eyes of the investigation and represents the cognitive mode. Laurent, the local police commissioner, remains in his office, where he receives information and hypothesizes. To be sure, Wallas creates hypotheses, as we have seen (often about the modalities of observation), and Laurent perceives and remembers. But Wallas's method is observation, while Laurent's is inference. The commissioner conjures up a series of hypothetical scenarios: Dupont committed suicide, was killed by his ex-wife or by his housekeeper, or by Wallas, or died of a heart attack, or was shot by his illegitimate son. He tests each scenario against the known facts, eliminating those contrary to the data. Since reports and testimony are his sole source of knowledge, he makes inferences about the relative validity of these. Operating almost entirely in the hypothetical mode, he solves the crime, just as Wallas "solves" it on the more pragmatic, cognitive level.

Dupont, the supposed victim, is, as previously noted, not dead. While Wallas is reinspecting the "murder" room, some twenty-four hours after the crime, Dupont slips back into his house in search of certain papers. Fearing that the murderer is again waiting for him in his little upstairs study (a hypothesis based on a door Wallas left unlocked downstairs when he came in), Dupont bursts into the study, revolver in hand. Expecting the murderer's return himself (an unfortunate hypothesis), and seeing a gun aimed in his direction, Wallas shoots Dupont dead. The fact that "the detective did it" makes a delightful parody of standard crime fiction. But when Wallas surmises at last (anagnorisis!) the identity of his victim, now truly dead, he phones Laurent at headquarters, only to hear the commissioner announce the results of his hypothetical analyses: "J'ai fait une découverte—vous ne devineriez jamais! Daniel Dupont! Il n'est pas mort du tout!" (V, 6, p. 254); "I've made a discovery—you'd never guess! Daniel Dupont! He isn't dead at all!"

Wallas's fatal assumptions—that, if someone enters the house furtively, it is the murderer, that the gun pointed at him will fire (readers know that it cannot), are untested hypotheses arising directly from cognitive perceptions: quietly approaching footsteps, a door that bursts open, a light that flashes on, a gun. Wallas, moving about in "reality," must operate very close to the cognitive mode, his perceptions producing projects, which are thwarted or abetted by the causation of random circumstance, or sidetracked by the "halo of error and doubt" that surrounds objects and separates the perceived from the comprehended. Yet he discovers Dupont alive and standing before him at approximately the same moment when Laurent reaches his correct conclusion; Wallas perceives but does not comprehend. Shut away in his office, Laurent is less affected by immediate causation and more able to grasp a causal function. Thus it is that Laurent can comprehend but not perceive. The lesson to be derived from the double "error" seems not unoptimistic. Laurent is not faced with psychological questions like the premeditation problem facing Meursault's prosecutor, but he does better with "the facts" than Denizet. Despite the divorce between psyche and reality, it would seem that the mind can formulate on occasion relatively valid hypotheses about its own perception of the real. We must, however, be willing to accept and evaluate new data, and be flexible enough to reformulate even our most cherished hypotheses when the information requires it. With patience and care, successive hypotheses will, like an asymptote, approach ever nearer to the truth. It is unlikely (perhaps technically impossible) that the hypothetical mode will ever attain the truth, however, for, by the time one comprehends reality, it has changed. "He isn't dead at all!" is the solution to the problem, but it comes too late to be "true," to stay Wallas's finger on the trigger. Wallas would have to perceive and comprehend at the same time to avoid the killing. The time between perception and comprehension is too long to provide for useful reactions. But the hypothetical mode holds some promise in securely stable situations, or with highly predictable processes. Laurent, because he does not "see," errs in treating the transitory as static. Still, he would have hit the bull's eye, had not the target moved.

Like Laurent, readers of the novel receive their information in indirect voice and, in order to understand, create hypotheses about it. Perhaps the best known, brilliantly put forward by Bruce Morrissette,[6] holds that the text is a reworking of the Oedipus myth, and thus that Dupont is Wallas's long-lost father. The twisted causal chain that leads Wallas to the fatal encounter with Dupont would be, in that case, an example of the ironic mythical causation evoked in chapter eight above. As Morrissette demonstrates, the novel is awash with mythical allusions, references to Thebes, the Corinth road, the riddling Sphinx, killed, rescued, and ungrateful children, etc. It is also replete with examples of textual reworking (for one example among many, Wallas "reworks" the Fabius fantasy to interview the busybody), the process of mythic fiction. Is Morrissette's hypothesis "correct"? It fits all the mythic details, but what of the other information? The problem is perhaps perceptible in the headlines of a newspaper Wallas scans in an idle moment (I, 3, pp. 64–65). They read: (1) "Grave accident de la circulation sur la route de Delf" ("Serious traffic accident on the Delf road"); (2) "Le Conseil se réunira demain pour l'élection d'un nouveau maire" ("Council meets tomorrow to elect new mayor"); (3) "La voyante abusait ses clients" ("Fortuneteller abuses her customers"); (4) "La production des pommes de terre a dépassé celle des meilleures années" ("Potato production exceeds previous annual records"); (5) "Décès d'un de nos concitoyens" ("Local man dies"). The fifth article is the official announcement of Dupont's "murder": it is myth-related only if he is a Laius figure. The first three can all be read to suggest events in the myth, thus tending to confirm the mythic character of number five. But the fourth headline? Prior to anagnorisis and atonement, according to Sophocles's version of the myth, famine rather than plenty characterized Theban agriculture. Should astute readers allow one apparently out-of-place detail to destroy a hypothesis that fits the other four? This is precisely the sort of question faced by the intradiegetic Laurent; the smallest crack—"la plus petite faille"—as the text reminds us with mock sententiousness on several occasions, can destroy an otherwise perfect project. In fact, the *narration* appears to be producing a *récit* with sufficient causes to encourage the Oedipal interpretation, but with enough contrary and irrelevant information to prevent absolute confirmation. If so, despite the static character of the text, the hypothesis remains an interesting inference, separate from the novel's reality, a comprehension that cannot perceive all the details, such as headline number four.

The *narration* suggests in many ways that the hypothetical mode produces problematic results for characters and readers alike. To enjoy the phenomenon, one need only sketch, while reading, a map of the city in which the crime occurs, showing Wallas's peregrinations. Enough details are provided for relatively accurate depiction of the principal streets and landmarks, with compass bearings and an approximation of scale, for we know how fast Wallas walks the first morning, and for how long. Still, the order in which the information is given will oblige amateur cartographers to work in pencil, with frequent recourse to the item that holds the title role, as natural but erroneous assumptions need to be erased in favor of ever more nearly accurate hypotheses. Likewise, bits of our own reading must, at times, be effaced and replaced, when the voice of the narrator, who might have told us how to read, has been eclipsed or ellipsed or erased. One can read, for example, the first sentence of the Fabius fantasy as straightforward narrative (cognitive mode, indirect voice), until the clues that Wallas is imagining this tale sink in. The entire initial passage of chapter III (pp. 141–43) can be attributed to the narrator; not until "Ici Laurent s'arrête" ("Here Laurent stops") are we aware whose mental representations we are reading. Unless a clever guess was made early on, readers will need to "erase" and reformulate the "point" of this passage, its role in the novel, after reading it through. The source of the passage, its "first cause"—a narrator recounting, a character thinking, etc.—is fundamental to readers' hypotheses about its meaning. The foregrounding of the hypothetical mode in this novel points to the importance of causal hypotheses in reading and in daily life, and to their problematical nature. Our other "detective stories," *La Bête humaine* and *L'Etranger*, also evoked the problems with hypothesizing and privileged the "eyewitness" account (of the narrator, of Meursault) over the hypothetical reconstructions (of Denizet, of the prosecutor); *Les Gommes* suggests that eyewitnesses, with inadequate grasp of causal chains, are at least as apt as the hypothesizers to make incorrect decisions.[7]

Like hypotheses, counterfactuals have a causal structure, but they are rare in *Les Gommes*. Wallas's final regrets are an example: "Dans son extrême fatigue, des bribes de sa journée perdue viennent encore le tourmenter: '. . . et si, à ce moment-là, j'avais pensé à . . . et si j'avais . . .'" (Epilogue, p. 259; "In his extreme fatigue, bits and pieces of his wasted day return to torment him: '. . . and if, right then, I had thought of . . . and if I had . . .'"). The grammatical structures suffice to evoke the mode, which is itself the substance of our hero's thought; the ellipses eclipse the useless absent causes, now absent from the text as well as from Wallas's reality.

Causal vocabulary functions within mental representations (particularly in the hypothetical mode) and between them (notably to designate the origin of a cognitive representation), just as in more traditional novels. It abounds in *Les Gommes*, although much of it is of the less obvious variety (e.g., "c'est très rare qu'un cambrioleur . . . se trouble, *à* la vue du propriétaire, *au point de* se croire obligé de *le tuer*," [I, 5, p. 80; emphasis mine]). According to Allott and Tremewan,[8] *parce que* occurs only eight times in the novel, and *car* only thirty-four times, most often in Laurent's meditations, where the word *cause* (twenty occurrences) seems at its most frequent. *Par* recurs more than three hundred times, often to express agency (e.g., "réveillé par ses cris," [Prologue, p. 29]), but not always ("Par où était-il passé?" [Prologue, p. 28]). Agents here, of course, are more often hypothetical ones than in traditional fiction, and the verbs *devoir* and *pouvoir* return with relative frequency to mark the hypothetical mode (e.g., "La balle a dû dévier," [III, 5, p. 172]; "On a pu lui raconter souvent cette journée," [II, 6, p. 137]), although hypotheses are quite often stated as fact (e.g., "Il a eu peur, surtout," [I, 5, p. 80, for "Il a dû avoir peur"]). Of the obvious causal vocabulary, *pour* is the most common term, expressing intention (e.g., "pour masquer son énervement—et le maîtriser en partie—il se force à cette modération exagérée," [IV, 6, p. 216]); *pour* occurs over five hundred times, and, although it is not always causal, its frequency (averaging twice per page) suggests the importance of prediction and project in the novel. Projects may be either cognitive or hypothetical (inferring the intentions of another), but there subsists a framework of fictional "reality" to which most hypotheses in *Les Gommes* can be compared.

To summarize, then, causal reasoning is the motive force of mental representation in the hypothetical and counterfactual modes. When such representations are imitated in a text, the text advances by means of expressed or inferable causation. In the cognitive mode, cause is present at its origin, and its nature differs by tense. Memory is stimulated by perception, imagination, or by other memories. Perception is (presumably) stimulated by an exterior "object"—light, sound, etc. Prediction arises from desire (project) or from fear, and from understanding resulting from combinations of perception, memory, and hypothesis. The imaginary mode, internally free of logical causation, may spring from memory, perception, desire, fear, or from no precise stimulus at all. With the exception of texts composed entirely in the imaginary mode (of which we will examine an example), causal language (*récit*) and causal inferences (*histoire*) connect mental representations in the "new" French fiction just as they did events in the more traditional texts; they now allude more frequently to *conditions* than to the determining *causes* of traditional fiction, however.

Mental-representation fiction tends to reproduce, by different modalities, the fundamental causal structures we have seen before. *Les Gommes* produces a parodic form of mythic structure, with, as its myth, the traditional detective story (crime and solution), of which *Oedipus Rex* serves as the partial prototype. Simon's *La Route des Flandres* has elements of Proustian structure, liberating readers within the space of the text. The most common pattern is doubtless the "fragmented" or "broken-line" model, suggesting kinship between much mental-representation fiction and its existentialist predecessors.

Daphne Patai[9] has carefully charted the interplay of tenses in the cognitive mode in Butor's *La Modification*—perception, memory, and project, with the final intervention of the imaginary mode in Léon's "fantasy"—noting that, within the novel, "Butor has utilized a traditional (temporally sequential) form as well as a new fragmented one." The fixed train route from Paris to Rome and the processes of the modification provide the linear substratum, while the alternating and increasingly conflictual interaction of perception- and memory-stimulated recollections and both general and specific projects fragments the sequence of mental representations, as well as Léon's identity.

In *Les Fruits d'or* (1963), Nathalie Sarraute creates a series of literary conversations at Parisian parties, all of which concern a fictive novel called "Les Fruits d'or." The famous Sarrautian subconversations—interior monologues sparked within a character by a verbal encounter and usually simultaneous with it—transform the conversations into mental representations, perceptions giving rise to more voluminous hypotheses and imaginations. Causation is thus at work in microcosm, as the spoken words engender subjective images in the unidentified conversationalists themselves or in witnesses to the discussions. The subconversations are most often metaphoric in character, expressing the sensation that what is happening in the verbal exchange is comparable to another sort of activity. As I have argued elsewhere,[10] the subconversational metaphors in this text most often evoke elements of what has been called "animal" behavior: dominance-and-submission games, territoriality, peck order, and herd psychology. For these salon or cocktail-party conversations are only ostensibly concerned with the artistic merit of "Les Fruits d'or"; they are at bottom the personal power ploys of a would-be intellectual élite, using literary conversation as a means to demonstrate superiority. The psychological effects of their calculated utterances, on themselves and on others, emerge in the subconversational metaphors: X dominates Y, or Z joins Y's "harem." With one or two exceptions, it is impossible to determine the identity of speakers or listeners; it is even probable that nearly every chapter has an entirely new cast of characters. Such fragmentation makes impossible any objective determination that the discussions are presented in chronological order.

Yet, in the early chapters, "Les Fruits d'or" is virtually unknown; further along, it is admired by the intellectual élite, which is imposing its judgment upon others; still later, the book is the talk of Paris, "all the rage," while at the end it drops into nearly universal indifference. This progression itself suggests linear, chronological development. And the text reveals that, despite fragmentation, a kind of double causal law is at work on this larger scale: the first part of the law suggests that one's power is measured by the number of intelligent people upon whom one can impose one's opinions; the second part holds that superiority resides in difference, in one's ability to distinguish oneself from the masses. Thus a following is good, but a nearly all-inclusive following is undesirable. The popularity of "Les Fruits d'or" is dependent upon the operation of this double law: passing favorable judgment upon the novel is, at first, a sign of rallying (or submitting) to the leaders, while later on, when everyone has rallied, the opinion makers no longer wish to be associated with it. This two-part causation produces the curve of the book's rapid rise to popularity and its still more rapid decline, reproducing, from the level of animal behavior, the "K extinction curve," by which population biologists describe the "crash" that follows too sudden an increase in population in animal and insect colonies.[11] The functioning of this curve in the novel is, of course, based on a causal principle; a law of increase with an upper threshold that triggers an immediate decrease is a causal matrix providing a high degree of predictability. Thus, despite the fragmented mental representations that make up the text, traditional causation, reinstated at the metaphorical level, gives the novel a linear ("broken-line") structure.

A series of fragmented mental images conjoin in linear progression in Robbe-Grillet's *La Jalousie* (1957)[12] as well, as the narrator evolves from suspicion to jealous frenzy. The best-remembered marker of progression is the mental representation of the centipede: finger length on page 62, it "grows" to the size of a dinner plate, page 163. That jealousy is the cause of these mental transformations is inferable from the obsessive memories always uniting A. . . and Franck, while separating the Other, who is obviously A. . .'s husband and the narrator. The growing jealousy feeds upon a succession of disconnected memories: A. . . talking to Franck about a book they are reading; the crackle of a comb through A. . .'s thick, long hair; A. . . perhaps passing a note to Franck; A. . .'s chair placed closer to Franck's than to her husband's; Franck, in a virile and protective gesture, killing the centipede that frightens A. . .; A. . .'s day in town with Franck, an absence prolonged unexpectedly until the next morning, and so on. These memories generate the hypotheses which cause the linear substratum; that A. . . and Franck are engaged in a love affair, that the trip to town was really a tryst, despite the explanation of car trouble the pair offers upon return. Linear progression is there in time (marked by the changed position of the pillar's shadow upon the porch where the narrator ruminates) as well as in the rising jealous passion; the multiple memories, and the imaginations they inspire, produce the linear *histoire*, a line of progression which in turn infuses the distinct mental representations of the *récit* with ever more violent imagery.

As these examples indicate, the continuous, causal, linear vectors and curves come into being as constituents of the *histoire* (or of the *narration/lecture* in the case of *Les Gommes*), as a creation of readers' inferences. These inferences (readers' hypothetical mode) are conditioned by lexical data in the *récit* (e.g., metaphors in *Les Fruits d'or*, contrast of comparable items early and late in *La Modification* and *La Jalousie*). Once the linear hypothesis is formulated by readers, it creates an expectation (project) which bears upon our perception of subsequent data in the *récit*, for we are no longer "open-minded," but in search of confirmation in each new element of the *récit* for our linear hypothesis. Thus, as we advance, we tend increasingly to foreground confirming details and to background the others, a mechanism we observed *ex post facto* in the Oedipal reading of *Les Gommes*. Such closedmindedness, which would be ill-advised in scientific observation, is not necessarily undesirable in the reading of fiction, or even in criticism, for reasons I will indicate in the conclusion.

In mental-representation fiction however, causality is not solely a matter for reader inference. It can also exist within the *récit*, linking mental representations explicitly to one another by means of triggers (*déclencheurs*) and shifters (*embrayeurs*) which function intermodally and intramodally.

Certain triggers operate intervocalically for readers, as well as intramodally for characters. Thus, so long as we are not entirely in the imaginary mode, a causation of sorts remains alive and well in the *récit* itself. But such causality exists as a *condition* of passage from one mental representation to another, rather than as a force entailing the shift; it therefore provides, as we have noted, virtually no predictive capacity, although it helps to explain after the fact. Causal functions in mental-representation *récits* are well illustrated in *La Jalousie* and in Simon's *La Route des Flandres*.

The narrator of *La Jalousie* loses his openmindedness in a manner akin to that ascribed to readers above. As he broods, for example, upon A. . .'s failure to return home after the day in town with Franck (perhaps he is recalling the anguished night spent in her absence), he catches sight of the stain on the dining room wall, left by the crushed centipede. This perception triggers the memory of Franck's manly gesture, using his napkin (*serviette*) to smash the little beast, crushing its fallen body again on the floor. But this time, instead of squashing it on the tiles (*carrelage*) of the dining room floor as in the previous obsessive accounts of this memory, he tramples the myriapod on "le plancher de la chambre" (p. 166; "the bedroom floor"). His *serviette* now designates a hand towel, which he hangs up near the wash stand: imagination has transferred Franck from dining room to hotel room. A. . .'s presence there is suppressed, but someone is waiting for Franck in bed, clutching the sheets, as A. . . had clutched her knife when she glimpsed the centipede. Drawing the mosquito netting around them, Franck climbs into bed; then, in his haste to reach his goal, we are told, he accelerates the pace, and the jolts become more violent. A sex scene? Obviously. But with the shifter "jolts" (*cahots*), we slip into another mental image, of Franck driving his car home on the rutted dirt road at night (presumably with A. . . ?), hitting a sinkhole at top speed, crashing into an embankment: "Aussitôt des flammes jaillissent" (p. 167; "Immediately flames spring up"). Two hypotheses explaining why A. . . has not returned (hotel room tryst, serious accident on the road) fuse together through the common language of a shifter phrase, just as Franck-killing-the-centipede became Franck-the-hotel-room-adulterer. At this point, however, they are more than hypotheses, for the logical connections have disappeared between images, replaced by associations, which are the causal connectors either of memory (but the narrator could not "remember" these scenes) or of imagination, the basic mode of the passage.

The causal chain which conditions the development of the text passes from present cognitive (wall stain) to past cognitive (scene that caused the stain), to a past hypothetical quickly colored by the vivid images and illogical connectors of the imaginary mode. Movements of this kind from perception to imagination, through words each belonging to two semantic fields (*serviette, cahots*), are not, however, ends in themselves: the emotion involved in the imaginary mode returns to the point of departure, coloring the narrator's perception of reality; it is this sort of effect that increases, for example, the apparent size of the stain left by the centipede.

Imagination is an even more powerful contaminant of memory, which often lacks objective confirmation. Toward the end, the narrator, unable to confirm or to confound his hypothesis of an adulterous affair between A. . . and Franck, recalls their animated conversation about a novel they have both read but which he has not. His memory of the conversation (p. 216) is a confused jumble of contradictory sentences. Since it is extremely unlikely that A. . . and Franck could be in such utter disagreement about the *histoire* of a conventional novel, we must lay the contradictions at the door of the narrator's imagination. As it is a question of a financially sound (or shaky) corporation, and of predecessors and successors, honest or dishonest, in the corporate management, one may hypothesize that the narrator is associating randomly the book's plot with his own marriage. The half-remembered snatches of conversation are now contaminated by imagination, as the imaginary mode impinges upon the cognitive, which triggered it. The narrator's conditioned trajectories, from memory to hypothesis and imagination, and thence back to memory or perception, parallel the succession of mental states in a reader involved in constituting a fictional text.

In *La Route des Flandres*, the only perceptions of the narrator (Georges) are those of the bedroom in which he is spending a night of love with Corinne. The rest is, superficially at least, reminiscence: memories of defeat, capture, transport to and life in a Nazi prison camp; memories of memories, things remembered as a prisoner about his former French commanding officer, Captain de Reixach, a distant relative, and about the captain's wife, Corinne, with whom Georges now lies; memories of family legends and stories associated with the bedroom, which the narrator has only heard in indirect voice. The novel begins in the past cognitive, and only gradually do we become aware of the narrator's intradiegetic identity and present situation, and of the relationship of that situation to the flood of reminiscences which make up the novel. Readers' hypotheses about the text slowly approach and finally grasp the kernel of perceived reality at the center of the construction.

But the linear text itself advances through remembrances, by a series of associations, which are the "causal" structure of memory. Here again, shifters represent the passage from one remembrance to the next. Doubtless the most evident of these are related to virginity. De Reixach, very "old nobility" and "old cavalry," had died on horseback, leading his decimated mounted unit against the invading Panzers. Georges, a surviving member of the unit, has a clear mental image of his captain's glorious final pose, horse rearing, sabre aloft:

> . . . un instant l'éblouissant reflet du soleil accroché ou plutôt condensé, comme s'il avait capté attiré à lui pour une fraction de seconde toute la lumière et la gloire, sur l'acier virginal . . . Seulement, vierge, il y avait belle lurette qu'elle ne l'était plus, mais je suppose que ce n'était pas cela qu'il lui demandait espérait d'elle le jour où il avait décidé de l'épouser. . . . (P. 13)

> (. . . for an instant the dazzling reflection of the sun caught or rather condensed, as if he had captured drawn unto himself for a fraction of a second all the light and the glory, on the virgin steel . . . Only, a virgin, it had been ages since she had been one of those, but I suppose that wasn't what he asked of her expected from her the day he decided to marry her. . . .)

Thus the association *virginal-vierge* conditions the shift from the captain's heroic death to his marriage to Corinne. Later, we will recognize as the prime cause of all the "Corinne" memories, and of the erotic images which seep as if by osmosis into other recollections of other times, the presence of Corinne in his bed: present perception is also facilitating the glide from one memory into the next.

However, the memory of the early years of de Reixach's marriage is not, we soon discover, in direct voice. Georges has learned about them from Iglésia, a fellow member of the cavalry unit and fellow prisoner during the war, who had been the jockey for de Reixach's string of race horses, and who had had no qualms about cuckolding his future captain, in the horse barns, with the ever-eager Corinne. Yet the detailed images derived from such accounts (pp. 22–25, 51–54, 137–54, 166–69, 174–83) go far beyond the general comments of Iglésia in the narrator's actual memory (pp. 49–51, for example). Thus, "Et cette fois Georges put les voir, exactement comme si lui-même avait été là" (p. 144; "And this time Georges could see them, exactly as if he had been there himself") represents a transition from memory, the remembered words of an account of a competition between Iglésia and de Reixach, to imagination. Georges's mental representation includes color, clothing descriptions, facial expressions, attitudes, bits of conversation, representing what it might have been like to be present the day de Reixach took his jockey's place, riding in a race, as his jockey had replaced him, "riding" Corinne. But the associations remain operative (e.g., mounting a horse, mounting a sexual partner), interconnecting memory, present perception, and imagination, so that the imagination is constrained by a kind of causal probability: these people, in this situation, would have doubtless behaved in this way. Accounts of events, and the narrator's acquaintance with all the participants, prohibit wild flights of fancy: Georges is approaching a hypothesis. For, in a sense, these imaginings are to form the basis for the justification of one of a series of hypotheses formulated early in the text: when de Reixach assumed his statuelike pose in the face of enemy fire, he was perhaps (a) enjoying a noble, heroic death, or maybe (b) seeking to draw enemy fire toward his unit, hoping that Iglésia would be killed—a cuckold's revenge—or, more probably (c) drawing fire upon himself, committing suicide (pp. 14–17). Other hypotheses in the text concern possible reasons for suicide on his part, and for other suicides—ancestral, political, national—and the relationship of sexual satisfaction and dissatisfaction to the death wish and to the general entropic disaggregation reaching culmination in World War II.

These hypotheses develop discontinuous thematic strata within the text, which the reader's memory can collect into at least four themes: the suicide of a nineteenth-century ancestor, de Reixach's death, the fall of France in 1940, and the accompanying disintegration of European culture. As these thematic strands are connected by association in the narrator's mind, the text itself begins to cause or condition reader reaction to its structure in two primary ways.

First, in almost Proustian fashion (de Reixach falls in battle into an intertext, as it were, smack in front of a "perfumed, springtime hedge of hawthorns," [p. 314]), mental images trigger other mental images, causing the text to advance. As readers assimilate the system of associations, they may begin to move about in the space of the text, as with Proust, whenever later images (such as that of the less-than-virginal Virginie) trigger their own memories of themselves mentally creating earlier ones (such as the glint of the sun on the sabre's "acier virginal"). In a stricter sense, of course, when we collect bits of text to constitute a "theme," or associate similar images, we are moving about, not in the space of the text, but in that of our memory of it. This is, then, an example of intervocalic shift, when present reading (indirect voice) triggers our memories (direct voice) of assimilation, of our imagination fleshing out a spare linguistic tale, as the narrator had vivified in imagination Iglésia's accounts.

Second, as readers become aware of the spatial nature of the text, they recognize that there is indeed no movement, except perhaps the rhythm, the repeated (and therefore "static") movements of Georges's copulations with Corinne. The microcosmic triggers that advance the text from one mental representation to the next are not creating a space but exploring a preexisting space. The awareness that imagination penetrates our perception of all accounts of the past, indeed infuses human memory (is any narrator "reliable"?), invalidates them as grounds for the justification of our inferences. We may constrain imagination sufficiently to formulate memory-based hypotheses, but not enough to justify them. For the truth value of hypotheses depends upon the soundness of objective, logical causation, which can coexist only with movement. The text rarely tells us which details are remembered and which imagined; it is likely the narrator has no greater certainty about such things than do the readers. Indeed the novel ends on this uncertainty, as Georges again recalls de Reixach's (mock?) heroic posture just before he was killed:

> Mais l'ai-je vraiment vu ou cru le voir ou tout simplement imaginé après coup ou encore rêvé, peut-être dormais-je n'avais-je cessé de dormir les yeux grands ouverts en plein jour bercé par le martèlement monotone des sabots des cinq chevaux piétinant leurs ombres ne marchant pas exactement à la même cadence de sorte que c'était comme un crépitement alternant se rattrapant se superposant se confondant par moments comme s'il n'y avait plus qu'un seul cheval, puis se dissociant de nouveau, se désagrégeant recommençant semblait-il à se courir après et cela ainsi de suite. . . . (P. 314)

> (But I did really see it or believe I saw it or simply imagine it after the fact or even dream it, maybe I was sleeping had never stopped sleeping with my eyes wide open in broad daylight rocked by the monotonous pounding of the five horses' hoofs stomping their shadows not advancing exactly in the same cadence so that it was like an alternating

ratatatat catching up superimposing blending at times as if there were now but a single horse, then separating once again, disintegrating starting it seemed to chase each other again and so on like that. . . .)

Hypotheses, memory, and imagination blend, like the shadows of the horses, and their hoofbeats, as punctuation falls away, allowing each phrase to melt into its successor. Like the precious Leipzig library, the carefully collected and preserved record of expanding human wisdom which proved powerless against the bombs that destroyed it (pp. 222–25), memory, infused with imagination, is unable to act or guide action, useless as a tool for explanation, prediction, or project.

Of the two oft-noted tendencies that structure this novel, aggregative and disaggregative, the former (by means of which, for example, we compare the Leipzig library to Georges's memory) relies solely on the principles of comparison and psychological association. Having lost its modal purity, memory cannot serve as the basis for hypothetical reason, in which the causal assumption forms the ground of movement and action. Readers can construct in memory four main "themes" in parallel lines (as Marcel's memory did the Combray walks), so that a note struck on any one of them resonates on all the others. But with causation limited to the little triggers of psychological association, only the *récit* can advance: the *histoire* is static.

Belief in the potential validity of the causal assumption, and therefore of the hypothetical mode for readers, at least, if not for characters as well, appears a necessary condition for an *histoire* that advances, that moves with direction. The *histoire* of *La Jalousie* can be said to move forward insofar as causality is at work: suspicion generates imagination, which provokes even wilder imagination, whence frenetic jealousy, and so on. One cannot advance along *La Route des Flandres* as *histoire*, only rise higher above it, for an ever broader view of its preexisting totality.

More recent mental-representation novels have tended to exclude the cognitive and hypothetical modes and to dwell almost entirely in the imaginary. One thinks of the later novels of Marguerite Duras, beginning approximately with *Le Ravissement de Lol V. Stein* (1964)—with the exception of her presumably autobiographical *L'Amant* (1984), in which inference returns in force. In *Dans le labyrinthe* (1959), with its famous multiple beginning (Outside it's raining . . . ; Outside it's sunny . . . ; Outside it's snowing . . .), Robbe-Grillet situates us in the freely associating mind of an inferred narrator-author, who tests out meteorological settings until one is found to generate the desired (by whom?) thematics. The famous loop in his *La Maison de rendez-vous*,[13] in which the image of a person in a printed picture leaves the frame and eventually finds herself in position to become a potential observer of the picture, typifies the sort of implausibility that is the hallmark of imaginary-mode fiction. Even though the vocabulary remains quite referential (one can of course visualize clearly each phase of the loop), the temporal relationship among the elements displays a certain "real-world impossibility": it is causality that is out of joint.

As a mental-representation text composed entirely in the imaginary mode, Robbe-Grillet's *Souvenirs du triangle d'or* (1978)[14] will serve to exemplify the exclusion of traditional causation from the novel. Some meager grounds remain, as we shall see, for causal inferences about the *narration* on the part of readers, but the absence or implausibility of causation in the *récit* precludes the constitution in readers' minds of a meaningful *histoire*. An "*histoire*" subsists, in that one can visualize or reconstitute each of the "scenes" described, but the absence of inferable causal relationships among them precludes the kind of meaningfulness of which we have been speaking. There are no narratorial perceptions to cause memories (the word *souvenirs*—"memories"—in the title, in the absence of plausible relationships, seems an ironic reference to the contamination of memory by imagination) or to stimulate projects, no valid hypotheses, no facts on which to base counterfactuals. We read simply a series of mental images, a number of which are neurotically erotic, violent, or sadistic—almost always with women as victims. A text made up entirely of imaginary-mode representations gains certain attributes lacking in works with reality-referential elements, but it also loses interesting characteristics found in novels in which cause and effect play a role. Since the absence of a structuring device may often be as informative as its presence, a survey of the "losses" and "gains" in this apparently extreme sort of fictional structure will provide an instructive conclusion to this chapter. What major narrative concepts are lost in mental-representation fiction limited to the imaginary mode?

1. *The identity of the narrator.* When a narrative consists of causally interrelated or interrelatable events, or of causally associated mental representations, readers are justified in presuming that the narrative voice retains a consistent identity. While the narrator may undergo change within certain parameters (*La Nausée*, *La Jalousie*), we expect her or him to be the "same" person. When the text presents simply a series of implausible

imaginings, none of which have consequences in any of the others, there is no reason, beyond our traditional habits, to suppose that a single, constantly identical narrator is speaking to us from the printed page. True enough, there is sufficient parodic (or pseudoparodic—without objective standards, one cannot tell) pornography in *Souvenirs du triangle d'or*, it seems to me, to lead one to posit a narrator of obsessive tendencies. But there is quite enough material of other kinds—scenes of incarceration and escape, of exploration and investigation, of bouncing balls and pearls bouncing on a mirror—to leave that hypothesis unconfirmed. As if to reinforce our doubts, the "narrator's" name seems to change as well. On page 46, he appears to be "Franck" (later known as the police official "Franck V. Francis," a.k.a. "Francis Lever," a.k.a. "Francisco Franco"); on page 91, however, the narratorial "I" meets Franck, although we will be told on page 101 that Franck V. Francis is indeed "le narrateur." Later, a female "character" ("Lady Caroline") narrates a segment (pp. 154–68) in which she has some of the experiences previously attributed to a male identity, until she becomes again a "third person," at which point all the characters we meet, including Franck, are presented in "third person" for a time. One narrative voice splits into two before our eyes as he criticizes his own "narrative" act ("Ne me faites pas rire," [p. 198]; "Don't make me laugh"). When narrators do remain "themselves" throughout a text, there is a presumed cause for it, as I suggested earlier with respect to the surrealist novels; in these shifting sands, where causation cannot be presumed, constant narratorial identity cannot be presumed either.

2. *The concept of character.* Characters have traditionally been defined either in terms of "traits" (whether these are named in the *récit* or inferable from their recounted actions) or as functions of plot structure called *actants*.[15] Without causality, there can be no "plot," no actions of consequence; as a result, the linguistic imitations of persons which inhabit texts like *Souvenirs* can scarcely be analyzed as *actants*. One might see the narrator as consequentially active and construe an *histoire* which would be: "The narrator imagines . . ." followed by the text of the novel. But, if the narrator is not necessarily the "same" person, such an *histoire* is meaningless and the "narrator(s)" undefinable as "character(s)." The concept of character "traits" presupposes a certain essence or constancy of identity of dubious validity in *Souvenirs*. Gender does appear to remain consistent throughout (a notion which gains increased significance because of the shifting, causeless structure); men are men and women, women; but sex alone defines categories

rather than individuals. One would be hard put to find the complex or paradigm of traits required for the depiction of an individual character, beyond the attributes of gender. Imagination is free, and there is therefore no cause for a human entity to retain any constant set of traits, even contradictory ones, in the imaginary mode.

3. *The notion of fictional reality*. The causal implausibility of "events" that marks *Souvenirs* as a text in the imaginary mode also deprives it of the benchmark of reality. For example, the "narrator" supposedly sees, from his seat in a seaside café, a naked adolescent girl on horseback, riding up the beach at water's edge. When she has passed behind him, a triad of hunters arrives in the same direction. As soon as they too are behind the "narrator," a shot rings out, followed by screams, which a second shot silences, and by the sound of some sort of "body" falling into the water (pp. 10–12). One may infer causation, that the hunters have shot the girl, but the "narrator" fails to turn his head, so as to be able to provide an eyewitness account, and the "event," if it is one, has no further consequences in the novel. Implausibility itself does not destroy fictional reality, so long as the "laws" of causality are not tampered with. A science fiction text may be implausible, but it will provide causes and effects consistent with its own system. In fairy tales, a pumpkin may become a coach, but only according to the rules: fairy godmothers may cause such things, but no one else can; an internally consistent causal system still functions. In *Souvenirs*, causes remain absent. Why did the hunters fire? Why did the narrator refrain from looking? What were the results of the supposed murder? In a world in which people can sometimes pass Alice-like[16] through a looking glass (pp. 112–13), readers have no use for their common sense and life experience in making the inferences essential to the constitution of a meaningful *histoire*.

4. *The concept of time*. *Souvenirs du triangle d'or* is composed, like much mental-representation fiction, largely in the present tense, which wavers often ambiguously between description and narration. With no causes and effects to order the mental images, readers are at sea in the question of chronology. Did the scene on the beach occur before or after the imprisonment? (Which scene on the beach? Whose imprisonment?) Logic, in the absence of causal connectives, cannot distinguish "before" from "after." Interrogators ask the imprisoned male, near the end of the novel, to provide a chronological summary, thus pointing ironically to the meaninglessness of time in the text. The prisoner obliges, spreading the contradictory "events" of the fiction (and a few new ones) over a period of eight hours and

thirty-six minutes, divided into twelve-minute segments. This imposition of a temporal "order" on incongruous "events" in the present tense endows them with the stasis of stop-action photography, to which I have alluded, but it does nothing to connect or organize them, or to render them plausible: it merely derides the concept of temporality. The time in which the "events" may be said to have taken place is the time it took to imagine them. But who imagined them, if not the reader? Fictional time and reading time are no longer distinct concepts.

5. *The notion of predictability*. Without reality-based causation, we obviously have no capacity for predicting what might or might not happen in coming segments of the *récit*. Curiosity (desire to know what will turn out to have happened), and suspense (desire to know what will happen)[17] must therefore also remain inoperative in such texts as *Souvenirs*. Predictability allows us to determine that a character is in danger, or that a revelation about the past is forthcoming. Lack of knowledge, which is the basis for both curiosity and suspense, is a prime attribute of this text, but knowledge here is not simply deferred but absent. So, in the knowledge that we will not acquire knowledge, we perceive curiosity and suspense as idle.

6. *The notion of explicability*. Having perused all the words of the text, readers cannot connect the "events" (*qua* events) in any order which will render them comprehensible in relation to one another. Thus, if we have continued to read out of a belief that all would eventually come clear, we have erred.

7. *Traditional narrative units*. Narratologists distinguish in traditional novels certain crucial events, which determine by causation the direction of the text (they are called *noyaux* or "kernels"), and those lesser, though enriching, events that could be eliminated "without disturbing the logic of the plot," and which are termed *catalyses* or "satellites."[18] The absence of causation eliminates all notion of "plot" in Forster's sense by definition, and with it the distinction between *noyaux* and *catalyses*. Since movement and change are present in *Souvenirs*, it remains possible to speak of "events" (or "imagined events") in the text. Few of them, however, can be said to have "consequences," although most of them are potentially consequential. As a result, at first reading, it remains difficult to determine when an event ends, for its potential effect hangs fire. Likewise, beginnings of events are difficult to pinpoint, since one tends to suspect that unstated antecedent reasons for them must exist. Thus, there is "no telling" what the

boundaries of events might be, for in a sense there is "no telling" in the novel at all.

8. *The notion of importance.* At one point in the narrative, young Angélica, operating on orders from Lady Caroline, has gotten herself arrested by a person purporting to be a police inspector named Franck. But is he really with the police?

> Dans la Cadillac noire qui l'emmène à vive allure, Angélica essaie en vain de résoudre cette grave question. Par instant le coeur lui manque, en brusques bouffées brûlantes, à la pensée qu'elle vient de commettre une faute impardonnable: si ce prétendu inspecteur était en réalité le faux médecin? (P. 171)

> (In the black Cadillac that is speeding away with her, Angélica tries in vain to resolve this grave question. At times, her heart falters for an instant, in sudden burning bursts, at the thought that she has just committed an impardonable sin: what if this self-styled inspector were in reality the false doctor?)

In the absence of causal connectives, nothing can be of consequence; no questions are therefore "grave," and there are no "impardonable sins"— indeed, no sins at all, since judgment would reinstitute causation in the text. As figments of the imagination, little Angélica and her burning palpitations remain unimportant. Words like "grave," "impardonable," and especially "en réalité," in this realm of shifting "character" identity, acquire a special irony unattainable in cognitive-mode texts. Perhaps the most amusing example of it occurs when the narrator of the moment is instructed, in preparing his final chronology, to leave out "useless details" (p. 225).

In addition to this peculiar irony, *Souvenirs du triangle d'or* gains, as an imaginary-mode text, other distinctive characteristics. Since no continuous *histoire* can be constituted, readers' hunger for structure drives them mercilessly toward the *narration*. Internal repetitions and intertexts attain increased significance as the only remaining clues to potential order. Among the internal repetitions are the limited number of settings, which perforce recur. Indeed, each time the décor changes, we appear to be in a new mental representation, so that series of potentially comparable narrative units can be envisaged on the basis of setting: beach, prison, temple of the secret society, and so on. Recurring images, of bouncing white spheroids, for example, and of triangles, provide further ground for comparison. Triangles emerge in the title, in the image of the pediment of a Greek-style temple, in the references to the upper front of a woman's pointed shoe, in images of the exposed pubic hair of females, and in the name of the "Société du Triangle d'or" ("Society of the Golden Triangle"), accused, in imagination at least, of sponsoring sadistic orgies. All occurrences are at least distantly sex-related. Even the pediment contains as a frieze an inverted equilateral triangle with an eye in it, set on end on the vertical axis; little imagination is required of readers to see in the frieze a schematic representation of the female genitalia. The recurrence of erotic and voyeuristic imagery might suggest the periodic return of desire, here employed as a structuring device.

The intertexts also attain exceptional significance as indices of order: allusions to Robbe-Grillet's own early fiction (*Les Gommes*, *Le Voyeur*, *La Jalousie*), as well as to *Alice through the Looking Glass* and to Valéry's *Cimetière marin* (quoted on p. 112). Since the girl "character," who, at this point, passes through the "peau de panthère et chlamyde trouée" which is the surface of a mirror, bears the name "Temple," it is tempting to undertake a reading of the text as a dark-side parody of the famous poem. The occasional sea imagery, and the "temple" headquarters of the secret society provide further encouragement. "Cruel Zeno's" paradoxes about stasis and movement are inherent here in the present-tense conflict between narration and description, between the successive fantasies and the final imposed "chronology." If Valéry's poem traces an evolution from belief in eternal, rational order governing human existence to the understanding that life is an interplay of irrational, dynamic, and mortal forces, his imagined "Temple du Temps, qu'un seul soupir résume," is "dead in the water" before the end of the poem. But instead of finding, like Valéry, beneath the surface of the soul, in the fear of death, an emotional and quasiexistential reason for attempting to live and act, Robbe-Grillet's text uncovers in introspection the hideous dynamic of sadistic desire (which one might associate with the "panther") and the masochism relatable to the pilgrim wearers of the ragged "chlamyde." The inactivity of neurotic imagination would replace, in such a reading, existential choice and action.

The golden triangle of the title might also refer to the Pythagorean mysteries, to the secret order of the universe, or perhaps to the logical structure of abstraction or of the syllogism. Symmetries in triangles, trajectories, and mirror images also suggest structural order, or the before-and-after of Pythagorean metempsychosis. Psychoanalytical readings are disappointingly easy, the "ego" having bothered little with censorship; and if this is the text of a dream, whose dream is it (cf. Alice's problem with the Red King)? Since the inferred author is free, in the imaginary mode, to present any images in any order, the *narration* need not represent a consistent intent: readers are equally free to attribute significance to any aspect of repeated images or of intertexts and to structure them all at will in a *lecture*. We are left, in the virtual absence of a syntagmatic axis, with the pseudotask of constituting an unverifiable paradigmatic one. And gone is the pleasure to be derived from the discovery of an author's skill in creating entities that combine temporal and eternal functions in a text. In its place remains the reader's free but inconsequential creation.

One escape from such futility is to read the text as text, remaining as close as possible to syntax and signifiers and restraining the imagination from embroidering on the signifieds. The evil experiments of the scurrilous Dr. Morgan may be described as "expériences sur les comportements oniriques tertiaires" (p. 184); "experiments on tertiary (REM) oneiric behavior"—but they are also "textual experiments" (p. 155; "expériences textuelles"). While in context readers can scarcely fail to note the potential substitution of the near-rhyme "sexuelles" for "textuelles," the book is not only a succession of separate dreams, like separate pearls bouncing off a mirror (described as an "experiment in structural organization," [p. 103]), but an experiment in the texture, in the weaving together, of words. So it is, for example, that the "narrator" in his jail cell perceives a yellow object and a red one, which, we are told, would produce "une orange, qui ne saurait donc tarder à paraître" (p. 149; "an orange, which can therefore not be long in making its appearance"). Sure enough, in the next fantasy, Lady Caroline finds, in her bathing cabin at the beach, "a large, perfectly spherical orange" (p. 151; "une grosse orange parfaitement sphérique"). Words generate words on the level of individual signifiers, independently of a generalized meaning of the text. Such generation would appear caused only if one could infer the inferred author's intent.

Novels of mental representation continue to make use of causal elements for unifying and structuring purposes, for the constitution of a definable syntagmatic axis, so long as the mental representations involve the cognitive or the hypothetical mode. In the former, a series of unrelated perceptions is conceivable, but in practice, characters' memories begin to connect them by associations, which will become the causes of later recall. In the future cognitive, the inherent perceived inevitability is causal in nature. The hypothetical mode, the domain of inference, uses causation as its essential logic.

But the imaginary mode, the realm of fantasy and dreams, escapes internal causation, and with it not only a major structural armature, but primary tools of meaning production. As the basis for explanation and for inferable intent, causation has served as a source of metonymic understanding, as a fundamental determiner of meaning in fiction. It is precisely this linear, "narrative" notion of meaning that imaginary-mode texts undertake to subvert. Their intent, if we can infer it, is to revitalize fiction on other, nonnarrative grounds, free at last from causal chains.

Notes

1. See Dorrit Cohn, *Transparent Minds: Narrative Modes for Presenting Consciousness in Fiction* (Princeton: Princeton University Press, 1978) for a thorough analysis of linguistic imitations of mental representations. Her notions of "consonance" and "memory monologue" are quite relevant to this chapter.

2. Claude Simon, *La Route des Flandres* (Paris: Editions de Minuit, 1960), p. 199. Future references in the text are to this edition.

3. I use the terms in the sense of Seymour Chatman, *Story and Discourse* (Ithaca: Cornell University Press, 1978), pp. 43–145; see especially pp. 96–107.

4. Alain Robbe-Grillet, *Les Gommes* (Paris: Editions de Minuit, 1953). Further references in the text are to this edition.

5. The causal effect of the imaginary mode can occur, of course, only in a fictionally "real" world. In novels composed entirely in the imaginary mode, the causal function on the level of the *histoire* is tenuous or absent.

6. Bruce Morrissette, "Oedipe ou le cercle fermé: *Les Gommes*," in his *Les Romans de Robbe-Grillet* (Paris: Editions de Minuit, 1963), pp. 37–75.

7. Although *L'Etranger* privileges Meursault over the prosecutor, the narrator's

account is hardly above suspicion (chapter nine, above). Such doubt about an eyewitness account situates the work clearly between the Zola and Robbe-Grillet texts.

8.   Figures in this paragraph are obtained from Ken Allott and Peter Tremewan, *Les Gommes d'Alain Robbe-Grillet: index verborum et table des fréquences* (Paris, Geneva: Champion, Slatkine, 1985).

9.   Daphne Patai, "Temporal Structure as a Fictional Category in Michel Butor's *La Modification*," *French Review*, 46, 6 (May 1973), 1117–28.

10.   Roy Jay Nelson, "Territorial Psychology in Nathalie Sarraute's *Les Fruits d'or*," *Symposium*, 35, 4 (Winter 1981/82), 307–23.

11.   Nelson, pp. 320–22.

12.   Alain Robbe-Grillet, *La Jalousie* (Paris: Editions de Minuit, 1957). Further references in the text are to this edition.

13.   Alain Robbe-Grillet, *La Maison de rendez-vous* (Paris: Editions de Minuit, 1965), pp. 35–38.

14.   Alain Robbe-Grillet, *Souvenirs du triangle d'or* (Paris: Editions de Minuit, 1978). Further references in the text are to this edition.

15.   Chatman, pp. 107–45, outlines the notion of "character" as defined by theorists from Aristotle to Todorov, with a refutation directed at extreme structuralist positions. "People," in *Souvenirs du triangle d'or*, function almost as "settings," as defined in the latter part of Chatman's chapter.

16.   Lewis Carroll's *Alice in Wonderland* and *Alice through the Looking Glass* are both imaginary-mode stories (not fairy tales), but they are provided with cognitive-mode frames, which are their contact with "reality" and their cause. This is an essential structural difference from *Souvenirs du triangle d'or*.

17.   The definitions are drawn from Meir Sternberg, *Expositional Modes and Temporal Ordering in Fiction* (Baltimore: Johns Hopkins University Press, 1978), p. 65.

18.   See Roland Barthes, *L'Aventure sémiologique* (Paris: Editions du Seuil, 1985), pp. 175–83. See also Chatman, pp. 53–56.

Conclusion

Les séquences proaïrétiques vont bientôt toutes se fermer, le récit mourra. Que savons-nous d'elles?

(Soon the proaïretic sequences will close; the tale will die. What do we know about them?)

—ROLAND BARTHES

. . . c'est parce que nous savons l'irréversibilité du devenir que nous pouvons reconnaître le mouvement réversible, le changement simple, réductible à une équivalence réversible entre cause et effet.

(. . . it is because we know the irreversibility of becoming that we can recognize reversible movement, simple change, reducible to a reversible equivalency between cause and effect.)

—PRIGOGINE AND STENGERS

Temporal plurality, inherent in the new physics,[1] finds its echo, of course, in our insertion of cause and effect into the levels of narrative. This heuristic device has revealed the fundamental notions of plausibility and connectedness as dependent upon readers' relationship to the text, suggesting the usefulness of describing additional levels.

The distinction among traditional levels should be nowhere more apparent than in the closing pages of the preceding chapter. All fiction is by definition, for the *narration*, imaginary; imaginary-mode fiction does not begin, however, until the *récit* undertakes to imitate the process of imagining. It does so by multiplying implausibilities. Now, as our readings of texts indicate, the implausible does not reside in the names of entities:

speech is not implausible, nor are white rabbits. But when Alice's white rabbit begins to produce speech, a serious implausibility arises; it is not the entities but the relationships among them that may be implausible. Even then, one would be hard put to prove that any relationship is inherently implausible; relationships become implausible only in comparison to some standard, which is usually life experience (although, in science fiction, it might be an imaginary system, such as the peculiar physics of the planet Xyron). Relationships among entities, if they occur across time, invariably presuppose a causal element or its absence; passing through a mirror (*Souvenirs du triangle d'or*) or recovering completely from a four-story fall (*L'Assommoir*) seems to presuppose the obliteration of the constraints of physics as they apply to human anatomy. And the standard of plausibility, as a component of the condition of inference, therefore also functions causally.

We may conclude, then, that the causal assumption is critical to the perception of plausibility/implausibility in texts. We may also conclude that the causal hypothesis is the mode of insertion of the verisimilar into the temporality of narrative. Even though readers may recognize as familiar the entities of a text, unless causal predictability or explicability defines the relationship among entities, the story will appear to deviate from the realistic.

In addition to "incorrect" causality (the implausible), our device also uncovers disconnectedness among temporally related fictional phenomena. It is only apparent when we assume that causal relationships are to be expected; once again, comparison with life or literary experience is operative. There is potential misunderstanding involved in pointing out (as in the last chapter) gaps and disconnectedness in imaginary-mode texts, through comparison to standards of narrative that are inapplicable to them; the aim there, of course, was not understanding but demonstration of difference. But in texts that do not mimic imagination, that include, even minimally, elements of the cognitive or hypothetical modes, comparison with a standard is invited, for these modes presuppose the existence of a fictional "reality." When the *récit* imitates these modes (remembering, perceiving, projecting, hypothesizing), the fundamental existence of the "real" is implied, and thus "real" temporal relationships: causation. It was obvious, for example, that the narrator of *La Jalousie* could not be remembering certain scenes and must therefore be imagining them; despite the emphasis on imagination in that work, enough cognitive data surface to make causal assumptions possible in interpretation. Like plausibility/

implausibility, perception of connectedness/disconnectedness in temporal narratives is dependent upon readerly causal hypotheses.

Reading for causality thus also clearly demonstrates the creative importance of readers to texts. The choice of the standards of connectedness and plausibility against which narratives are measured is entirely the reader's. Readerly inference, based on individual life experience, gauges the implausible and fills the gaps. Texts do not create their readers, nor readers texts: making a story is a cooperative enterprise. It is time to agree, as the physical scientists have done, that we are, in studying texts, both actors and observers in the production of meaning, partially creators of the texts we describe.[2]

Now that analysis of unmediated mental representations in recent texts has led (see chapter ten) to their categorization by voice, mode, and tense, I am equipped to return to my initial description of causation in narrative levels and to expand it in terms of the mental representations of readers. For, as the foregoing analyses suggest, a novel, as it is read, comes to exist on at least five levels:

$$
\begin{array}{ll}
\text{Real author} \left\{
\begin{array}{l}
\text{Indexic author} \text{------------------------------} \textit{Narration} \\
\text{Inferred author} \text{------------------------------} \textit{Histoire (1)} \\
\end{array}
\right. \\
\text{Real reader} \left\{
\begin{array}{l}
\text{Narrator/Reader} \text{------------------------------} \textit{Récit} \\
\text{Inferred reader} \text{------------------------------} \textit{Histoire (2)} \\
\text{Indexic reader} \text{------------------------------} \textit{Lecture} \\
\end{array}
\right.
\end{array}
$$

In this light, narrator and reader share the *récit*, united in the encoding-decoding relationship, which already implies for the reader an active, interpreting role. The *histoire* acquires its true double nature, both as a series of events provided by the inferred author, and as a series of events existing as a mental representation of a reader, with inferred causal connections filling, where possible, any gaps. *Histoire (1)* precedes (theoretically, but not really, as we shall see) and is a condition of the account given by the narrator, while *histoire (2)* arises later, as a result of that account. The levels of *narration* and *lecture* stand in symmetry, on either side of the communicative act. While readers may ask questions of the *narration* (for example, "Why am I being told this?"), they obviously need direct none to the *lecture*. Indeed, readers may well infer that it is rather the author who infers the (prospective) reader and is curious about his or her (future) *lecture*. We might assume that the author has asked, "Why is this being read?" or "Why is this being read in this way?" Although some answers to these questions surely lie outside the text, in the needs and propensities of real, individual readers, the inference that authors inform their stories with an eye to predetermining the answers as much as possible by means of the text is an interesting one.

Adoption of a causal bias obviously tends to privilege "authors" as prime movers and first causes. That is not to say, however, that they deserve (or desire) this distinction. The name on the title page can be read to designate the funnel through which pass the multiple ideological, cultural, and psychological codes inherent in language. Diachronic comparisons that point to an increasingly definitive divorce between psyche and the material world can be read quite ideologically. Both middle-class individualism, for example, which propounds each person's ability to create her or his own destiny, and collectivist theories, which seek to predict the inevitable outcome of the social and economic struggle, share some common causal assumptions; both must now admit of increased uncertainty. Explicability and predictability, as components of ideology on the right and the left, can be fruitfully explored through literary texts seen as artifacts,[3] but the apparently growing impetus to weed out trustworthy causal inferences from novels, despite the procausal bias inherent in language, seems to be a part of a more general development; Heisenberg's uncertainty principle appears at work not only in physics but in anthropology and elsewhere. If the fictional shift is part of a broadly based cultural phenomenon, then the concept of "author" must be taken to represent the influence of major social and scientific principles.

Still, whether authors really infer reader reaction, or whether cultural codes inherent in fiction merely imitate such inferences, texts work as if authors of traditional novels were correctly inferring that causation in *histoire (2)* would operate in the same direction as that in *histoire (1)*, that is to say chronologically, cause before effect. But causation in the *lecture* functions both chronologically, with respect to the text, and antichronologically. Since the *lecture* may induce causation operating in both directions at once, it differs from the *récit*, which may present causes and effects either in one order or the other, but not in both simultaneously. A phrase in the text may impel readers backward, to reexperience or reevaluate a past-cognitive mental representation that arose in response to preceding pages. So it is with Proust's "Mort à jamais?" or with "Ici Laurent s'arrête," which, in *Les Gommes*, makes us reconstitute the source and sense of the preceding passage; so it is even with the second term of a metaphor. Lexical data may likewise lead readers to form, hypothetically, a mental image of what is yet to happen in the *histoire* (the revelations of Jacques Lantier's homicidal mania, for example, or Michel's pronouncement that Marceline was, in his eyes, "damaged goods"). Once readers believe they understand what is afoot in the *narration*, they may impose a general interpretation upon a text as they read, so that it colors both their memories of what has been read and their reading of what is to come. Reference, in *Les Gommes* to a sketch of a Greek temple in a stationer's window may impel readers to bring together their memories of past references to ancient Greece in the text, and, on that basis, having hypothesized an Oedipus connection, to read ahead with the Theban king in mind, foregrounding details useful to the mythic reading and backgrounding the rest. Thus a single reference may plunge readers at once into the past and the future cognitive, the hypothesis having become for them a "sure thing."

When readers' hypotheses about the *narration* become projects, readers are, as we have noted, "closed-minded," and the *récit* undergoes reduction in the *lecture*. This is not of itself an evil, but a process of narrowing inherent in reading. No one remembers a *récit*; many of us recall in detail a few *histoires*; and most can give in a few sentences the general purpose— intent of *narration*—of a great number of novels. Having inferred the tendency toward closedmindedness in readers, authors can structure their texts to use it or to circumvent it. It is natural that, given Lantier's sex-related murderous impulses, readers will expect the engineer to do Séverine in. The text works, for a time, to thwart that expectation, as the lovers spend night after night together in relatively uneventful bliss. A long and satisfying affair is required to reopen readers' eyes to other possibilities, so that the timing of the murder, at least, will produce a degree of essential shock and surprise. In its lexical data, *Les Gommes* encourages a certain closedmindedness about the Oedipus legend as matrix; since the central conflict of the *histoire* reveals, however, the importance of remaining open-minded and flexible in the formulation of hypotheses, it is reasonable to expect that the inducement of a closedminded reading should also serve to unmask the inherent weakness in such a *lecture*. And indeed there is much in the text to discourage an Oedipal *lecture*, from the fact that the murder comes during the investigation and not before, to the extreme "stretching" of evidence necessary to conclude that Dupont is Wallas's father. Play with the closedminded expectations of readers is evident as well in the techniques of causal surprise we have uncovered in Zola and which are common in traditional fiction: cumulative causation, interference of series, reversals (Virginie and Gervaise; Roubaud jealous, then not jealous). These all presuppose readerly inferences that will be at least partly erroneous. In this game of mirrors, of hypotheses about hypotheses, the critic must be a closedminded reader too, so as to experience the effects of authors' inferred inferences about the inferences of potential readers. In order to construct the five-line diagram of narrative levels (that is to say, in order to exist outside it), the critic must once have dwelt within it, taking cognizance at first hand of each level.

Operating from the perspective of poetics, and without considering the inferential mechanisms of a level of *lecture*, Tzvetan Todorov shrouds a vital insight in what appears to be a false causal paradox.[4] Noting the transitive nature of causality, he remarks that causation can operate in both directions when psychological causes of physical action are involved. Do actions serve to reveal the psychological traits of characters (the view of Henry James in *The Art of Fiction*), or do the traits exist merely to prepare and explain the actions? In the paradigm X kills Y, is the focus on the subject (Jamesian stance) or on the predicate? Todorov begins by admitting both possibilities as distinct, calling the subject-focus mediated causality ("causalité *médiatisée*"), and the predicate-focus immediate causality ("causalité *immédiate*"). When the subject is in focus, the action is simply exemplary of a character trait; when the predicate dominates, the character trait arises rather as a modality to allow for or to explain the action. So far, so good. Then Todorov raises the paradox:

> Un trait de caractère n'est pas simplement la cause d'une action, ni simplement son effet: il est les deux à la fois, tout comme l'action. X tue sa femme parce qu'il est cruel; mais il est cruel parce qu'il tue sa femme. L'analyse causale du récit ne renvoie pas à une origine, première et immuable, qui serait le sens et la loi des images ultérieures; autrement dit, à l'état pur, il faut pouvoir saisir cette causalité hors du temps linéaire. La cause n'est pas un *avant* primordial, elle n'est qu'un des éléments du couple "cause-effet" sans que l'un soit par là-même supérieur à l'autre. (Pp. 80–81)

(A character trait is not simply the cause of an action, nor simply its effect: it is both of them at once, just as with action. X kills his wife because he is cruel, but he is cruel because he kills his wife. Causal analysis of stories does not look backward toward some first and immutable origin, which would be the meaning and the law of all the subsequent images; in other words, ideally, we must be able to lay hold of this causality outside of linear time. A cause is not a primordial *before*; it is merely one of the elements of the "cause-effect" couple, without one being for this reason superior to the other.)

This analysis reduces virtually to zero the "mediated/immediate" distinction of the earlier argument and thereby opens doors to causal problems we have been trying to solve.

Todorov's conclusion contains an essential insight. On the *lecture* level, cause and effect come into being at the same instant, because the reader discovers not two things but one: a relationship. For, as I have stressed, neither a cause nor an effect can be perceived as such until a reader has identified the other partner in its "couple." But this simultaneity is not obtained through a special perceptive effort ("we must be able"); it is a sine qua non of causal reading. It holds true for all categories of such relationships: for physical causes of physical effects (e.g., Coupeau is injured, in *L'Assommoir*, because he falls from a rooftop); for physical causes of psychological effects (Michel's attitude toward life is changed in *L'Immoraliste*, for example, as a result of a tubercular infection); for psychological causes of physical effects—Todorov's specific instance (in *La Bête humaine*, Lantier murders Séverine because he is deranged, and Denizet has Cabuche and Roubaud falsely convicted because of arrogance, pride, and a closedminded refusal to accept Roubaud's confession); and for psychological causes of psychological effects (e.g., the narrator's imaginings in *La Jalousie* make him more jealous, as his increased jealousy reciprocally spurs his imagination). While readers are always aware of the condition or event that will become a cause (or an effect) before they are conscious of the other "half" of the causal couple, it is only at the moment when they infer a connection that cause and effect acquire their identity as such in the *lecture*.

Yet despite the inevitable unity of the causal couple on this level, the notion of anteriority tends to persist in *histoires* (1) and (2). The unitary relationship of the *lecture* is usually by nature one of temporal priority and directional movement: A produces (is a condition of, contributes to the production of) B. Ability to lead readers to infer the direction of transitivity is a major communicative tool on the author's workbench—or among the potentialities of texts. Leaving aside the logical nonessentials of Todorov's paradox (one can be cruel without killing one's spouse, or kill one's spouse without being cruel—accident, euthanasia, etc.), it can be of fundamental importance to a text that readers infer correctly (from the author's point of view) whether a murder produces or exemplifies a character trait. The very "point" of *L'Etranger* hinges on it. Imagine a reader who, after perusing the account of the funeral and the following day's swim and date with Marie, determines that Meursault is inherently cruel (or "pathologically insensitive" or "lacking in regard for human life"). The murder of the Arab will, for that reader, appear to be caused by an inherent trait: it provides only one more example of the character's preexisting cruelty. But such a reader, if he or she existed, would have adopted the prosecutor's view before the text revealed it, thus destroying the ironic problematics inherent in the clash of opposing versions of events. For the text to reveal its irony, one must perceive, not that Meursault kills because he is cruel, but that he becomes cruel, in the eyes of the prosecutor and the jurors, because he kills. The text requires that this be, in part I, an example of *causalité immédiate*: temporal priority and direction of derivativeness are crucial. So it is with Proust's Marcel: if his involuntary memories are viewed primarily as results of an inherent character trait, then individual readers may presume that they lack it, and that they cannot know themselves the joys of such epiphanies. The text would thus lose its expansiveness, which arises from causal directionality. Marcel becomes a rememberer because he remembers, because he happens upon the keys to remembrance; in this direction, discovery is open to us all.

Perception of mediated causality (the opposite direction), where it exists, is equally essential. The "testing events" we observed in *L'Immoraliste* and *La Porte étroite* serve to reflect the degree of change, if any, in the traits of characters. The traits exist first, having accomplished their relative changes, and they determine events, which exemplify them. Likewise, Michel "kills" Marceline because he is (has become) cruel. The death crowns the list of Michel's heedless and egocentric actions; it puts the spotlight on him, not on her, and prompts a moral revaluation of his "liberation." Only when we learn of her demise can we perceive the causal couple, but when we do so, the derivativeness is inherent in it: cruelty → death. Mediated causality is the essence of *Le Paysan de Paris* and of *Nadja* as well, where each "event" is the result of a preexisting trait in the narrator: "Breton's" unconscious creates *Les Détraquées* in *Nadja*, just as "Aragon's" creates the Parc des Buttes-Chaumont. To infer the opposite would be to attribute magic properties to places and events, which is delightful, but also to leave the narratorial voices neutral and uninteresting, which is to miss the point. When causality is mediated, as in these examples, it provides a measure of what I have been calling *predictability*; when causation is immediate, it yields rather *explicability*.

This is not to say that causal direction is never ambivalent in the *histoire*. But it only becomes so as a result of tactics of the *narration* embodied in the *récit*. Whether memory feeds imagination, or imagination memory, is a moot point in *La Jalousie*. Do the qualities of otherness in the pebble impart the sensation of nausea to Roquentin's hand, or does the feeling of nausea create the perception of otherness in the pebble? These are examples of interaction, with derivativeness flowing both ways. A text can choose such ambivalence, but it is not a condition of causal expression, even when the psychological and the physical interact. The ambivalence, when it is perceived, is not "outside of linear time": it is grasped as a simultaneous interaction occurring at a point, or over a period, on the timeline of the *histoire*. And when it is grasped, the comprehension takes place in the *lecture*, a developing interpretation of the novel, which has a timeline and a causality of its own. The *narration*, "inferring" reader reaction, selects ambivalence or unidirectionality in order to cause (so we may infer) a specific *lecture*.

The preceding analysis is based on inferred authorial hypothesis: $A \Rightarrow$ Critic ($B \Rightarrow$ Author [$C \Rightarrow$ Reader ($X \rightarrow Y$)]). C is a necessary condition—causal vocabulary, an easily bridgeable gap in the *histoire*, etc.—for the reader's inference of the derivation of Y from X. B is the necessary condition—an element of the author's experience—for authorial inference of the reader's hypothesis, if the reader perceives C. But, if there is to be a critic, she or he must function as a reader, with a reader's tools; thus A is identical with C, but it leads to a different inference. The difference depends on the fact that the "reader" is here transforming *histoire (1)* into *histoire (2)*, working across the single level of the *récit*, while the "critic" is at a further remove, constituting a hypothetical *narration* from the level of *lecture*. This summarizes the argument for the derivation of the levels. The interplay of mirrors appears when we realize that C (and therefore A) derive(s) from B, which includes an understanding of readers and their hypothetical mode. Thus, if causation most often functions unidirectionally along the horizontal timeline of the *histoire*, it acquires reflexive characteristics when it operates vertically, across the levels of narrativity. This is so even for the "reader" in our algorithm, for the inference that $X \rightarrow Y$ is derived from

C, and C is derived from inferred authorial desire to create the inference $X \rightarrow Y$.

Yet C has a double derivation. Our conditions for inferences about the stories we read are derived from our individual life experience, as well as from strategies embodied in the texts. Readerly experience—including reading, as a subset of it—provides the standards for plausibility and connectedness, for verisimilitude and credibility. Cultural codes are not the exclusive property of the coded text; they enter into the decoding as well, for textual strategies are not the sole determiners of the inferences readers will make. The reader, armed with prior knowledge and acquired assumptions, conscious or unconscious, breaks the cycle of the inferential game of mirrors, giving them something to reflect. The experiential component of each condition for inference is thus remarkably "important," in the special sense this study has been giving to the term.

If I have foregrounded the reader's hypothetical mode, it is because it is our means for apprehending causal relationships in novels. But the imaginary mode is by far the most useful and creative tool readers have for appreciating stories; theories of reading wisely focus on its operation. Left to its own devices, imagination is free. Narrative fiction both inspires and restricts it, tightening the tension between liberty and constraint. Along with precise and detailed descriptions, causation provides a primary constraint to the imagination, usually unidirectional in character, helping to channel our imaginations along a specific path.

Yet unlike precise description (indirect voice, cognitive mode), causal relationships involve at least a degree of imaginative freedom, because we perceive them in the hypothetical mode, a step closer to the imaginary. Should a narrator tell us the heroine's blouse was rose-beige, readers would be obliged to believe and never suggest that it was, in fact, aqua. But if the narrator adds that she wore it to please her mother, readers may decide to accept or reject this interpretation, thus forming hypotheses about the insight and reliability of the narrator. Even the heroine's own causal statements are open to readerly doubt. While readers' hypotheses are restricted by the text, they are nonetheless a step removed from the cognitive, which is heavily constrained by the incontrovertible *Ding-an-Sichheit* of fictional reality. Hypotheses are by definition unproved and therefore supplantable in the light of further information, which may come from the text or arise in our imagination.

My few, brief statistical forays into the realm of causal vocabulary suggest that it is unreliable as a measure of the text's domination over the unifying activity of readerly inference. Part I of *L'Etranger* abounds in obvious causal terms, yet critics find almost unanimously that causal connections are lacking in the series of events it depicts. The fact is that, since causality is a function of readerly inference, horizontal (story line) causality achieves definitive "existence" only in *histoire (2)*. Causality in the *récit*, as an expression of the narrator's inferences (or lies, or misconceptions) is a measure of narratorial reliability rather than of functioning causation. Since causality is an interpretive mental grid, characteristic of the hypothetical and counterfactual modes, no causal statement is inherently true; readers must judge the conditions for inference and weigh that judgment against the import of the causal vocabulary. Despite the fact that Michel is only slightly more explicit about causation than Jérôme, *La Porte étroite* supports far more diverse causal readings than does *L'Immoraliste*: the complex textual components of the conditions of readerly inference are at the basis of the difference. While readers may indeed be influenced by (their interpretation of) what characters or narrators say about causes and effects, they retain a curiosity about the "real" causes lurking behind the words—as Foucault so skillfully puts it in another context:

> . . . par delà les énoncés eux-mêmes l'intention du sujet parlant, son activité consciente, ce qu'il a voulu dire, ou encore le jeu inconscient qui s'est fait jour malgré lui dans ce qu'il a dit ou dans la presque imperceptible cassure de ses paroles manifestes. . . .[5]

> (. . . behind the utterances themselves, the intention of the speaking subject, his conscious activity, what he meant to say, or also the subconscious interplay that came to light in spite of him in what he said or in the almost imperceptible crack in his actual words. . . .)

What then occurs in the transformation of *histoire (1)* to *histoire (2)*? Answers obviously vary from one real reader to the next. It appears likely, however, that each reader imagines events in his or her own way, perhaps "hearing" voice timbre and intonations in conversations, "seeing" facial expressions, clothing, gestures, actions performed, fleshing out the linguistic bones of the *récit*. Then, to constitute the text, readers conjoin these images, by "substitution" (mental assembling of images in which the same characters, actions, or settings participate), by comparison (mental uniting of lexically and thematically related elements), and by causal inference. In traditional stories, such inferences are drawn virtually by instinct, as we reach for a familiar light switch, out of assumption of need for an explicable world, in which our predictions have a better than average chance of success. Indeed, we are normally conscious of hypothesizing, of imposing a causal grid upon fictional events, only when two conditions apply: (1) our involvement with the characters' predicaments is such that we feel a need to predict, and (2) we are hesitant about our hypotheses. In part I of *L'Etranger*, for example, the second condition applies (it is hard to know what is coming next), but the first does not: foresight and understanding never seem required to "save" our hero, who appears at no real risk at all until his final meeting with the Arab beneath the relentless sun. In more traditional texts, such as most Zola novels, the first condition often obtains, while the second does not. Readily explainable events in verisimilar settings leave readers confident of their immediate inferences. And realistic fiction, following the "rule of prepared consequentiality," normally avoids contradicting these inferences.

Indeed, it is far more difficult for a text to *prevent* the application of causal connectives to a series of fictional events, if the text is grounded in the cognitive or hypothetical modes. To this end, a series of causally unrelated happenings must be devised, or at least, if they are all causally related to an underlying condition, they must not cause each other. This is what we have observed in *A rebours* and *La Nausée*, where blockers mark the end of each development, followed by a shift to a different situation. Causal constraints (such as the credible, explicit denial of any causal connection between events, as in *Nadja*) may deter the reader's penchant to infer causality. The farther we roam from the familiar (*A rebours*, perhaps) or toward the imaginary mode (*Souvenirs du triangle d'or*), the less likely readers will probably be to impose automatic causal assumptions. Texts often manage, by clever manipulation of readers' desire for causal comprehension, to create curiosity and suspense, anticipation and fear (which are, after all, functions of predictability) in readers, to create a "reasonable" or an "absurd" world, and to determine which events will be perceived as more or less important. Or, by making causal comprehension impossible (*Souvenirs*), an inferred author may eliminate such traditional attributes from a text. Successful manipulation of inferred readers' hypothetical mode on the level of the *histoire* is a prime determinant of what we call "novel structure," and of the esthetic effects texts produce.

Creating the textual conditions for inference, by leaving more or less easily filled gaps between events, is the principal means of "expressing" causation in the *histoire*. But whether or not texts undertake to "express" causation on the level of *narration* is a different matter. The manipulation of which I have just spoken, for example, forms a part of the *narration*: do texts expect us to be aware of it? Fictional conventions seem to presuppose such awareness. Certain texts, through the depiction of a gloomy, rainy day, create foreboding, based in part upon the conventional understanding (understanding, therefore, of the intent of *narration*) that dire events happen, in fiction, in such weather. Often, however, for creation of curiosity, irony, or surprise, the *narration* needs to conceal its manipulations, as *L'Assommoir* screens Virginie's evil purposes (and thus the *narration*'s esthetic ones) until the ironic reversal springs shut like a trap upon the unwary reader. As with the creation of an *histoire (2)*, the development of a *lecture* is accomplished by inference; indeed, a *lecture* is the inference of *finalité*, of a causal principle, inherent in a *narration*. Here again, the reader's penchant is to hypothesize, and the motivation is the desire to comprehend the reason for telling a tale, for telling it in a particular manner, or for inventing specific events in its *histoire*. Creation of implausible or unexplainable events, as we have seen, is a dependable means of encouraging *narration*-level inference by the reader. Proust, by creating for readers a role parallel to that "lived" by his author-narrator, by taking advantage of the intervocalic shift (as does Simon later on), actually manages to reproduce in us the experience of the intent of *narration*. In mythic texts, the myth is itself a prime factor in the purpose of *narration*, and "authors" of such works must desire that a specific *lecture* be achieved. A degree of causal implausibility or improbability at the level of the *histoire* (*La Faute de l'abbé Mouret* or *Regain*, for example) can encourage readers to develop, in the *lecture*, the allegorical elements "concealed" in the *narration*. Devices inspiring readers to generalize from specific instances (such as providing partial generalizations in characters' statements—old Gisors's philosophical conclusions in *La Condition humaine*, the insightful conversations between Tarrou and Rieux in *La Peste*) serve to stimulate exploration of the *narration* for creation of a mythic *lecture*. In general, reader discovery of the "secrets" of the *narration* appears essential both for mythic texts and for texts of philosophical pretensions. The intent of *L'Etranger* includes a proper *lecture*; so does that of *La Nausée*, even though such a *lecture* uncovers the paradox which invalidates the ending of the *histoire*. Of course, *La Paysan de Paris* and *Nadja* are virtually meaningless in their *histoires* alone; only on the *lecture* level can possible links be forged to point to underlying meaning.

Narrative meanings need not be conclusive; *Les Gommes* appears to mean, for example, that its status as a mythic text must remain problematical; *La Porte étroite* and *L'Etranger*, along with many other modern French texts, encourage plural readings, a multivalent *lecture*. But in any case *lectures* expand novels from the world in which their characters live into our world. Certain texts encourage this expansion; others do not (although our hypothesizing minds usually expand them anyway, despite all). Causal inference is the basic means of the expansion: even when we read them as *récits spéculaires*, when our *lecture* makes spatial comparisons along elements of the text on the principle of the matrix, we sense an intent to conceal/reveal the comparability of the elements, on the part of some narrational authority, who wages intellectual battle with us, from whose *narration* we wrest our *lecture*.[6]

The existence of narrative levels creates the conditions for causal ironies between levels. We have seen them at work in mythic stories, where the eternal and immutable causation of mythic destiny (*narration*) makes sport of the petty, specific pseudocauses of characters' reality (*histoire*). The unreliable narrator is also a source of causal irony (e.g., *La Porte étroite*), where the explanations given (*récit*) are at odds with a likely *histoire*. Causality can be a theme as well as a structuring device; we have focused on this duality in *La Bête humaine* and *L'Etranger*, but it is almost a constant in traditional fiction. It can create ironic distance between causality as concept in the *histoire* and expressed cause and effect in the *récit*. Ironic distinctions can arise as well between the *récit* and the *narration*, as we have noted in *La Nausée* (Roquentin's "possession" of the Absurd, born of his ability to name it, contradicts the inferred author's representation of absurdity), and in *Souvenirs du triangle d'or*, when the discourse calls for the elimination of "useless detail" in its own "summary" (*récit* fails to understand—and therefore must understand—the intent of *narration*). Irony exists between *histoire* (1) and *histoire* (2) only when a character, not the narrator, says or thinks something the reader does not believe. Each of these ironies is recovered in a *lecture*. But the *lecture* itself seldom appears to stand in ironic relationship to other levels, since few readers stand apart from their *lecture* (therefore on still another level: *métalecture*?) sufficiently to see it as ironic difference. Yet this irony too exists in potential. The construction/ deconstruction of the Oedipal reading in *Les Gommes* can place Oedipal closedmindedness (*lecture*) in ironic disjunction with the *narration*, as this latter reveals the weakness of the reading it fosters. Definition of such interlevel irony should be a feature of causal analysis.

It would create an amusing symmetry if I could argue that my five-line diagram of levels depicted a real temporal and causal sequence. In the beginning, then, would be the *narration*, an idea-intent, which would give rise to an *histoire*, which would engender the *récit* to tell it; the *récit* would generate an *histoire (2)* in the mind of a reader, which would lead in turn to a *lecture*. But that is an obvious counterfactual. Novels can without question begin as *histoires* and generate their *narrations* concurrently with their *récits*. It is quite feasible also to start with the *récit*, as Nadja does: "Two, two what? Two women. What do they look like?" etc., allowing the *récit* to bring the *histoire* to light, in which the author may discover at last a *narration* in his or her own *lecture*. In one sense, the *récit* precedes and causes *histoire (2)*. But, from another viewpoint, the *récit* as read is concurrent with the generation of imagined events and their interpretation in readers' minds. In mid-novel, already a sizable portion of the *histoire* exists for readers, while a large segment of the *récit* is still "inexistent," unknown to them. The *histoire* which exists for us at the midpoint of a novel is, of course, still fluid, subject to revision as we alter our hypotheses on the basis of later data. But all our efforts will be bent toward making it congeal, and to that end we will be building a *lecture*, also fluid, hypothetical, aimed at grasping the purposes behind the *histoire*. The *lecture* is thus expanding concurrently with the generation of *histoire (2)* and interacting with it. To be sure, the *lecture* needs the data from *histoire (2)* to exist, but it does not require all the data and may begin growing from a few early events. As it begins to solidify, making the reader "closed-minded," it influences the mental elaboration of the *histoire*. So it is that, as readers recognize the Gervaise-Virginie reversal in *L'Assommoir* as an element of esthetic intent, they may foreground in their *histoire (2)* aspects of symmetry in the two events, losing sight of the great quantities of unsymmetrical detail. While a *lecture* is necessarily indexic of an *histoire (2)*, and not *vice versa*, a specific *histoire (2)* may be informed by a connate *lecture*.

So, despite our assumption for purposes of inference that each of the levels has causal priority over those below it in the diagram, such priority is not necessarily temporal in practice. This again points to the radical simultaneity of the causal relationship, perceived as a unit, with directional derivativeness inherent in it. Thus, even if we "know" by external means that a given *récit* preceded its *narration* in its author's mind, the causal assumption impels us to presume the *narration*'s preexistence, somewhere in the authorial subconscious. Such presumption may be unwarranted, and the causal assumption therefore unjustified in the vertical dimension. But just as the imposition of the causal grid is indeed warranted in the horizontal dimension in those texts that provide receptors for it, it seems to me that those texts that mimic convincingly an authorial presence (through a relatively obvious intent of *narration*, and through selection of causal options in *récit* and *histoire*) incite readerly collaboration in creation of the author, as well.

Rarely are *lectures* complete at the end of a first reading; they may continue to harden, like the arteries of the venerable, through several readings of a text. But when final solidification sets in on a reader's *lecture* level, the text is dead for that reader.

Admittedly, a text is considerably stiffened when its structure has been satisfactorily described. But as structures themselves are a product of posthypothetical closedmindedness, hope remains for new readers and new hypotheses: generalized *rigor mortis* among all readers of a well-drawn text is fortunately rare. For the impulsion toward causal hypothesizing is a dynamic, the essential constituent of narrative continuity.

Causal dynamics provide, however, but one view of narrative structure, one whose peculiar traits are movement, directionality, inferential incompleteness, and linearity. But lines can espouse many forms. My examples have uncovered the following principal types, which can exist, of course, in combination.

1. Rectilinear causation: the long, easily inferable causal chains of traditional fiction.
2. Explicitly branching structures: dead-end sidetracks leading off from a causal "main line," as in Huysmans.[7]
3. Implicitly branching structures: the "main line" effaced, with the branches alone remaining, as indicators of absence (Aragon, Breton).
4. Curviform causation: Proust's self-referential "Möbius strip," which is also partly brachiate.

5. Parallel causal structures: the ironic parallel of *narration* and *récit* typical of mythic narrative read as allegory, including portrayal of allegory as problematical (*Les Gommes*).
6. Fragmented structure: Sartre, Camus, and the "broken line"; Sarraute; Robbe-Grillet's *La Jalousie*.
7. Nonlinear structure: absence of causation in the essentially nonnarrative fiction of total immersion in the imaginary mode (Robbe-Grillet's *Souvenirs du triangle d'or*).

Types two through six, associated with "modernist" fiction, tend to undermine readerly assurance about the validity of causal concatenations in narrative. They find ways to use language for the subversion of causation inherent in language. The more frequent selection of intradiegetic narrators leaves causal hypotheses in their *récits* increasingly more problematical, until, with the appearance of type seven, a perhaps postmodernist strategy, readers are limited to the sole noncausal mode of narratorial mental representation.

If other types of causal structure can exist, they surely will, and probably do already. But causality remains a system, involving minimal rules of perceived relationship and directionality: the freedom of my seventh type is a "causal structure" only in its decision to exist in the absence of causal strictures. The interest of this "canon" of standard structures will be, I hope, its potential for comparison, which can reveal deviant and/or combinatory structures in other texts. We have observed combination in Proust and in *L'Etranger; La Route des Flandres* reveals elements of the brachiate track-and-sidetrack structure, in Proustian parallel, although the sidetracks are themselves segmented and redistributed, according to the principles of association, along the wandering timeline of mental representations in conditioned sequence.

If there is anything seminal in this volume—that is to say, anything that might cause others to think in causal terms in their reading and research—it should therefore lie in what turns out to be absent, or perhaps implausible, in these pages. The essential is always in the gaps, generative in criticism and in theory as in fiction and in life of fertile hypotheses. Each inference requires as its cause a Lacanian "desire," a conatus to know, which surfaces in the intervals between segments of the metonymic chain, and a condition or conditions for belief. As the condition approaches proof, hypothesis becomes project, then solidified knowledge. The delight in literature, as in other aspects of living, resides in the penchant for solidity, a desire that can survive only in the presence of generative doubt. The line of *lecture* and of life continues only so long as there are gaps in the *histoire* or in the *narration*, cracks to be bridged, only so long as one cannot yet cry, with Balzac's moribund Balthazar: "EUREKA!"

Notes

1. Ilya Prigogine and Isabelle Stengers, *La Nouvelle Alliance: Métamorphose de la science* (Paris: Gallimard, 1979), pp. 274–77.

2. For the distinctions between "the reader" and the textual construct called "the narratee," see Gerald Prince, "Introduction à l'étude du narrataire," *Poétique*, 14 (1973), 178–96. On the scientist as "actor" in the observation of material phenomena, see Prigogine and Stengers, pp. 222–33, 278.

3. The problem is perhaps more readily addressed from the opposite standpoint: belief in "chance"; on this question, see Erich Köhler, *Der literarische Zufall, das Mögliche und die Notwendigkeit* (Munich: Wilhelm Fink Verlag, 1973).

4. Tzvetan Todorov, *Poétique de la prose* (Paris: Editions du Seuil, 1971), pp. 78–85. The subsequent reference is to this edition.

5. Michel Foucault, *L'Archéologie du savoir* (Paris: Gallimard, 1969), p. 39.

6. The notion of inferred textual purpose is often apparent in Ross Chambers's specular approaches to fiction; see his *Story and Situation* (Minneapolis: University of Minnesota Press, 1984), pp. 64–70 and *passim*.

7. Authors' names in this list are shorthand references to texts analyzed in preceding chapters; obviously, all texts of a given author need not adopt the same causal structure.

Appendix A
Relative Frequency of Causal
Vocabulary in Gide's *L'Immoraliste*
and *La Porte étroite*

The survey of causal vocabulary in the two novels is based on a sampling of pages. Each text fills 104 pages of the Pléiade edition of Gide's *Romans, récits et soties, oeuvres lyriques* (Paris: Galimard, 1958). For analysis, 10 pages were selected at random from the first 52 pages of each work and 10 more from the second 52 to constitute the 40-page sample. In the second 10 sample pages from *La Porte étroite*, 4 were intentionally chosen at random from pp. 581–98, to insure proportional inclusion of Alissa's diary. The sample consists, then, of these pages: *L'Immoraliste*, pp. 376, 381, 386, 392, 395, 396, 397, 407, 412, 416, 421, 434, 437, 441, 444, 445, 450, 460, 471, 472; *La Porte étroite*, pp. 514, 515, 519, 521, 526, 528, 534, 542, 543, 545, 547, 548, 550, 557, 562, 566, 586, 592, 595, 598. The findings may be summarized as follows, with the understanding that the numbers of occurrences, given the potential for stylistic variation from page to page, are useful for drawing only the most general conclusions.

Typology of Causal Expression

1. "METALANGUAGE" OF CAUSALITY: *à cause de, causer, cause* (IM, 2; PE, 3).

2. CAUSAL CONJUNCTIONS: *parce que, car, puisque, comme* (when causal), *pour que, de sorte que, [c'est] que, [d'autant plus] que* (IM, 9; PE, 17).

3. CAUSAL PREPOSITIONS: *par, de* (when causal, and *en* in replacement), *à* (when causal, and *là* in replacement), *pour* plus cause, *pour* plus intent, *pour* plus result, *en . . .-ant* (expressing means), *à la faveur de, à force de, selon* (causal) (IM, 105; PE, 73). Illustrative examples: (Causal *de*) "la gêne de sentir accrochées l'une à l'autre nos mains moites," p. 557; (*de* expressing agency) "Charles . . . le calmait de la parole," p. 416; (*en* in replacement) "la joie qu'elle en eut," p. 395. (Causal *à*) "peut-être quelque ressentiment gênait-il mon affection pour ma tante, à la voir manifester pour la cadette de ses nièces une prédilection très marquée," p. 514. (*Pour* plus intent, causal when the intention bears fruit) "je me couche au milieu du jour pour tromper la longueur morne des journées," p. 471. Frequency in major

subcategories: *par* (IM, 15; PE, 15); *de* (*en*), (IM, 42; PE, 25); *à* (*là*) (IM, 10; PE, 7); *pour* (IM, 33; PE, 22).

4. VERBS OF TRANSITIVITY: all transitive, nonreflexive verbs designating a modification (IM, 214; PE, 225).

5. SPECIAL CAUSAL VERBS: causal *faire* (*faire* plus infinitive, *faire* [*en sorte*] *que*); verbs of volition that achieve a result (*vouloir, se décider à, chercher à*, obeyed imperatives); verbs of obligation (*devoir* expressing obligation, *falloir, forcer*); verbs of transformation (*faire* or *rendre* plus adjective); verbs of permission when a modification is thereby effected (*laisser, permettre*) (IM, 59; PE, 52). Frequency of causal *faire*: IM, 15; PE, 9.

6. PRESENT PARTICIPLES AND OTHER ADJECTIVES designating the cause of a specified effect (IM, 25; PE, 18). Illustrative examples: "voyant sa détresse, j'ajoutai moins brutalement, 'Tu m'aideras'," p. 386; "Désoeuvré, plein d'angoisse et d'impatience, après avoir laissé Abel, pour tromper mon attente, je me lançai dans une longue course," p. 534.

7. NOUNS designating the cause of a specified effect (IM, 11; PE, 1).

8. ADVERBS OF LOGICAL CONCLUSION: *donc, ainsi, alors, aussi* (when causal) (IM, 13; PE, 8).

9. EXPRESSIONS OF DEGREE evoking causality: *tant; si . . . que; tel . . . que; à ce point que*, etc. (IM, 14; PE, 18). Illustrative examples: Pity, says Michel, "m'emplit si violemment, que je ne pus retenir mes larmes," p. 376; Jérôme, speaking of Alissa, declares, "O Juliette! la vie avec elle m'apparaît tellement belle que je n'ose pas . . . comprends-tu cela? que je n'ose pas lui en parler," p. 519. (Such expressions evoke a threshold of causation, below which the consequences— here, Michel's tears, Jérôme's feeling of interdiction—would have been lesser or nonexistent, but which, when reached, allows a specific event to be triggered.)

10. TEMPORAL EXPRESSIONS evoking cause (IM, 10; PE, 15). Illustrative example: Jérôme, referring to Aunt Félicie, says, "Dès qu'elle fut partie, la maison put se recueillir," p. 514. (Jérôme indicates that her absence is a necessary condition for the household's tranquillity.)

11. SPATIAL EXPRESSIONS evoking cause (IM, 12; PE, 9).

12. EXPRESSIONS OF PUTATIVE CAUSALITY: *mettre sur le compte de, sembler venir de, soit que . . . soit que . . .* (IM, 4; PE, 1).

13. STANDARD PARATAXIS: implied causality between events juxtaposed in the *récit* (IM, 41; PE, 29). Illustrative examples: (same sentence) "Inutile d'aller plus loin, dit Marceline; ces vergers se ressemblent tous," p. 392; (succeeding sentences) "Arrachez-moi d'ici; je ne puis le faire moi-même. Quelque chose en ma volonté s'est brisé," p. 471; (within three sentences) Marceline staggers, p. 460, and two sentences later Michel hastens to her side. (Although causation may be inferred across a still greater interval than two or three sentences—e.g., Lucile's

flight, p. 504, may be causally related to Alissa's apparent fear of her heredity and of physical passion, pp. 585–86—causation can scarcely be seen as implied by the *récit* without juxtaposition, which suggests "intent to imply."

14. CONVERSATIONAL PARATAXIS: implied causal relationships in reported conversations between one character's speech and another's response (IM, 12; PE, 40).

TOTALS (IM, 531; PE, 509): 1040.

Appendix B
Comparison of Causal Vocabulary in Zola's *L'Assommoir* and in Gide's *L'Immoraliste* and *La Porte étroite*

Relative frequency of causal vocabulary in Zola's *L'Assommoir* is based on a sample of pages from the *Oeuvres complètes* edition, volume 3 (Paris: Cercle du Livre Précieux, 1967). The sample was selected by dividing the novel into 7 49-page segments. Three pages were selected at random from each segment; 1 page was eliminated at random from the pages thus designated to form the 20-page sample. It consists of the following pages: 615, 640, 647, 658, 663, 667, 724, 731, 746, 755, 762, 783, 805, 809, 870, 879, 880, 895, 901, 929.

Figures given for Gide refer to the number of occurrences in the total sample for both *L'Immoraliste* and *La Porte étroite* shown in appendix A; figures in parentheses indicate the percentage of the total number of occurrences in each sample to be found in each category.

Comparative Typology of Causal Expressions

CATEGORY	GIDE		ZOLA	
	No. of Occurrences	Percentage	No. of Occurrences	Percentage
1. "Metalanguage" of causality	5	(0.5%)	8	(1%)
2. Causal conjunctions	26	(3%)	45	(7%)
3. Causal prepositions	178	(17%)	113	(18%)
4, 5. Causal verbs	550	(53%)	232	(38%)
6. Causal participles, adjectives	43	(4%)	28	(5%)
7. Causal nouns	12	(1%)	7	(1%)
8. Adverbs of logical conclusion	21	(2%)	13	(2%)
9. Causal expressions of degree	32	(3%)	17	(3%)
10. Causal temporal expressions	25	(2%)	23	(4%)
11. Causal spatial expressions	21	(2%)	10	(2%)
12. Expressions of putative cause	5	(0.5%)	1	(0%)
13. Standard parataxis	70	(7%)	66	(11%)
14. Conversational parataxis	52	(5%)	50	(8%)
Totals	1040	(100%)	613	(100%)

Two causal expressions in *L'Assommoir* are particularly worthy of note, the first because it is totally absent from the Gide sample (appendix A), and the second because it returns with some frequency in the Zola text. The first is *histoire de* (e.g., "Puis, un soir, ayant de la monnaie, ils s'attablèrent et burent un saladier de vin à la française, histoire de se raffraichir," [p. 895]; "Then one evening, since they had a little change in their pockets, they sat down at a table and drank a bowl of wine the French way, just to cool off"). This particularly colloquial term expressing motivation exemplifies the working-class flavor of the narrator's diction and seems at odds with the very "literary" verb tenses (past definite) of the *récit*, in a way that Gide's lexicon would seldom permit. It may signal a "lapse" into (almost) free indirect discourse, as if the portion of the sentence containing it came from the mind of the characters (Gervaise and Coupeau in the example given): this is the pretext they give for drinking, not the true cause. Such shoddy causal logic is not uncommon among *L'Assommoir*'s characters.

And Zola's narrator seems especially fond of the construction: *ne . . . plus . . . sans*. The *ne . . . plus* indicates a change, points out an "effect." The *sans* implies the nature of the change (from "not always" to "always"), but no cause is given (e.g., "Elle ne passa plus devant la porte d'un bal sans entrer," [p. 895]; "now she never passed a dance hall door without going in"; here, Gervaise is seeking her daughter, but for deeper motivations—alcohol is available in dance halls—readers are thrown back upon the *histoire* to infer them.) *Ne . . . plus . . . sans* evokes a "now always" state of affairs, akin to the "static," "described" scenes that abound in the novel (the Assommoir Tavern, Gervaise in her laundry, Gouget at his forge, the saint's-day banquet, Gervaise scrubbing floors, attempting prostitution in the streets, etc.), which come into existence without clear causal links to the past at the level of the *récit*. Relatively common in *L'Assommoir*, this construction tends to fragment the causal chains, sending us to the *histoire* to infer causation.

FUNCTION	NUMBER OF OCCURRENCES										
	parce que	causal *comme*	*à cause de*	*puisque*	*car*	*c'est pour cela que*	causal *ainsi*	*donc*	*par suite*	Totals	Per-centage
Causes of inconsequential effects	25	5	6	2	2	0	0	0	0	40	37
"Evasive" explanations	12	6	0	0	1	1	0	0	0	20	19
Inferences	2	1	1	0	0	0	0	0	0	4	4
Speculations	0	0	0	3	1	0	1	1	1	7	6
Substantial causes	6	1	4	2	1	0	1	0	0	15	14
Consequential explanations of Meursault's psychic states	3	0	0	0	1	0	0	0	0	4	4
Text-referential causes	6	0	1	0	0	1	0	0	0	8	7
Causal judgments by other characters (direct or indirect discourse)	7	1	1	0	0	1	0	0	0	10	9
Totals	61	14	13	7	6	3	2	1	1	108	100

(Summary: analysis of data in Ignace Feuerlicht, "Camus's *L'Etranger* Revisited," *PMLA* 78, 5 [Dec. 1963], 612.)

Works Cited

Albérès, R.-M. "Introduction [to Zola's *L'Assommoir*]." In Emile Zola, *Oeuvres complètes*, 3. Paris: Cercle du Livre Précieux, 1967, pp. 591–97.

Allott, Ken, and Peter Tremewan. *Les Gommes d'Alain Robbe-Grillet: Index verborum et table des fréquences*. Paris, Geneva: Champion, Slatkine, 1985.

Anscombe, G. E. M. "Causality and Determination." In *Causation and Conditionals*. Ernest Sosa, ed. London: Oxford University Press, 1975, pp. 63–81.

Aragon, Louis. *Le Paysan de Paris*. Paris: Gallimard, 1926.

Aristotle. *The Poetics of Aristotle*. S. H. Butcher, trans. London: Macmillan, 1936.

Barthes, Roland. *L'Aventure sémiologique*. Paris: Editions du Seuil, 1985.

———. *S/Z*. Paris: Editions du Seuil, 1970.

Bergson, Henri. *Oeuvres*. Paris: Presses Universitaires de France, 1959.

Booth, Wayne C. *The Rhetoric of Fiction*. Chicago: University of Chicago Press, 1961.

Borie, Jean. *Zola et les mythes, ou de la nausée au salut*. Paris: Editions du Seuil, 1971.

Bourget, Paul. *Le Disciple*. Paris: Nelson, [1911].

Brée, Germaine. *Gide*. New Brunswick: Rutgers University Press, 1963.

Bremond, Claude. *Logique du récit*. Paris: Editions du Seuil, 1973.

Breton, André. *Nadja*. Paris: Gallimard, 1963.

Brooks, Peter. *Reading for the Plot*. New York: Alfred A. Knopf, 1984.

Camus, Albert. *L'Etranger*. In his *Théâtre, récits, nouvelles*. Paris: Gallimard, Pléiade, 1962, pp. 1123–1212. Another edition: Germaine Brée and Carlos Lynes, eds. New York: Appleton-Century-Crofts, 1955.

———. *Le Mythe de Sisyphe*. In his *Essais*. Paris: Gallimard, Pléiade, 1965, pp. 89–211.

———. *La Peste*. In his *Théâtre, récits, nouvelles*. Paris: Gallimard, Pléiade, 1962, pp. 1213–1474. Another edition: Paris: Gallimard, 1947.

Carroll, Lewis. *Alice's Adventures in Wonderland, Through the Looking Glass, and The Hunting of the Snark*. New York: Carlton House, n.d.

Chambers, Ross. *Story and Situation: Narrative Seduction and the Power of Fiction*. Minneapolis: University of Minnesota Press, 1984.

Chatman, Seymour. *Story and Discourse: Narrative Structure in Fiction and Film*. Ithaca: Cornell University Press, 1978.

Claudel, Paul, and André Gide. *Correspondance, 1899–1926*. Paris: Gallimard, 1949.

Cocteau, Jean. *Les Enfants terribles*. Paris: Arthème Fayard, 1951.

Cohn, Dorrit. *Transparent Minds: Narrative Modes for Presenting Consciousness in Fiction*. Princeton: Princeton University Press, 1978.

Concalon, Elaine. "Les Récits d'André Gide: Essai d'analyse actantielle." *Modern Language Notes*, 90 (May 1975), 590–96.

Culler, Jonathan. *On Deconstruction*. Ithaca: Cornell University Press, 1982.

Dällenbach, Lucien. *La Récit spéculaire: Essai sur la mise en abyme*. Paris: Editions du Seuil, 1977.

Davies, John C. *Gide: L'Immoraliste and La Porte étroite*. London: Edward Arnold, 1968.

de Faria, Néide. *Structures et unité dans "les Rougon-Macquart"*. Paris: Nizet, 1977.

Deleuze, Gilles. *Différence et répétition*. Paris: Presses Universitaires de France, 1968.

———. "Introduction [to Zola's *La Bête humaine*]." In Emile Zola, *Oeuvres complètes*, 6. Paris: Cercle du Livre Précieux, 1967, pp. 13–21.

de Man, Paul. *Allegories of Reading*. New Haven: Yale University Press, 1979.

Eco, Umberto. *The Role of the Reader*. London: Hutchinson, 1979.

Feuerlicht, Ignace. "Camus's *L'Etranger* Revisited." *PMLA*, 78, 3 (December 1963), 606–21.

Fitch, Brian. *L'Etranger d'Albert Camus: Un texte, ses lecteurs, leurs lectures, étude méthodologique*. Paris: Larousse, 1972.

———. "Narrateur et narration dans *L'Etranger* d'Albert Camus." *Archives des Lettres Modernes*, 34 (1960), 1–48.

Flaubert, Gustave. *Correspondance*. Paris: Gallimard, Pléiade, 1980, vol. 2.

Forster, E. M. *Aspects of the Novel*. New York: Harcourt, Brace, 1927.

Foucault, Michel. *L'Archéologie du savoir*. Paris: Gallimard, 1969.

Frazer, Sir James George. *The Golden Bough*. New York: Macmillan, 1935, vol. 4.

Frohock, W. M. *André Malraux and the Tragic Imagination*. Palo Alto: Stanford University Press, 1952.

Gautier, Théophile. *Jettatura*. In his *Romans et contes*. Paris: Charpentier, 1923, pp. 137–270.

Genette, Gérard. *Figures*. Paris: Editions du Seuil, 1966.

———. *Figures II*. Paris: Editions du Seuil, 1969.

———. *Figures III*. Paris: Editions du Seuil, 1972.

———. *Nouveaux Discours du récit*. Paris: Editions du Seuil, 1983.

Gide, André. *Les Caves du Vatican*. Paris: Gallimard, 1922.

———. "Faits divers." *Nouvelle Revue Française*, 30 (1ᵉʳ juin 1928), 839–49.

————. *Les Faux-monnayeurs*. Paris: Gallimard, 1925.

————. *L'Immoraliste*. In his *Romans, récits et soties, oeuvres lyriques*. Paris: Gallimard, Pléiade, 1958, pp. 365–472.

————. *Journal, 1889–1939*. Paris: Gallimard, Pléiade, 1951.

————. *La Porte étroite*. In his *Romans, récits et soties, oeuvres lyriques*. Paris: Gallimard, Pléiade, 1958, pp. 493–598.

————. *Si le grain ne meurt*. In his *Oeuvres complètes*, 10. Paris: Gallimard, 1936, pp. 27–445.

————. *Thésée*. In his *Romans, récits et soties, oeuvres lyriques*. Paris: Gallimard, Pléiade, 1958, pp. 1413–53.

Giono, Jean. *Regain*. Paris: Bernard Grasset, 1930.

Godel, Robert. *Les Sources manuscrites du Cours de linguistique générale*. Geneva, Paris: Droz, Minard, 1957.

Greimas, A.-J. *Sémantique structurale*. Paris: Larousse, 1966.

Hobsbaum, Philip. *A Theory of Communication*. London: Macmillan, 1970.

Holland, Norman N. "Unity Identity Text Self." In *Reader Response Criticism from Formalism to Post-Structuralism*. Jane P. Tompkins, ed. Baltimore: Johns Hopkins University Press, 1980, pp. 118–33.

Hume, David. *A Treatise of Human Nature*. Oxford: Clarendon Press, 1888.

Huysmans, Joris-Karl. *A rebours*. Paris: Fasquelle, 1955.

Iser, Wolfgang. *The Act of Reading: A Theory of Aesthetic Response*. Baltimore: Johns Hopkins University Press, 1978.

Jakobson, Roman. *Essais de linguistique générale*. Nicolas Ruwet, trans. Paris: Editions de Minuit, 1963.

Jameson, Fredric. *The Political Unconscious*. Ithaca: Cornell University Press, 1981.

Jennings, Chantal Bertrand. *L'Eros et la femme chez Zola*. Paris: Klincksieck, 1977.

Kant, Immanuel. *Kritik der reinen Vernunft*. Heidelberg: Georg Weiss, 1884.

Knecht, Loring D. "A New Reading of Gide's *La Porte étroite*." *PMLA*, 82, 7 (December 1967), 640–48.

Köhler, Erich. *Der literarische Zufall, das Mögliche und die Notwendigkeit*. Munich: Wilhelm Fink Verlag, 1973.

Leefmans, Bert M.-P. "Malraux and Tragedy: The Structure of *La Condition humaine*." *Romanic Review*, 44, 3 (October 1953), 208–14.

Lévi-Strauss, Claude. *Anthropologie structurale*. Paris: Plon, 1958.

Mackie, J. L. "Causes and Conditions." In *Causation and Conditionals*. Ernest Sosa, ed. London: Oxford University Press, 1975.

Maillet, Henri. *L'Immoraliste d'André Gide*. Paris: Hachette, 1972.

Malraux, André. *La Condition humaine*. Paris: Gallimard, 1933.

March, Harold. *Gide and the Hound of Heaven*. Philadelphia: University of Pennsylvania Press, 1952.

Matthews, J. H. *Les Deux Zola*. Geneva, Paris: Droz, Minard, 1967.

McClelland, John. "The Lexicon of *Les Caves du Vatican*." *PMLA*, 89, 2 (March 1974), 256–67.

Michotte, Albert, et al. *Causalité, permanence et réalité phénoménales*. Louvain: Publications Universitaires, 1962.

Morrissette, Bruce. *Les Romans de Robbe-Grillet*. Paris: Editions de Minuit, 1963.

Nelson, Roy Jay. "Gidean Causality: *L'Immoraliste* and *La Porte étroite*." *Symposium*, 31, 1 (Spring 1977), 43–58.

———. "Malraux and Camus: The Myth of the Beleaguered City." *Kentucky Foreign Language Quarterly*, 13, 2 (1966), 89–94.

———. "Territorial Psychology in Nathalie Sarraute's *Les Fruits d'or*." *Symposium*, 35, 4 (Winter 1981–82), 307–23.

Nietzsche, Friedrich. *Der Wille zur Macht*. In his *Nachgelassene Werke*, 15. Leipzig: E. G. Nauman, 1901. Translation: *The Will to Power*. Walter Kaufmann and R. J. Hollingdale, trans. New York: Random House, 1967.

———. "Uber Warheit und Lüge im aussermoralischen Sinn." In his *Werke in drei Bänden*, 3. Munich: Carl Hanser Verlag, 1956, pp. 309–22.

Noyer-Weidner, Alfred. "Structure et sens de *L'Etranger*." In *Albert Camus 1980*. R. Gay-Crosier, ed. Gainesville: University Presses of Florida, 1980, pp. 72–85.

O'Brien, Justin. *Portrait of André Gide*. New York: Alfred A. Knopf, 1953.

Olrik, Hilde. "La Théorie de l'imprégnation." *Nineteenth-Century French Studies*, 15, 1 & 2 (Fall-Winter 1986–87), 128–40.

Pariente, Jean-Claude. "*L'Etranger* et son double." *Revue des Lettres Modernes*, 170–174 (1968), 53–80.

Patai, Daphne. "Temporal Structure as a Fictional Category in Michel Butor's *La Modification*." *French Review*, 46, 6 (May 1973), 1117–28.

Peirce, C. S. *Philosophical Writings of Peirce*. Justus Buchler, ed. New York: Dover Publications, 1955.

Pfromm, Rüdiger. *Revolution im Zeichen des Mythos: Eine wirkungsgeschichtliche Untersuchung von Louis Aragons "Le Paysan de Paris"*. Frankfort-am-Main: Peter Lang, 1985.

Prigogine, Ilya, and Isabelle Stengers. *La Nouvelle Alliance: Métamorphose de la science*. Paris: Gallimard, 1979.

Prince, Gerald. *A Grammar of Stories*. The Hague: Mouton, 1973.

———. "Introduction à l'étude du narrataire." *Poétique*, 14 (1973), 178–96.

Proust, Marcel. *A la recherche du temps perdu*. Paris: Gallimard, Pléiade, 1954, 3 vols. Translation: *Remembrance of Things Past*. C. K. Scott Moncrieff and Frederick A. Blossom, trans. New York: Random House, 1924, 1927. 2 vols. Rpt. 1941.

Queneau, Raymond. *Zazie dans le métro*. Paris: Gallimard, 1959.

Raoul, Valerie. *The French Fictional Journal: Fictional Narcissism/Narcissistic Fiction*. Toronto: University of Toronto Press, 1980.

Ricardou, Jean. "Miracles de l'analogie (aspects proustiens de la métaphore productrice)." In *Etudes proustiennes II*. Paris: Gallimard, 1975, pp. 11–42.

Ricoeur, Paul. *Finitude et culpabilité*. II, *La Symbolique du mal*. Paris: Aubier, Editions Montaigne, 1960.

Riffaterre, Michel. *Semiotics of Poetry*. Bloomington: Indiana University Press, 1978.

Rimbaud, Arthur. *Oeuvres*. Paris: Presses Universitaires de France, 1950.

Ripoll, Roger. *Réalité et mythe chez Zola*. Paris: Honoré Champion, 1981.

Robbe-Grillet, Alain. *Les Gommes*. Paris: Editions de Minuit, 1953.

———. *La Jalousie*. Paris: Editions de Minuit, 1957.

———. *La Maison de rendez-vous*. Paris: Editions de Minuit, 1965.

———. *Souvenirs du triangle d'or*. Paris: Editions de Minuit, 1978.

Russell, Bertrand. "On the Nature of Cause." In his *Mysticism and Logic*. New York: W. W. Norton, 1929, pp. 180–208.

San-Antonio. *Ça tourne au vinaigre*. Paris: Fleuve Noir, 1956.

Sartre, Jean-Paul. "Explication de *L'Etranger*." In his *Situations I*. Paris: Gallimard, 1947, pp. 99–121.

———. *La Nausée*. In his *Oeuvres romanesques*. Paris: Gallimard, Pléiade, 1981, pp. 1–210.

Serres, Michel. *Feux et signaux de brume: Zola*. Paris: Bernard Grasset, 1975.

Shattuck, Roger. *Proust's Binoculars: A Study of Memory, Time, and Recognition in A la recherche du temps perdu*. New York: Random House, 1963.

Siebers, Tobin. *The Mirror of Medusa*. Berkeley: University of California Press, 1983.

Simon, Claude. *La Route des Flandres*. Paris: Editions de Minuit, 1960.

———. *Le Vent. Tentative de restitution d'un retable baroque*. Paris: Editions de Minuit, 1957.

Soelberg, Nils. "Le Paradoxe du JE-narrateur: approche narratologique de *L'Etranger* de Camus." *Revue Romane*, 20, 1 (1985), 68–97.

Stendhal. *Le Rouge et le Noir*. Geneva: Cercle du Bibliophile, 1971.

Sternberg, Meir. *Expositional Modes and Temporal Ordering in Fiction*. Baltimore: Johns Hopkins University Press, 1978.

Suleiman, Susan Rubin. *Authoritarian Fictions: The Ideological Novel as a Literary Genre*. New York: Columbia University Press, 1983.

Tacca, Oscar. "*L'Etranger* comme récit d'auteur-transcripteur." In *Albert Camus 1980*. R. Gay-Crosier, ed. Gainesville: University Presses of Florida, 1980, pp. 87–98.

Taine, Hippolyte. *Histoire de la littérature anglaise*. Paris: Hachette, 1873, vol. 1.

Todorov, Tzvetan. *Grammaire du Décaméron*. The Hague: Mouton, 1969.

———. *Poétique de la prose*. Paris: Editions du Seuil, 1971.

Valéry, Paul. "Regards sur le monde actuel." In his *Oeuvres*, 2. Paris: Gallimard, Pléiade, 1960, pp. 911–1158.

Zola, Emile. *L'Assommoir*. In his *Oeuvres complètes*, 3. Paris: Cercle du Livre Précieux, 1967, pp. 599–943.

———. *La Bête humaine*. In his *Oeuvres complètes*, 6. Paris: Cercle du Livre Précieux, 1967, pp. 23–297.

———. *La Faute de l'abbé Mouret*. In his *Oeuvres complètes*, 3. Paris: Cercle du Livre Précieux, 1967, pp. 19–270.

———. *Le Roman expérimental*. In his *Oeuvres complètes*, 10. Paris: Cercle du Livre Précieux, 1968, pp. 1175–1401.

Index

Absurdity, 16, 32, 34, 38, 76, 120, 143–45, 149–72, 219, 221

Adjectives and participles, causal, 11, 23–24, 25, 56, 228, 230

Albérès, René-Marill (pseud. for René Marill), 37–38, 41, 42, 43

Algorithm: for inferred authorial hypothe-·sis, 216–17; for inferred causality, 8–9, 153; Saussure's, 7

Allegory, 137–47, 220, 224. *See also* Myth

Analepsis, 95, 96

Anscombe, Gertrude Elizabeth Margaret, xxiv–xxv, 5, 9, 11

Anticausal strategies, xxviii, 219; in absurdist fiction, 150, 152, 154–56, 159–63, 170; in allegory, 141–146; in episodic novels, 105–16; in fragmented "new" novels, 190–91; in imaginary-mode texts, 189, 199–206; in Proust, 125, 133–34. *See also* Causal block

Antichronology: antichronological reading in Proust, 134; in hypothetical reasoning, 179; inverted logic in Camus, 170; in *lecture*, 211; in *narration*, 93–97; in Nietzsche, xvii–xviii; in Sartre, 152–53, 155, 157; in Zola, 68–69, 82, 83–84. *See also* Causal logic

Aragon, Louis (pseud. for Louis Andrieux), 111–13, 119, 215, 221, 223

Aristotle, 4, 103

Association, psychological, 110, 124–34, 193, 195, 196–97, 198, 205

Author, 60, 69, 104, 110, 112–13, 120, 138, 141, 143, 150, 153, 220, 223; as dispositions of intentionality in texts, 9, 13; inferred existence of, 7, 92; inferred inferences of, 210–12, 216–17; as linguistic codes, 211; multiple identities of, 12–18. *See also* Indexic author; Inferred author

Barthes, Roland, xxii, 4, 27, 228

Baudelaire, Charles, 109, 134

Bergson, Henri, xx–xxi, 109

Bernanos, Georges, xviii, 151

Booth, Wayne C., 7, 12, 13

Borie, Jean, 51, 98

Bourget, Paul, 103–5

Bremond, Claude, 5

Breton, André, 111, 113–19, 120, 215, 219, 221, 222, 223

Brooks, Peter, xxix, xxx, 140–41

Butor, Michel, 69, 190, 192

Camus, Albert, 9–10, 98, 132, 139–40, 143–44, 145–46, 149, 150, 157–72, 175, 186, 188, 215, 218, 219, 220, 221, 224, 232